INVENTORY OF THE COLONIAL RECORDS OF TEXAS
1821–1837

Prepared by
The Historical Records Survey
Division of Women's and Professional Projects
Work Progress Administration

No. 3
Municipality of Brazoria County, 1832–1837

(Brazoria County Courthouse
Angleton, Texas)

WPA Records

Heritage Books
2025

HERITAGE BOOKS

AN IMPRINT OF HERITAGE BOOKS, INC.

Books, CDs, and more—Worldwide

For our listing of thousands of titles see our website
at
www.HeritageBooks.com

A Facsimile Reprint
Published 2025 by
HERITAGE BOOKS, INC.
Publishing Division
5810 Ruatan Street
Berwyn Heights, MD 20740

San Antonio, Texas
Historical Records Survey
June 1937

International Standard Book Number
Paperbound: 978-0-7884-7768-3

Preface

The Historical Records Survey has for its purpose the dis-
covery, preservation, and making accessible of basic materials for
research in the history of the United States.

Following the establishment of the Survey in November, 1935,
by executive letter of President Roosevelt, Dr. Luther H. Evans
as National Supervisor extended it to every state in the Union.
The Survey was begun in Texas on March 14, 1936, with J. Frank
Davis, State Supervisor of Writers' Projects, as ex-officie State
Supervisor and Ike Moore as Assistant State Supervisor. The state
office was established and continues to be at the Smith-Young Tower,
San Antonio. Under Mr. Moore's direction the Survey was carried
to all parts of the State. Area and district offices were established
in Abilene, Amarillo, Austin, Beaumont, Big Spring Brownwood Dallas,
El Paso Fort Worth, Houston Laredo, Marshall Palestine San Angelo,
San Antonio Tyler Uvalde, Waco, and Wichita Falls. Field workers
on May 15, 1937, had entered 175 counties.

In November 1936, upon the separation of the Survey from the
Writers' Projects, Mr. Moore became State Supervisor and Charles W.
Hodges Assistant State Supervisor.

A chief work of the Survey in Texas has been the inventorying
of state, county, and municipal archives. Historically, records
found in Texas county courthouses may be divided into three parts:
Spanish records, covering the period from 1718 to 1821; colonial records, 1821-1836; and county records, 1837 to the present.

Because of their historical importance, detailed attention has
been given to the colonial archives. One of the most complete sets
of such records now extant is housed in the Brazoria County courthouse at Angleton. Brazoria County is roughly the successor of the
Mexican Municipality of Brazoria, the division of government whose
records are listed in this book. This Inventory includes all extant
records of the municipality from its creation on April 28, 1832, to
the beginning of county government under the Republic of Texas on
February 20, 1837; and miscellaneous records dating from 1787 to
1837. An inventory of the records of Brazoria County, 1837--, is
now being prepared by the Historical Records Survey.

The Inventory is divided into four groups on the basis of
contents: (1) land records, (2) marriage records, (3) estates, and
(4) court records. The land records consist of two volumes, Record of
Spanish Deeds, which contains copies of the original instruments in
Spanish, and Transcribed Spanish Records, which contains English
translations of the original instruments. Marriage records comprise
bonds, agreements, and contracts, which were accepted until the
religious ceremony could be performed by a Catholic priest. Estates
include cases probated or containing instruments prior to February
20, 1837. The general probate papers of Brazoria County were ex-
amined for these, Court records contain five separate dockets,
alcalde court papers, and proceedings of the District Court of
Brazoria County in cases begun before February 20, 1837.

Preface

   With one exception (a file docket and fee book without dates
or case numbers), the Historical Records Survey has prepared an
index for each of the entries in the Inventory. A general index
has been made that includes all proper names appearing in the
Inventory, nearly 1,000 in all.

   It was extremely difficult to make an accurate list of proper
names since the spelling is often contradictory and the handwriting
is not always legible. The effort of the colonists to conform to
Mexican customs often made them attempt to modify proper names to
fit the Spanish pronunciation. Care has been taken to check the
names against each other and against contemporary documents.
Louis J. Wilson, of Angelton, an authority on the history of
Brazoria County, rendered valuable assistance in checking spelling.

   Claud Keltner, of Houston, Area Supervisor of the Survey, made
the initial inventory February 2--17, 1937. Mr. Keltner, Mr. Moore,
Mr. Hodges, Mrs. Virginia Smith Huff, and Mrs. Mary Fall Clee edited
the field notes.

   The cooperation of H. R. Stevens, County Clerk, Miss Jimmie
Patterson, District Clerk, Bob Monarch, Deputy County Clerk, and
Arrington Farer, Deputy District Clerk, all of Brazoria County, was
invaluable, and is gratefully acknowledge.

San Antonio, Texas.   Ike Moore
May 15, 1937   State Supervisor

                                       Luther H. Evans
                                       National Supervisor
                                       Historical Records Survey

Table of Contents

Illustration

Map showing boundaries of the Municipality of Brazoria.......   1

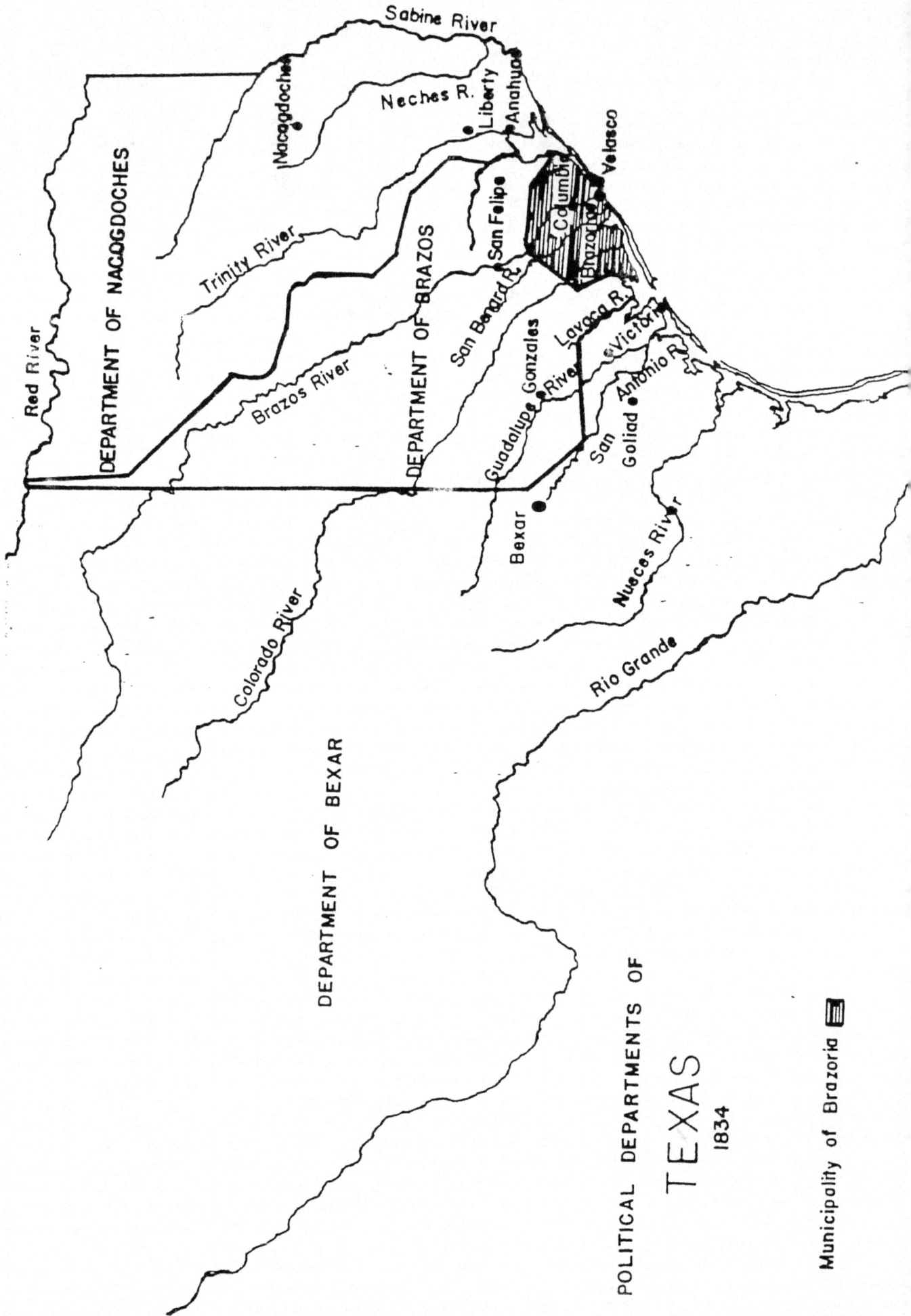

POLITICAL DEPARTMENTS OF

TEXAS

1834

Municipality of Brazoria

1.   Historical Sketch of the Municipality of Brazoria

A.   Republic of Mexico, 1823-1835

Lying below the regular routes of travel used by the Spanish, the region near the mouth of the Brazos River was not occupied by white men until the beginning of colonization by Anglo-Americans under the leadership of STEPHEN F. AUSTIN. This section was first organized in 1832 by the Congress of Coahuila and Texas as a political subdivision called the Municipality of Brazoria. The limits of the municipality included a portion of present Galveston, Matagorda, Wharton, Harris, and Fort Bend Counties, and all of present Brazoria County. The name of the municipality is a simple derivative of the name of the Brazos River, which in Spanish means arms.

After making the first settlements along the Brazos River near the present town of Washington in November, 1821, several of Austin's original colonists, "The Old Three Hundred," moved down the Brazos within the limits of what became in 1832 the Municipality of Brazoria. Among the leaders of this group was JOSIAH H. BELL, Austin's confidential agent, who moved southward in 1823. (E. C. BARKER, The Life of Stephen F. Austin, 42, 108)

An imperial decree of February 18, 1823, authorized Austin to organize the colonists into militia companies, assign lands to them, and administer justice until the government for the colony coule be established. The provisions of this decree were re-affirmed April 14, 1823, by the Constituent Congress, which succeeded the Mexican emperor Agustin Iturbide. (BARKER, Feadings in Texas History, 104) Each colonist was allowed one labor (177 acres) of farming land, and one league (4,428 acres) of grazing land. (Ibid., 108) As most of the colonists combined cattle-raising with farming, they received the maximum number of acres.

Recognizing that the Spanish government could not immediately extend local government into the section selected by Austin for colonization, Governor ANTONIO MARTINEZ had instructed Austin in August, 1821, to "cause all the colonists to understand that until the government organizes the government organizes the authority which is to govern them and administer justice, they must be governed by and be subordinate to you." (Ibid., 103-104; see also BARKER, The Life of Stephen F. Austin, 35)

Local courts were established in August, 1823, when Governor JOSE FELIX TRESPALACIOS, the first Mexican governor of Texas, divided the colony into two judicial districts, one on the Colorado River and the other on the Brazos, with an alcalde to administer justice in each. Later Austin divided the Brazos district, creating a third, which was known as the San Felipe district. (BARKER, Readings in Texas History, 104-105)

Austin governed the colony and administered justice as nearly in conformity with established laws as he could determine. The organization of theAyuntamiento of San Felipe after the election of February 3-4, 1828, established constitutional local self-government for the first time in the colony. (BARKER, The Life of Stephen F. Austin, 210)

The ayuntamiento divided the colony into several precincts for the administration of justice, and appointed a comisario to serve in each. The duties of the comisario were similar in some respects to those performed by a justice of peace in the United States at that time. One of these precincts, known as the Precinct of Victoria, was established for the lower portion of the colony in 1829. (HENRY SMITH, "Reminiscences of Henry Smith," Southwestern Historical Quarterly, XIV, 30) ALEXANDER HODGE served as comisario for this precinct during 1829. (Marriage Records, Brazoria County Archives, Angleton, Texas) Other comisarios of the precinct were ASA BRIGHAM and HENRY SMITH. (Docket for the Precinct of Victoria, Brazoria County Archives. HENRY SMITH, "Reminiscences of Henry Smith," Southwestern Historical Quarterly IX, 30) This court continued to administer justice until an alcalde court was established in 1832.

Unstable political conditions in Mexico soon disturbed the even flow of life in the colony. ANASTACIO BUSTAMANTE, a "bigoted, unprincipled, military chieftain," and vice president of Mexico, supplanted the more liberal VICENTE GUERRERO in 1830. Once in power, BUSTAMANTE inaugurated sweeping changes, which were generally performed under the authority of the Law of April 6, 1830. (JOHN HENRY BROWN, History of Texas, I, 248-249) This law restricted further colonization from the United States except in two colonies, provided for the establishment of customhouses at several Texas towns to collect duties imposed on foreign imports, authorized the establishment of convict colonies in Texas, and forbade American colonists to settle within twenty leagues of the boundary of the United States or ten leagues of the coast. (BARKER, The Life of Stephen F. Austin, 296-326. Full text in JOHN and HENRY SAYLES, Early Laws of Texas, I, 55-56) In the fall of 1830 BUSTAMANTE dispatched military units to Texas to enforce the Law, establishing garrisons at Anahuac, Teran, Nacogdoches, Velasco, and other towns. Two of these garrisons were commanded by former Americans, Colonel PETER ELLIS BEAN at Teran and Colonel JOHN DAVIS BRADBURN at Anahuac. (BARKER, The Life of Stephen F. Austin, 327)

Serious trouble arose at Anahuac during the early part of June, 1832, between settlers from the vicinity of Liberty and Colonel BRADBURN. J. FRANCISCO MADERO had previously been sent to Liberty by the government to issue titles for lands. Soon after BRADBURN'S arrival at Anahuac, he determined to collect duties imposed under the Law of April 6, 1830, and arbitrarily canceled the titles issued by MADERO. BRADBURN arrested and imprisoned two popular leaders of the settlers, WILLIAM BARRETT TRAVIS and PATRICK G. JACK. This aroused the colonists to action, and they laid siege to Anahuac. As soon as the news spread through Texas, the more impetuous men of several communities rallied to the support of the colonists at Anahuac, but before these units arrived, Colonel JOSE DE LAS PIEDRAS, military commandant, came from Nacogdoches to deal with the colonists. PIEDRAS agreed to turn the prisoners over to civil authorities for trial, to pay for the property seized by BRADBURN, and to endeavor to obtain BRADBURN'S removal. (BARKER, The Life of Stephen F. Austin, 386-287)

This agreement was not made known in time to prevent trouble, and an armed clash between the Texans and the Mexican authorities occurred at Velasco, a few miles below Brazoria, on June 26-27, 1832, when the colonists attempted to move two cannon by way of the Brazos River to the aid of their countrymen besieging Anahuac. (G. P. GARRISON, Texas, 177) Colonel DOMINGO DE UGARTECHEA, commandant at Velasco, prevented the colonists from moving the cannon, and the aroused Texans attacked the Mexican garrison at Velasco, and captured the fort. During this encounter, known as the Battle of Velasco, seven Texans and thirty-two Mexicans were killed Three other Texans died from wounds. (HENRY SMITH, "Reminiscences of Henry Smith," Southwestern Historical Quarterly, XIV, 43)

During this unsettled period the Congress of Coahuila and Texas attempted to maintain local government for the lower portion of Austin's colony by creating the Municipality of Brazoria. (H. P. N. Gammel, Laws of Texas, I, 307) The town of Brazoria, which had been designated as the capital of the municipality, was an important commercial center about fifteen miles above the mouth of the Brazos. Mrs. MARY AUSTIN HOLLEY, writing from Bolivar, Texas, during December, 1831, thus de-scribed the town:

> Too much must not be expected of Brazoria. It is
> not located in a prairie, where nothing was to be done
> to prepare the foundation of the rising city, but to
> mark off its lines with compass and chain; but upon a
> wooded elevation of peachland, as it is called. This
> spot was chosen as the most commanding and healthful,
> besides combining other advantages.... One street
> streaches along the bank of the Brazos, and one parallel
> with it farther back, while other streets, with trees
> still standing, are laid out to intersect these at right
> angles, to be cleared at some future day, as the wants
> of the citizens may require.... A speedy settlement and
> a rapid growth in population and importance, are cal-
> culated upon with certainty. Nor will these calculations
> appear unreasonable, when we consider that it is but
> three years since the first tree was cut, and it now con-
> tains fifty families, many of which are of the first
> respectability. (MARY AUSTIN HOLLEY, Letters of an
> Early American Traveller, edited by MATTIE AUSTIN HATCHER, 117)

Historical Sketch of the Municipality of Brazoria

Under provisions of the decree of April 28, 1832, the Congress of Coahuila and Texas defined the boundaries of the municipality and designated the capital:

The Congress of the State of Coahuila and Texas, has thought proper to decree as follows:

Art. 1. In the Southern portion of the municipality of Austin a new municipality shall be formed, of which the town of Brazoria shall be the capital.

Art. 2 The limits of the said municipality shall be as follows: Commencing at the mouth of Clear Creek on Galveston Bay, following the principal branch of said creek to its source; thence southwesterly in a straight line to the confluence of Guajolote Creek and the river San Bernard; thence due southwest to the distance of five leagues west of the Colorado; thence to the source of Trespalacios Creek, decending said creek to its entrance into Matagorda Bay; thence following the beach upon the coast northward and eastward to the place of beginning.

Art. 3 The Executive shall accord the proper measures in order that the inhabitants of Brazoria at the approaching elections for new Ayuntamientos, may proceed to elect the Ayuntamiento established by law. (Gammel, Laws of Texas, I, 308)

Uncertain political conditions in Texas during the summer and fall of 1832 prevented the immediate execution of this decree. The Ayuntamiento of San Felipe de Austin was instructed to supervise an election of officers for the Municipality of Brazoria. Evidently the election was held sometime during the early part of 1833, at which the following officers were elected: HENRY SMITH, alcalde, R. R. ROYALL and WILLIAM H. WHARTON, regidores, and WILLIAM ECKEL, sindico procurador, or marshal. (Ayuntamiento of Brazoria to)place not given), May 13, 1933. Bexar Archives, University of Texas Library) Captain JOHN AUSTIN was selected to supervise the election and make the proper reports. Captain AUSTIN died during the severe cholera epidemic which followed the flood on the Brazos River in June, 1833, failing to make the reports before his death. (HENRY SMITH, Brazoria, to Ayuntamiento of Brazoria, first Monday of October, 1833. Bexar Archives)

MIGUEL ARCINIEGA, Political Chief of the Department of Bexar, questioned the legal status of the Ayuntamiento of Brazoria and asked for instructions when it became apparent that Captain AUSTIN'S reports were not among his private or public papers. (M. Arciniega, Bexar, to Srie. Del Despo. del S. G. de Estado, Monclova, August 26, 1833. Bexar Archives)

Historical Sketch of the Municipality of Brazoria

The difficulties which the municipality experienced during
its first year were summarized by HENRY SMITH in a letter to the
ayuntamiento:

At a regular meeting of the Ayuntamiento for the
District of Brazoria here at the Alcalde office on the
first monday of October 1833. Present HENRY SMITH Prest.
R. R. ROYALL 1st Rigidor WILLIAM H. WHARTON 2nd Regidor
WILLIAM ECKEL SYNDICO Procurador absent from indisposition
--The following official communication from the President
was read--

To the illustrious Ayuntamiento for the Jurisdiction
of Brazoria.

Gentlemen.

It is with feelings of the deepest regret I have to
inform you that every effort on the part of Your Illustrious
body to be put in Correspondence with the Political Chiefs
of this Department has proved abortive.--The year is now
growing to a close and the time for holding the Election
near at hand. It therefore becomes our duty as the re-
presentative of the people to prepare the way for our
successors, in order that the inconveniences and disadvantages under which WE have had to labor during the
present year be removed. I have recently learned the
reasons why we have not been put in official correspondence
with the Political Chief of this Department. A letter
under date of the 22nd Sepr. for the Alcalde of Austin
called on the Ayuntamiento of that Municipality to have
the returns of Election from this district sent up for
recognition, that the secretary of that body Mr. SAMUEL M.
WILLIAMS called on Capt. JOHN AUSTIN who was appointed by
the Ayuntamiento of Austin to hold the Election in this
Jurisdiction and make the returns to the proper Authoit-
ies, that Capt. AUSTIN informed him he could not that no
regular list had been kept, or if it had it was lost or
mislaid, since which time, Capt. AUSTIN has unfortunately
died (who was the only person authorised) and an examination of his Archives proves the fact that no list of the
Election had been kept, which renders it entirely out of
our power at this late period, under all the circumstances
to prevent similar evils and inconveniences the next year
without adopting some efficient means to procure from the
proper authorities an appointment of some proper and
suitable person to preside at the ensuing election who will
be authorised to make the proper returns.--The resolution
adopted and forwarded to the Chief of Department some time
during the past Spring, praying to be either recognised or
disolved as an unconstituted body, have been received from

that quarter--I would therefore recommend to your considera-
tion the propriety of calling on the Ayuntamiento of Austin
who are officially known as a body corporate to and as in
this procurement in order that the disadvantages and inconveniences encountered, and suffered by us this Year be
not entailed on our successors--And in as much as the time
will be too short, probably, to effect this object in time
to hold the election at the Constitutional time, I suggest
the propriety of requesting the Alcalde of Austin who is
officially known and recognised, to authorise and make such
appointment of a proper and suitable person here as he with
the consent of the Ayuntamiento may think proper to recommend to the proper authorities, to be appointed to preside
and make the corresponding return, and thereby render the
returns official--

    With sentiments of the highest regard and consideration
I remain Gentlemen

                                        Yr obst
                                        Henry Smith
                                        President
                                        (rubic)

(Henry Smith to Ayuntamiento of Brazoria, Brazoria, the
first Monday of October, 1833. Bexar Archives)

An editorial by JOHN WHARTON, published in The Advocate of
the People's Rights, Brazoria, February 22, 1834, summarized
the achievements of HENRY SMITH as alcalde of the Municipality
of Brazoria:

    I call attention to the subjoined extract from the
valedictory address of HENRY SMITH, Ex Alcalde. Are we so
illiberal, so devoid of principal, and justice as to per-
mit one man to bear the whole of the public burden. We
ought to recollect that HENRY SMITH was brought out for
office of Alcalde without his approbation or knowledge,
that the office was not a lucrative one, that he discharged
the duties with ability and fidelity.... Who is to pay the
expense that will attend the prosecution and trial of
Stone... I trust if no other cause will have effect, that
shame alone will impell the good people to pay their por-
tions of the public expense.. .

    It is a fact well known to all (said SMITH), that this
district has been recently organized, without revenue, or
the means to raise it, other than taxation, and that some
revenue must be required to defray the public expenses, all
will admit. This ayuntamiento has, from time to time, made
such levies as seem to them equitable...these levies all
reamin uncollected - the first dollar has not yet been
received.......

Historical Sketch of the Municipality of Brazoria

Officers elected for the Ayuntamiento of Brazoria on January 1, 1834, were EDWIN WALLER, alcalde; WILLIAM H. WHARTON and Captain HENRY S. BROWN, regidores; and PEYTON R. SPLANCE, sindico procurador. (JOHN HENRY BROWN, Life of Henry Smith, 23) These officers dispatched a communication to the Ayuntamiento of Goliad on January 2, 1834, urging that municipality to delay action intended to secure separate statehood for Texas, hoping that the provisions of the Law of April 6, 1830, would be repealed and no further oppression attempted. (EDWIN WALLER, WILLIAM H. WHARTON, HENRY S. BROWN, PEYTON R. SPLANE, and HENRY SMITH, Brazoria, to Ayuntamiento of Goliad, Goliad, January 2, 1834 Bexar Archives) The Ayuntamiento of Goliad received this communication and their actions on it were reported to the political chief at Bexar. (JOSE MIGUEL ALDRETE, JUAN JOSE HERNANDEZ, and others of Ayuntamiento of Goliad, April 12, 1834. Bexar Archives)

Events were transpiring which prevented officers of the Ayuntamiento of Brazoria from diligently performing their civic duties. STEPHEN F. AUSTIN was arrested and imprisoned at Saltillo, Coahuila, on January 3, 1834, by Mexican authorities. (BARKER, The Life of Stephen F. Austin, 436) When word of his arrest reached Texas, a wave of indignation swept the country, arousing the citizens to vigorous protest. The Brazoria protest was forwarded July 31, 1834, to the Mexican authorities at Saltillo. (Ibid., 447. See also BARKER, Austin Papers, II, 1069-1070)

The officers of the Ayuntamiento of Brazoria were so lax in the performance of official duties that HENRY SMITH, Political Chief of the Department of Brazos, published the following notice: "Finding the ayuntamiento of this jurisdiction disorganized and feeling unwilling that it should lose its political existence.... The citizens are hereby notified that an election will be held on the 8th day of November(1834). .." (The Texas Republican, Brazoria, November 1, 1834)

On April 25, 1834, the Congress of Coahuila and Texas decreed that the name of the municipality be changed and the capital be moved

Sec. 7. THE CAPITAL OF THE MUNICIPALITY OF BRAZORIA SHALL BE REMOVED from the town of the same name to that of Columbia, situated three or four leagues above more or less.

Sec. 8. BRAZORIA CHANGED TO COLUMBIA. - Hereafter said municipality shall be denominated Municipality of Columbia. (SAYLES, Early Laws of Texas, I, 105; see also Gammel, Laws of Texas, I, 385)

This change was not entirely satisfactory to all citizens of the municipality, as evidenced by a petition to the ayuntamiento; "Praying the removal of the seat of justice from Columbia to Brazoria was presented on Monday the 2nd inst.....(The citizens were requested) to meet at the various polling places on Sunday the 22nd, for deciding the matter." (The Texas Republican (date uncertain) Notice dated February 7, 1835) No further reference is made to this election, but the result must have favored Columbia because the primary court continued to meet there. (Docket of the Primary Court of the Jurisdiction of Columbia, Brazoria County Archives)

In June, 1835, trouble again arose at Anahuac, this time between Captain ANTONIO TENORIO and the colonists over the collection of tariff duties. Travis was placed in command of the colonists, who quickly overpowered the Mexican garrison and sent TENORIO with his men to Mexico. (BARKER, The Life of Stephen F. Austin, 474-475)

The colonists were reluctant to commit an act which might be construed by the Mexican authorities as treason or the flouting of established government. A meeting held on June 28, 1835, at Columbia, over which WARREN D. C. HALL presided and BYRD B. WALLER served as secretary, affirmed the established authority of the political chief of the department and urged the citizens to support the constitution of their adopted country. At this meeting a permanent committee of safety was appointed, consisting of WARREN D. C. HALL, JOHN A. WHARTON, WILLIAM H. JACK, JOHN G. McNOEL, and GEORGE B. McKINSTRY. (BROWN, History of Texas, I, 293-294)

Local leaders, realizing that whatever grievances the colonists might have against the Mexican government concerned all of Texas, at a meeting in Columbia on August 15, 1835, declared themselves in favor of a consultation of all Texas to consider plans of action to bring relief. (Ibid., I, 305)

Considering the gravity of the crisis facing Texas, the citizens of Columbia addressed the following communication to the Ayuntamiento of San Felipe:

TO THE CHAIRMAN OF THE MEETING IN SAN FELIPE ON THE 14th OF JULY, 1835.

The Ayuntamiento of Columbia (Brazoria) have thought proper to address you the communication, and to send you five confidential citizens (viz. JOHN A. WHARTON, STERLING McNEEL, JAMES F. PERRY, JOSIAH H. BELL and JAMES NIGHT) to represent this jurisdiction, and to confer with you touching the matters of public concern, which now agitate the country....

Asa Brigham, P. of A.
W. H. Sledge Sec'y.

(The Texas Republican, July 18, 1835)

Out of this conference developed the movement for a consultation for all Texas to be held at San Felipe.

Before the consultation met, STEPHEN F. AUSTIN returned to Texas. He delivered the "keynote" address at a meeting in Brazoria on September 8, 1836, urging that a convention of all Texas was necessary. After the arrival of the Mexican army under General MARTIN PERFECTO DE COS on September 21, 1835, the Texans began to prepare openly for revolution. (BARKER, The Life of Stephen F. Austin, 479-481)

Committees of public safety were formed throughout Texas, and the colonists organized their military forces for the impending clash with the Mexican dictator SANTA ANNA. Two skirmishes occurred before the consultation assembled, one at Gonzales on October 2, 1835, and the other at Goliad on October 8, (Ibid., 484-485)

The fever for revolution, always strong in Brazoria, reached a new high level as actual hostilities took place. Prompted by their hatred for General COS, the "Volunteers" of Brazoria published the following notice in The Texas Republican, October 10, 1835:

$5,000 will be paid to the individual who kills or takes prisoner General MARTIN PERFECTO DE COS, and $500 will be paid for the arrest and detention in close custody of JOHN A. WILLIAMS who by the most infamous lying and by the production of forged letters from SANTA ANNA and COS prevented 66 volunteers from joining their countrymen at Gonzales.

Brazoria, October 5th, 1835   V O L U N T E E R S

Twenty-one candidates presented themselves for election as delegates from the municipality to the proposed consultation at San Felipe. Returns were received from Velasco, Brazoria, Columbia, and Chocolate; WILLIAMS did not report. The election was held October 10, 1835, and the following were selected: WILLIAM H. WHARTON, 152 votes; HENRY SMITH, 181; BRANCH T. ARCHER, 199; WARREN D. C. HALL, 192; JOHN A. WHARTON, 179; JOHN S.D. BYROM, 238; EDWIN WALLER, 170. (The Texas Republican, October 10, 1835)

B.   Provisional Government of Texas, 1835-1836

The Consultation outlined and approved a provisional government on November 13, 1835, and elected HENRY SMITH of Brazoria Provisional Governor. A General Council was formed from the delegates to conduct the affairs of government. (BARKER, Readings in Texas History, 160-161)

Historical Sketch of the Municipality of Brazoria

The General Council changed the name of the municipality of Columbia back to Brazoria on November 12, 1835:

> On motion of Mr. WALLER; WHEREAS: the late Jurisdiction of Brazoria was changed in name to that of Columbia and the seat of Justice removed to the town of Columbia, by the congress of Coahuila and Texas. Contrary to the wishes, inclinations and interests of a large majority of the citizens of that jurisdiction; therefore,
>
> BE IT RESOLVED that the name of said Jurisdiction be changed and hereafter called and known by its former name and the seat of Justice established in the town of Brazoria. (Gammel, Laws of Texas, I, 535)

On January 22, 1836, the General Council, as the Provisional Government of Texas, approved a decree opening courts in municipalities. The terms of this act were substantially the same as those which had been in force under the laws of Mexico. (Ibid., 1039)

Prior to this decree the General Council had appointed L. C. MANSON first judge, and ROBERT MILLER second judge, for the Municipality of Brazoria on November 28, 1835. (Telegraph and Texas Register, San Felipe, January 16, 1836) These actions were contemplated to maintain the even flow of justice until a permanent form of local government could be established.

The Municipality of Brazoria sent EDWIN WALLER, ASA BRIGHAM, JAMES COLLINGSWORTH, and JOHN S. D. BYROM to the Convention which met at Washington-on-the-Brazos on March 1, 1836. (Gammel, Laws of Texas, I, 508) These men were among the signers of the Declaration of Independence, which was presented to and ratified by the delegates on the following day, March 2, 1836.

During the general flight (Runaway Scrape) which took place in April, 1836, local government collapsed and did not completely function again until after counties were formally organized in 1837.

Provisional President DAVID G. BURNET appointed BENJAMIN C. FRANKLIN District Judge, District of Brazos, on June 15, 1836, to preside over a special district court with admiralty jurisdiction. This court met at Velasco to try a prize, the Brig Pocket, captured by the Texans off Velasco. The court condemned the ship and turned it over to the proper authorities. (C.T. NEU, "The Case of the Brig Pocket," Southwestern Historical Quarterly, XII, 276-295)

Instruments filed in civil and probate cases in Brazoria County, issued by Judge FRANKLIN during 1836 and 1837, indicate

that his court assumed general administration of justice until
Brazoria County was formally organized on February 20, 1837.
(Probate Records, Brazoria County Archives)

2. Governmental Organization and Records System

A. Republic of Mexico, 1832-1835

No well-defined uniform system of local government was
developed by Spain for her American colonies during her three
centuries of New World domination. She dealt with each locality
as a distinct problem, vesting colonial authority in viceroyalties
and audiencias. After the revolution of 1821, the internal
affairs of Mexico were so unstable that for over a decade local
government received little attention from central or state
authorities. Under these chaotic conditions STEPHEN F. AUSTIN
introduced American colonists into the territory assigned under
his empresario contract finally approved April 14, 1823.

Returning from Mexico City, AUSTIN tried to determine the
full extent of his authority and the form of local government
which would be granted his colony. In August, 1821, just before
the fall of the Spanish regime, Governor MARTINEZ had instructed
him: "You will cause all the colonists to understand that until
the government organizes the authority which is to govern them
and administer justice, they must be governed by and be subordinate to you." (BARKER, Readings in Texas History, 103-104) In
June, 1823, General FELIPE DE LA GARZA, the Mexican commandant
of the Eastern Interior Provinces, instructed AUSTIN to keep a
complete record of all trials and verdicts in capital crimes,
referring the same to the superior government at Saltillo,
Coahuila, for final approval. While awaiting confirmation of
sentences, prisoners were to be worked at hard labor on public
roads. (Ibid., 104) AUSTIN governed the colony and administered
justice under these instructions, as nearly in conformity with
established laws as could be determined, until local self-government was created. (BARKER, The Life of Stephen F. Austin, 98)

With the organization of the Ayuntamiento of San Felipe
de Austin by the elction of February 3-4, 1828, constitutional
local self-government was established for the first time in the
colony. (Ibid., 210) All of AUSTIN'S Colony was governed by
this ayuntamiento until the creation of the Municipality of
Brazoria on April 28, 1832, by the Congress of Coahuila and
Texas under Decree No. 196, Art. 3:

The executive shall accord the proper measures in
order that the inhabitants of Brazoria, at the approaching
elections for new ayuntamientos, may proceed to elect the
Ayuntamiento established by this law. (Gammel, Laws of
Texas, I, 418)

Governmental Organization and Records System

The ayuntamiento, long a part of the Spanish colonial system, was the administrative agency of local self-government. Elective officers were an alcalde, two or more regidores, and a sindico procurador. (Ibid., 145)

Dr. EUGENE C. BARKER in his study on the government of the colony explains:

> The duties of the ayuntamiento covered a wide range, including most of the functions of a modern city commission and some of those belonging to the county commissioners--to promote the establishment of hospitals, poor houses and educational and charitable institutions, and to administer them when established; to license qualified and properly certified physicians and druggists and prevent others from practicing; to appoint boards of health, inspect foods, markets, and drug stores, keep the streets clean, visit prisons, drain lakes and stagnant ponds, and wage continual war on every menace to the health of man and beast; to see that streets were straight and ornamented with shade trees, and wherever possible, paved and lighted; maintain roads and public buildings; preserve the forests; punish vagabonds, drunkards, idlers, and gamblers; promote agriculture, industry, and commerce; administer municipal funds, which, with the consent of the Governor and Legislature, might be raised by taxation; establish and supervise primary schools; and take the census every six months--these were the more important duties of the ayuntamiento. (BARKER, "The Government of Austin's Colony, 1821-1831", Southwestern Historical Quarterly, XXI, 23)

Ayuntamientos were required to file annually a report with the political chief (jefe politico) of the department, setting forth the condition of the community during their administration. (Gammel, Laws of Texas, I, 74) All estrayed stock was to be reported to the ayuntamiento, which should determine the owner and return it if possible; if not, dispose of it in the manner prescribed by law. (Ibid., I, 418) The Mexican Congress could require the ayuntamiento to collect taxes, organize and equip militia companies, and care for indigent free negro children. (Ibid., I. 169; see also BARKER, "Minutes of the Ayuntamiento of San Felipe de Austin," Southwestern Historical Quarterly, XXI, 299, 301)

The Ayuntamiento of Brazoria apparently did not function efficiently, as HENRY SMITH, political chief of the Department of Brazos, issued an order: "Finding the ayuntamiento of this jurisdiction disorganized and feeling unwilling that it should lose its political existence... The citizens are hereby notified that an election will be held on the 8th day of November (1834)...." (The Texas Republican, Brazoria, November 1, 1834) A few of the proceedings of the ayuntamiento have been discovered, consisting

mainly of broadsides issued either to protest the acts of the
Mexican Government or to call special meetings. (BARKER, Austin
Papers, II, 1069-1070)

For the administration of justice, Austin's Colony was divided
into precincts, over each of which a magistrate, who was called
variously comisario, alcalde, or primary judge, presided. HENRY
SMITH, while alcalde, said: "To make these terms a little more
intelligible, suffice it to say the Alcalde is a judicial officer
possessing great power, and is president of the Ayuntamiento when
in session--the whole body may be compared to the Mayor and
Aldermen of a city ..." (HENRY SMITH, "Reminiscences of Henry
Smith," Southwestern Historical Quarterly, XIV, 30) An alcalde
in the capital of a municipality combined the duties of president
of the ayuntamiento and magistrate of the alcalde court.

Alcaldes, as magistrates, were required to keep dockets and
registers of official acts, receive written petitions before
suits could be brought, issue proper summons, render judgements,
issue executions and require proper returns thereon. They had
original and final jurisdiction over cases involving amounts
less than ten dollars; with or without the assistance of arbitrators,
over amounts between ten and twenty-five dollars; and with
arbitrators over amounts exceeding twenty-five dollars. (D.W.C.
BAKER, A Texas Scrap-Book, 175)

Entries in the dockets, which contain summaries of court
proceedings, and the case papers indicate that jurisdiction of
these courts increased until they assumed original jurisdiction
over cases involving much larger amounts, In the case of CHARLOTTE
ROBERTSON, alias JACKSON, vs. ASA BRIGHAM and WILLIAM T. AUSTIN,
administrators for EDWARD ROBERTSON, March 12, 1834, the amount
involved was $2,300. (Docket, Jurisdiction of Brazoria, Case No.
120, 121, Brazoria County Archives) A judgement for $2,524.10
was confessed by WILLIAM T. AUSTIN on March 18, 1834. (E.W. GREGORY
vs. WILLIAM T. AUSTIN, Ibid., Case No. 94) Other cases involved
amounts ranging from a few dollars to several hundred.

The alcalde court also assumed probate jurisdiction over the
property of deceased persons, appointing appraisers and administrators and approving letters of administration. (Probate Records,
Brazoria County Archives)

The usual procedure in civil cases was to issue a notice to
both parties to effect, if possible, amicable settlement, or in
modern phraseology, "settle out of court." If the parties failed
to reach an agreement, the case was tried by the court before the
alcalde, alone or with arbitrators. Neither the plaintiff nor
the defendant was required to be present, but each had to be
represented by counsel or a responsible party. (Docket, Jurisdiction of Brazoria, Case No. 163, Brazoria County Archives)

Procedure was altered to fit unusual occasions, sometimes conforming with that of courts of the former residence of the alcalde EDWIN WALLER abrogated the procedure of the court in March, 1834, establishing the customs and practice of Louisiana:

At the March term of the Alcaldes Court for the Jurisdiction of Brazoria--The following order was entered by the court after consultation of all the causes at the bars: It was ordered that the old order of this Court be abrogated (X) and that the code of practice for the State of Louisiana be adopted as the rules of this Court so far as they are applicable and in conformity with the existing laws of this State And it was ordered that the same be adopted and conformed to as the rules of this Court from this time forward I certify the above

Edwin Waller
Alcalde
(Ibid., Case No. 122)

Upon the announcement of a judgement, an execution was granted, which was served by the executive officer of the court, who made a proper return thereon. Executions read surprisingly like those issued by modern court, and the officer's return was similar to present-day instruments. The court issued the usual executions, mandates, judgements, certificates, notices (citations), capiases, subpoenas, and other necessary court papers. Dockets of the court were similar to those of modern justices of peace, containing the names of the parties, number of the case, recapitulation of fees, names of attorneys, a brief statement of proceedings, and orders of the court.

A criminal code for Austin's Colony, approved May 24, 1824, dealt mainly with offenses committed by Indians, or by or against slaves; and provided for the return of fugitive slaves. Other provisions included penalties to be assessed against offenders committing crimes within the colony--murder, theft, gambling, profane swearing, drunkenness, cohabitation without marriage, counterfeiting or passing counterfeit money. Horse racing was excepted from the provision against gambling, because it was "calculated to improve the breed of horses." (BARKER, "The Government of Austin's Colony, 1821-1831, "Southwestern Historical Quarterly, XXI, 6)

Theft was punished by sentences to hard labor on public works. For amounts less than ten dollars the sentence was from one to three months; from ten to one hundred dollars, from one to two years. A culprit guilty of three offenses was first exhibited in a public place with a board on his head bearing the words "for theft." (Gammel, Laws of Texas, I, 166)

Governmental Organization and Records System

Alcalde HENRY SMITH summarized the fifficulties of a magistrate:

> Our laws respecting criminal proceedings were very
> defective and like most of the Mexican laws everything
> was sacrificed to forms... I had the right to arrest and
> if found necessary hold the prisoner in custody, but could
> not try and inflict punishment. By the law it was my
> province to take the testimony in the case and transmit it
> 800 miles to the seat of government to be investigated and
> tried by the Supreme Court.... This was not only in Crim-
> inal, but in Civil suits when taken up by appeal. (HENRY
> SMITH, "Reminiscences of Henry Smith," Southwestern
> Historical Quarterly, XIV, 32)

Only three criminal cases were discovered among the records surveyed: One for theft, State of Coahuila y Texas vs. CHEPHAS (Docket for the Precinct of Victoria, Municipality of Austin, 58, 68); one for trespass and assault, McGEE vs. DANIEL MILLICAN, September 23, 1835 (Alcalde Court Papers, Brazoria County Archives); and one in which the crime (presumably murder) was not named, People of the Jurisdiction of Brazoria vs. RUBEN P. T. STONE (Docket, Jurisdiction of Brazoria, Case No. 80, Brazoria County Archives) In the case against CHEPHAS, a free negro, the defendant's services were sold to repay his accuser for money stolen. In McGEE vs. MILLICAN, civil damages were recovered by the plaintiff. STONE was tried before a jury of twelve men selected from a jury panel of 48 freeholders, who sentenced him to receive 39 lashes to be applied to his bare back, to be branded with an M in his bare hand, and required him to leave the colony within ten days or be considered an outlaw. In these cases procedure was similar to that of a modern justice court, requiring that some informant come forward and make a statement; a brief examining trial was then held, which was followed by a formal jury trial if the evidence warranted it.

Capital crimes could be tried by the alcalde court but final sentence had to be approved by the superior court of the State of Coahuila and Texas, at Monclova, Mexico. The alcalde was required to send a transcript of the case to the superior court for final disposition. (BARKER, The Life of Stephen F. Austin, 87)

Under Decree No. 277, April 17, 1834, the Congress of Coahuila and Texas established "A plan for the better regulation of the Administration of Justice in Texas." A judicial circuit designated as "The Superior Judicial Court of Texas" established a superior court in each of the three political departments, Bexar, Brazos, and Nacogdoches. (Gammel, Laws of Texas, I, 364) THOMAS J. CHAMBERS was appointed superior judge for the Department of Brazos, and although he received thirty leagues (132,849 acres) of land for a year's salary, he never held a session of the court. DAVID G. BURNET was appointed late in 1834 and held several sessions. (JOHN HENRY BROWN, History of Texas, I, 262)

Under the provisions of this decree primary courts were established in each municipal capital, and a comisario who presided in each of the jurisdictions. (Gammel, Laws of Texas, I, 364) These courts were comparable to modern county courts-at-law and justice courts. They functioned until the Provisional Government of Texas was established October 16, 1835.

Dr. BARKER explains:

> The duties of the regidores and of the sindico procurador are nowhere clearly defined, the various Spanish and Mexican laws concerning the ayuntamiento assuming, apparently, that their functions were too well known to require statement. In general, the regidores may be compared with aldermen or city commissioners. They served on committees and looked after various branches of municipal administration, and in the absence of the alcalde the first regidor (ranked according to the number of votes received at election) acted in his place. The sindico seems to have been a sort of combination notary and city attorney. In addition to these officers, the alcalde appointed a sheriff, and the ayuntamiento chose a secretary, an official of more than usual importance because he had to serve as interpreter and translator in all relations with the superior authorities. (BARKER, The Life of Stephen F. Austin, 211)

AUSTIN assisted in securing the passage of a law establishing a state religion: "the Government of the Mexican Nation will protect the liberty, property, and civil rights of all foreigners who profess to the Roman Apostolic Religion, the established religion of the empire." (Gammel, I, 28; see also WILLIAM STUART RED, The Texas Colonists and Religion, 24-26) To be legal a marriage ceremony had to be performed by a priest of good standing. The colonists entered into a form of civil marriage through contracts, agreeing to present themselves to the first legal priest visiting the colony. These contracts were simple pledges, accompanied by bonds of sufficient amounts, that the parties thereto would comply with the laws of the state. (Marriage Records, Brazoria County Archives) They were usually subscribed to before the alcalde, but occasionally only witnesses attested the marriage contract.

Other provisions of the general laws enforced in the colony required posting notice of all strayed stock picked up and impounded, and registration of stock brands. (BARKER, "The Government of Austin's Colony, 1821-1831," Southwestern Historical Quarterly, XXI, 223-252) Unfortunately, none of these records were found for the Municipality of Brazoria.

Mexican authorities required AUSTIN to keep a register of all deeds, grants, and other instruments at the capital of the colony, San Felipe de Austin. On the first page was to be written, "Register of the documents and titles, issued in the first enterprise of colonization of the empresario, citizen STEPHEN F. AUSTIN, in Texas." At the close of each entry was to be written, "The foregoing instrument of writing, is literally copied from its original, which is on file in the archives of this colony; date and signature of the (land) commissioners, empresario, and alcalde, with assistant witnesses." (Gammel, Laws of Texas, I, 37) From the instruments in this register the settlers were later able to obtain copies of their deeds and grants to comply with an act of the Congress of the Republic of Texas validating land titles. The copies of deeds recorded in Record of Spanish Deeds, Brazoria County Archives, were made from instruments recorded in this register. Law required that all instruments be written on officially stamped paper, but the citizens of Austin's Colony were exempted from these provisions for ten years; so the majority of the records in the colonial archives of Brazoria do not bear this stamp. (Gammel, Laws of Texas, I, 207) Court papers follow the same general legal form of documents of present-day courts, and were usually properly acknowledged. A number of them were printed forms but the majority were handwritten.

B. Provisional Government of Texas, 1835-1836

With the establishment of the Provisional Government by the General Council, which grew out of the Consultation held at San Felipe on October 16, 1835, the Municipality of Columbia (Brazoria) was recognized. (Ibid., I, 508)

During the period which followed, local governments concerned themselves principally with raising and equipping troops for the Texas army in the conflict with Mexico, neglecting or paying only scant attention to their civic responsibilities.

The General Council passed a decree on January 22, 1836, creating courts of justice for the several municipalities. The decree stipulated that a term of court should be held once in each three months' period, the first judge of each municipality holding probate court on the first Monday of each month at the courthouse or the clerk's office. (Ibid., I, 1039) A notice published in The Texas Republican, Brazoria, March 2, 1836, indicates that probate court was held in the Municipality of Brazoria under the Provisional Government:

Primary court Jurisdiction of Brazoria

Housing, Care, and Accessibility of the Records

Whereas JOHN CHAFFIN has this day filed a petition in my office praying letters of Administration may be issued authorizing him to settle the estate of P. W. GORDON, late of the town of Columbia in said Jurisdiction.

All persons are hereby notified that unless objects are filed in my office within ten days the prayer of the petitioner will be granted upon his complying with the terms of the law.

> At office this 23rd Feb. 1836
> L. C. Manson
> Primary Judge

Two other petitions to settle estates were published at the same time. A careful study of the probate records in the Brazoria County Archives indicates that this probate court functioned until a special district court was established for the District of Brazos on June 15, 1836.

The Provisional Government established a district court for the Department of Brazos on March 12, 1836, with admiralty jurisdiction to try a prize, the Brig Pocket, but this court did not function because JAMES COLLINGSWORTH, who was appointed judge, declined to serve. DAVID G. BURNET, Provisional President of Texas, on June 15, 1836, appointed Judge BENJAMIN C. FRANKLIN to preside over this court, which condemned the brig and turned it over to the proper authorities. (C. T. NEU, "The Case of the Brig Pocket," Southwestern Historical Quarterly, XII, 276, 295)

In addition to performing this duty, Judge FRANKLIN held sessions of the court to deal with probate and civil cases. (District Court Records, Brazoria County Archives) Papers filed in a number of probate and civil cases indicate that this court functioned until Brazoria County was formally organized February 20, 1837, when the county and district courts assumed jurisdiction over cases within the county. An act of the Congress of the Republic of Texas on December 29, 1837, declared that judgments rendered by the alcalde and primary courts were valid, and ordered the new courts to continue cases initiated before the revolution. (Gammel, Laws of Texas, I, 1462)

3. Housing, Care, and Accessibility of the Records

Public records of the Municipality of Brazoria were taken over by Brazoria County when it was organized on February 20, 1837. These early documents formed the basis of the county records system, and offices established by the formation of county government assumed custody of the records of the municipality.

Many unbound instruments were filed haphazardly, without

logical arrangement or order. During the hundred years elapsing since the possession of these papers passed to the county, some were naturally misplaced or lost in the regular order of business; some during the removal of the county seat from Brazoria to Angleton on October 28, 1896; and others during the severe Gulf storm of 1932, which shattered the windows of the courthouse, blowing many loose sheets from the building.

Three dockets: Docket, Jurisdiction of Brazoria; File Docket; and A General Docket of All the Suits Instituted Before the Primary Court of the Jurisdiction of Columbia, 1835, are wrapped with heavy brown paper and marked Dockets, Municipality of Brazoria, 1834-1835. The Docket, Jurisdiction of Brazoria should be re-bound as the cover is badly torn and broken. The other volumes are in better condition. These dockets are deposited in a steel wall-cabinet along the north side of the county clerk's record room

Marriage records are filed with later licenses in a file box marked Old Marriage Bonds and Marriage Licenses. Miscellaneous papers of the alcalde courts are in a box marked Old Papers, No. 1. Two executions from the alcalde court are with current instruments in a box marked Executions Issued and Returned.

Probate papers are filed numerically by case numbers in six rows of file boxes in the record room of the county clerk's office. Each case is filed in a separate container bearing the number of the case. Case numbers may be secured by consulting the Index to Probate Cases (1832-1937), which is arranged numerically by case number, or by consulting the Index to Probate Cases (1832-1844), which is arranged alphabetically by the surname of the deceased person. Four other probate cases, those of Dr. JAMES GRANT, DAVID S. WALTMAN, JOHN McCROSKEY, and JOHN FADDIN, are filed in the container marked Old Papers, No. 1.

The file box marked Old Papers, No. 1 is in the county clerk's office in the upper tier of the row of file boxes, sixth from the right, in the center of the room; and one box, Executions Issued and Returned, is in the fifth tier from the bottom, eleventh box from the left end. It is necessary to use either a ladder or a chair to reach these boxes. The file box marked Old Marriage Bonds and Marriage Licenses is the first from the left, in the lower tier of boxes on the north wall, immediately below the boxes containing probate papers.

In the district clerk's office one file box marked Old Alcalde has two manila containers of records of the municipality. One is marked Alcalde Court Papers, and the other Exhibits, in 15491, CONLEY vs. ABRAMS. One docket, Docket for the Precinct of Victoria, Municipality of Austin, is filed with other dockets in the north counter-shelves in this office. The File Docket, Jurisdiction of

<u>Columbia</u>, comprises the last fifty-three pages of <u>Execution Docket</u>, Vol B, which is deposited with other execution dockets of the district court in this office.

Records of civil cases which originated either in the alcalde or primary courts or had their cause based on actions prior to February 20, 1837, are recorded in the first volume of a set of books titled <u>Final Record</u> in the district clerk's office. This volume is deposited in the upper tier, first row, in the set of counter-shelves. Civil cases are filed with other cases in file boxes along the east wall. The unbound records should be segregated and arranged in chronological order within respective titles, and filed in separate containers marked with titles. The dockets should be cleaned and re-bound to insure their preservation. The papers and dockets should be brushed with a soft camel's hair brush to remove dust, and brushed lightly with oil of cloves to guard against destruction by vermin. A few of the very badly torn records should be patched with transparent tape or glue. Some of the writing could be restored to its original clearness if treated by the proper method under the supervision of an expert versed in the use of restorative chemicals. By judicious care and treatment these instruments could be preserved indefinitely.

Besides the obvious value of these records to the historian of Colonial Texas, many of them are still used in court proceedings. In 1923, for example, the case of CONLEY vs. ABRAMS, No. 15491, required the use of many papers and transcripts from the dockets of these early courts.

4. List of Abbreviations and Symbols

adm.	administrator
adms.	administrators
agt.	agent
alph.	alphabetical, alphabetically
arr.	arranged
Art.	article
C.C.	county clerk
chron.	chronological, chronologically
D.C.	district clerk
exr.	executor
<u>Ibid</u>.	See nearest preceding reference.
no.	number
nos.	numbers
p.	page
pp.	pages
Sec.	section
vol.	volume
vols.	volumes
vs.	versus

List of Abbreviations and Symbols

x   by
--   to date

(   )   Titles of entries enclosed in parentheses are
                           supplied editorially when the title found was
                           inadequate.

Entry   Records are numbered throughout this Inventory
Numbers: in one series (1-13). Reference is made to an
                           entry by title and number: Record of Spanish
                           Deeds, 1.

Dates: First and last year dates covered by a
                           particular title are shown in the title-line
                           of its entry.

Condition: If no notation is made concerning the condition
                           of a record, it may be assumed to be excellent
                           or good.

Size: Size of containers is given in inches:
                           10 x 4½ x 2.

Legibility: The handwriting on early documents is not
                           always easily decipherable. The letters I
                           and J, S and T, D and O are often confusing.
                           Failure to dot the i makes it hard to dis-
                           tinguish from the e. The cramped style of
                           some writers makes it difficult to distinguish
                           the n and m, ii and ll, oo, and d.

Spelling of   Throughout the book names are shown as found on
Names: the documents, and as read. In the general
                           index variations appear in alphabetical
                           arrangement. Wherever possible full names and
                           initials have been secured and appear in the
                           general index

I. LAND RECORDS

1. RECORD OF SPANISH DEEDS, 1823-36. 1 vol.
Copies of land grants and deeds granted by Mexico to colonists, or transferred by the colonists among themselves, for land within the present boundaries of Brazoria County. Each instrument shows the name of grantor, name of grantee, date of instrument, amount of land involved, location and description of property, date of transfer, date of recording, and signature of county clerk. The instrument is written in Spanish; the acknowledgment by the county clerk is in English. Validity of title was established by the Constitution of 1836, and laws passed by the First Congress of the Republic of Texas, which required the recording of all deeds and grants by parties occupying land. Arr. chron. by date of recording. Alph. index (in English) by name of grantor. Handwritten. 500 pp. 18 x 12 x 2. C.C., office.

2. TRANSCRIBED SPANISH RECORDS, 1823-36. 1 vol
English translation of copies of land grants and deeds recorded in Record of Spanish Deeds, 1. The translation was made by F. TOUCHON, Houston, Texas, Spanish translator, and acknowledged by G.W. GALES, county clerk, Brazoria County, on September 1, 1893. Arr. chron. by date of recording, with deed nos. identical to those of the original instruments. Alph. index by name of grantor. Handwritten. 500 pp. 18 x 12 x 2. C.C., office.

The following direct alphabetical index by name of grantor, to deed number in Record of Spanish Deeds, 1, and Transcribed Spanish Records, 2, has been copied from the original index in the volumes.

(Grantor to Grantee)

ALSBURY, Hansen and H.A. to
  C.G. ALSBURY   424
ALSBURY, Horatio A. to
  S. KERETT   417, 421
ALSBURY, H.A. and H. to
  C.G. ALSBURY   424
AUSTIN, Elizabeth E. and W.T.
  to E.M.B. and H.L.B. ANDREWS 35
AUSTIN, E.E. and W.T. to E.
  JEFFERY   55
AUSTIN, Henry to E. ANDREWS,
  S. McNEEL, and C.D. SAYRE   1
AUSTIN, John to E. ANDREWS   38
AUSTIN, John to Wm. ECKEL   76
AUSTIN, John to E. JEFFERY and
  J.S.D. BYROM   128
AUSTIN, John to C.D.
  SAYRE   38, 44, 46
AUSTIN, John to T. YOUNG   51
AUSTIN, John and S.F. to
  C.D. SAYRE   48

AUSTIN, S.F. to heirs of
  J.H. and G.A. HAWKINS   57
AUSTIN, S.F. to James F.
  PERRY   168, 171
AUSTIN, S.F. to C.D.
  SAYRE   114
AUSTIN, S.F. and John to
  C.D. SAYRE   48
AUSTIN, W.T. and E.E. to
  E.M.B. and H.L.B.
  ANDREWS   35
AUSTIN, W.T. and E.E. to
  E. JEFFERY   55
BAILEY, J.B. to C.D.
  SAYRE   26, 29
BAILEY, J.B. by Henry
  SMITH, exr., to
  James WARE   204
BAIRD, James to G.B.
  McKINSTRY and J. AUSTIN 23

Lane Records

(Grantor to Grantee)

Lane Records

(Grantor to Grantee)

Mexican Government to
  William PRATER   158
Mexican Government to
  C.C. SMITH   83
Mexican Government to
  D. TALLEY   384
Mexican Government to
  George TENNEL   111
ORGAN, W. to J.H. POLLEY   132
PARKER, W. by T.W. DUKE,
  curator, to E. ANDREWS
  and C.D. SAYRE   52
PARKER, W. by T.W. DUKE,
  curator, to S.F.
  AUSTIN   122, 125
PARKER, W. by T.W. DUKE,
  curator, to John
  MILLICAN   200
PEYTON, J. C. to C.D. SAYRE   68
POLLEY, J.H. to S. CHANCE   130

RICHARDSON, Stephen to
  David H. MILBURN   262, 268
ROBERTS, William to
  Andrew ROBERTS   332
ROBERTS, W. to C. SMITH   88
ROBINSON, F. to E. CAPLE
  and O. PITTS   116
ROBINSON, F. to E. CAPLE   238
ROBINSON G. to James
  KNIGHT   290
SELKIRK, Wm. to S.F.
  AUSTIN   224
SMITH, C. to J. JONES   104
SMITH, C. to J.C. PEYTON   73
SMITH, Henry, exr. for J.B.
  BAILEY, to James WARE   204
WHITE, W.C. to S.F. AUSTIN   241
WILLIAMS, John S. to
  Oliver JONES   145

    The following reverse alphabetical index, by name of grantee,
to deed number in Record of Spanish Deeds, 1, and Transcribed
Spanish Records, 2, has been prepared by the Historical Records Survey.

(Grantee from Grantor)

ALSBURY, C.G. from H.A. and
  H. ALSBURY   424
ANDREWS, E., S. McNEEL, and
  C.D. SAYRE from Henry
  AUSTIN   1
ANDREWS, E. from John AUSTIN   38
ANDREWS, E., and C.D. SAYRE from
  W. PARKER by T.W. DUKE,
  curator   52
ANDREWS, E.M.B. and H.L.B. from
  W.T. and E.E. AUSTIN   35
ANDREWS, H.L.B. and E.M.B. from
  W.T. and E.E. AUSTIN   35
ANGIER, HALL, and BRADLEY from
  Mexican Government   275
ANGIER, S.F. from Mexican
  Government   278
AUSTIN, Emily M., and James
  F. PERRY from Mexican
  Government   162, 181
AUSTIN, Henry from
  William HARRIS   11
AUSTIN, Henry from Mexican
  Government   5, 7, 101, 228

AUSTIN, J., and G.B.
  McKINSTRY from James
  BAIRD   23
AUSTIN, S.F. from T.W. DUKE,
  curatory of W. PARKER
                            122, 125
AUSTIN, S.F. from
  Edward DICKINSON   217
AUSTIN, S.F. from Mexican
  Government   173, 245
AUSTIN, S.F. from Wm.
  SELKIRK   224
AUSTIN, S.F. from W.C.
  WHITE   241
BATTLE, M., M. BERRY, and
  J. WILLIAMS from Mexican
  Government   78
BELL, Josiah H. from
  Mexican Government   220
BERRY, M., M. BATTLE, and
  J. WILLIAMS from
  Mexican Government   78
BIGGAM, Francis from
  A. McFARLAN   143

24

Land Records

(Grantee from Grantor)

Lane Records

(Grantee from Grantor)

ROBERTS, Andrew from William ROBERTS	332	TENNEL, George from Mexican Government	111
SAYRE, C.D. from John AUSTIN	38, 44, 46	WALKER, JOHNSON, and BORDEN from Mexican Government	210
SAYRE, C.D. from S.F. AUSTIN	114	WARE, James from Henry SMITH, exr. of J.B. BAILEY	204
SAYRE, C.D. from S.F. and John AUSTIN	48	WILLIAMS, D.H. from CLARK and FOWLER, curators of Samuel CARTER	266
SAYRE, C.D. from J.B. BAILEY	26, 29		
SAYRE, C.D., E. ANDREWS, and S. McNEEL from Henry AUSTIN	1	WILLIAMS, J., M. BATTLE, and M. BERRY from Mexican Government	78
SAYRE, C.D., and E. ANDREWS from W. PARKER by T.W. DUKE, curator	52	WILLIAMS, John from John McCLOSKEY	215
SAYRE, C.D. from J.C. PEYTON	68	WHITE, W.C. from H. CURTIS, curator of J.F. LONG	406
SHELBY, David from S. MARSH	207		
SMITH, C. from W. ROBERTS	88	WHITE, W.C. from S.E. GROCE	241
SMITH, C.C. from Mexican Government	83	YOUNG, T. from J. AUSTIN	51
TALLEY, D. from Mexican Government	384		

II.   MARRIAGE RECORDS

3.   MARRIAGE RECORDS, 1829-36.   29 papers.
Original marriage bonds and contracts executed between parties under laws of Mexico permitting civil agreements until legal ceremonies could be performed.   Shows date of contract, name of man, name of woman, conditions of contract, amount of agreement, signatures of principals, signatures of witnesses.   The full texts of three contracts are given as examples.   Arr. chron. by date of instrument.   No index.   Index prepared by Historical Records Survey follows entries.   Filed in file box marked Old Marriage Bonds and Marriage Licenses.   C.C., office.

1829

No. 1.   Andrew ROBINSON and Mary G. ALLEN, Austin's Colony, Precinct of Victoria, March 17, 1829.   Marriage agreement.   Full text:

> Be it known that we, Andrew ROBINSON and Mary G. ALLEN, of lawful age of Austin Colony, wishing to unite ourselves in the bonds of matrimony and there being no Priest in the Colony to celebrate the same.   Therefore, I. Andrew ROBINSON, do agree to take and do hereby take Mary G. ALLEN to be my legal and lawful wife and as such to cherish, support and protect her, forsaking all others and keeping myself true and faithful unto ──── her alone.   And, I, Mary G. ALLEN, do agree and do hereby take

Marriage Records

Andrew ROBINSON to be my legal and lawful husband and as such to love, honor and obey him, forsaking all others and keeping myself true and faithful to him alone. We mutally bind ourselves to each other in the sum of five thousand dollars to have our marriage celebrated by the Priest of this Colony or some other priest authorized to do the same whenever an opportunity offers, all of which we promise in the name of God and in the presence of Alexander HODGE, Commissioner for the precinct of Victoria in said Colony and other witnesses present whereof we have hereunto set our hands this 17th day of March, 1829.

Witnesses

W. M. Ross
James Lynch

Andrew Robinson

                                                her
                              Mary   X   G. Allen
                                               mark

No. 2. Samuel HINCH and Leah Ann ALSBURY, Jurisdiction of Austin, April 21, 1829. Marriage contract.

No. 3. William E. ALCONR and Sarah KIGANS, Austin's Colony, Precinct of Victoria, July 2, 1829. Marriage contract.

No. 4. William BARRETT and Elizabeth WIENT, Austin's Colony on Brazos River, July 8, 1829. Marriage contract. Full text:

Be it known that we Will BARRETT and Elizabeth WIENT of lawful age of Austin Colony and State of Cuahula and Texas wishing to unite ourselves in the bonds of matrimony and there being no Priest in the Colony to Celebrat the same--Therefore I William BARRETT do agree to take and do hereby take Elizabeth WIENT to be my legal and lawful wife and as such to cherish support and protect her forsaking all others and keeping myself true and faithful unto her alone. And I Elizabeth WIENT do agree to take and Do hereby take William BARRET to be my leagal and Lawful husband and as such to love Honor and obey him forsaking all others keeping myself true and faithful unto him alone, and we also mutually bind ourselves to each other in the sum of five Thousand Dollars to have our marriage Celebrated by the Priest of this Colony or some other Priest Authorized so to do so soon as an opportunity offer, all of which we do promise in the name of God and in the presence of Alex-HODGE Commissario and the other witnesses Present in Testimony whereof we have hereunto set our hands on the River Brazzos this Eight Day of Jeuly in the year of our Lord 1829.

Margaret Canday
A. Hodge

William Barret

                                          her
                        Elizabeth   X   Wiant (sic)
                                         mark

1830

No. 5. James HODGE and Zulema KYRKENDALL, no place given, March 18, 1830. Marriage contract.

No. 6. Lima BARKER and Elizabeth STANDEFORD, Austin's Colony, Precinct of Victoria, November 4, 1830. Marriage agreement.

1831

No. 7. Henry F. NICHOLS and Leah BARCLAY, Austin's Colony, Precinct of Victoria, January 20, 1831. Marriage agreement.

1832

No. 8. Horace STRATTON and Ann R. JACOB, Tuscaloosa, Greene County, Alabama, month and day not given. Marriage agreement and settlement protecting the property of Ann R. JACOB.

1833

No. 9. Elisha MAXEY and Sally M. BOWLS, Department of Bexar, Jurisdiction of Brazoria, May 3, 1833. Marriage contract. Full text:

State of Coahula & Texas
Department of Bexar
Jurisdiction of Brazoria

To whomsoever these presents shall come be it known That we Elisha

MAXY and Sally M. BOWLS of lawful age of the above jurisdiction in Austin Colony, wishing to unite ourselves in the bonds of matrimony and there being no authority here competent to consumate the same--Therefor I Elisha MAXY do agree and by these presents do take Sally BOWLES to be my legal and lawful wife, and as such to love cherish support and protect, forsaking all other keeping myself true and faithful unto her alone--and I Sally M. BOWLES do agree and by these presents do take Elisha MAXY to be my legal and lawful husband such to love honor and obey forsaking all others keeping myself true and faithful unto him alone--And we do hereby mutually agree and bind ourselves to each other in the sum of five thousand dollars to have our marriage consumated by competent authority so soon as an opportunity offers-- All of which we solemnly in the name of God-- In the presence of Henry SMITH alcalde for the foregoing jurisdiction and undersigned witness--In testimony whereof we have hereunto set our hands in the above jurisdiction this third day of May in the year of our Lord eighteen hundred and thirty three.

S. Bowen   Henry Smith   Elisha Maxey
William R. Sandes   Alcalde   Sally M. Bowls

No. 10. Greenville McNEAL and Ann A. WESTALL, Department of Bexar, Jurisdiction of Brazoria, May 28, 1833. Marriage contract.

Marriage Records

No. 11   Jared E. GROCE and Mary Ann CALVIT, Department of Bexar, Jurisdiction of Brazoria, October 1, 1833. Marriage bond.

1834

No. 12.   Henry S. BROWN and Caroline SCOTT, Department of Bexar, Jurisdiction of Brazoria, January 9, 1834. Marriage agreement.

No. 13.   T. F. L. PARROTT and Elizabeth E. AUSTIN, Department of Bexar, Jurisdiction of Brazoria, January 28, 1834. Marriage contract.

No. 14.   William BAIRD and Margaret BRIDGES, Department of Bexar, Jurisdiction of Brazoria, March 14, 1834. Marriage bond.

No. 15.   William PAGE and Mariah H. OSBORN, Department of Bexar, Jurisdiction of Brazoria, July 24, 1834. Marriage bond.

No. 16.   Pickney S. McNIEL and Harriet COX (handwriting differs from 29), August 28, 1834. Marriage agreement.

No. 17.   Edward GALLEHER and Nancy C. RECTOR, Department of Bexar, Jurisdiction of Columbia, October 9, 1834. Marriage bond.

No. 18.   Franklin C. GRAY and Mary Ann PITTS, Department of Brazos, Jurisdiction of Columbia, November 12, 1834. Marriage contract.

1835

No. 19.   Robert D. MOORE and Ann C. HUNTER, Department of Brazos, Jurisdiction of Columbia, February 5, 1835. Marriage contract

No. 20.   Jesse K. DAVIS and Eliza DAVIS, Jurisdiction of Columbia, May 5, 1835. Marriage contract.

No. 21.   John JAMES and Sarah Ann COWAN, Department of Brazos, Jurisdiction of Columbia, September 17, 1835. Marriage bond.

No. 22.   Allen LARRISON and Susan STRINGFELLOW, Department of Brazos, Jurisdiction of Columbia, September 24, 1835. Marriage contract.

No. 23.   John B. COWAN and Mary McNEEL, Department of Brazos, Jurisdiction of Columbia, October 13, 1835. Marriage bond.

No. 24.   John WOODRUFF and Sally SMITH, Department of Brazos, Jurisdiction of Columbia, October 18, 1835. Marriage bond.

No. 25.   Josiah T. HARRELL and Margaret JAMESON, Department of Brazos, Jurisdiction of Columbia, October 29, 1835. Marriage contract and bond.

No. 26.   Edward W. ESTES and Mrs. Amelia WILSON, Department of Brazos, Jurisdiction of Columbia, December 13, 1835. Marriage bond.

Marriage Records

1836

No. 27. Thomas R. STIFF and Ann W. WINSON, Department of Brazos, Jurisdiction of Brazoria, February 10, 1836. Marriage Bond.

No. 28. John SHARP and Sarah Jane WHARTON, Department of Brazos, Jurisdiction of Brazoria, February 10, 1836. Marriage bond.

No date

No. 29. Thomas R. ERWIN and Harriet H. COX, (no place given). Marriage agreement.

The following list gives names of men who were parties to marriage agreements. Reference is to assigned number.

ALCORN, William E.	3	HODGE, James	5
BAIRD, William	14	JAMES, John	21
BARKER, Lima	6	LARRISON, Allen	22
BARRETT, William	4	MAXEY, Elisha	9
BROWN, Henry S.	12	McNEAL, Greenville	10
COWAN, John B.	23	McNIEL, Pickney S.	16
DAVIS, Jesse K.	20	MOORE, Robert D.	19
ERWIN, Thomas R.	29	NICHOLS, Henry F.	7
ESTES, Edward W.	26	PAGE, William	15
GALLEHER, Edward	17	PARROTT, T. F. L.	13
GRAY, Franklin C.	18	ROBINSON, Andrew	1
GROCE, Jared E.	11	SHARP, John	28
HARRELL, Josiah T.	25	STIFF, Thomas R.	27
HINCH, Samuel	2	STRATTON, Horace	8
	WOODRUFF, John	24	

The following list gives the names of the women who were parties to marriage agreements. Reference is to assigned number.

ALLEN, Mary G.	1	BARCLAY, Leah	7
ALSBURY, Leah Ann	2	BOWLS, Sally M.	9
AUSTIN, Elizabeth E.	13	BRIDGES, Margaret	14
CALVIT, Mary Ann	11	OSBORN, Maria H.	15
COWAN, Sarah Ann	21	PITTS, Mary Ann	18
COX, Harriet	16	RECTOR, Nancy C.	17
COX, Harriet H.	29	SCOTT, Caroline	12
DAVIS, Eliza	20	SMITH, Sally	24
HUNTER, Ann C.	19	STANDEFORD, Elizabeth	6
JACOB, Ann R.	8	STRINGFELLOW, Susan	22
JAMESON, Margaret	25	WESTALL, Ann A.	10
KIGANS, Sarah	3	WHARTON, Sarah Jane	28
KYRKENDALL, Zulema	5	WIENT, Elizabeth	4
McNEAL, Mary	23	WILSON, Mrs. Amelia	26
	WINSON, Ann W.	27	

III. ESTATES

4. PROBATE CASES, 1787-1869. 60 containers.
Original instruments, notices, and probate letters, which were used
in the administration of estates. Cases which were probated, or
contained instruments dated prior to February 20, 1837, are listed
below. An act of the Congress of the Republic of Texas on December
29, 1837, decreed that actions pending in the courts before the
revolution should be continued in the courts of the Republic.
(Gammel, Laws of Texas, I, 1462) It was a custom of the early courts
to assume charge of all real and personal property of deceased persons
who died intestate without heirs; consequently, a number of private
letters have been filed with case papers. Dates given in the title
lines are those contained in the papers, not the filing dates. The
case number may be secured from the list of estates following the
inventory of cases below. Each case is filed in a separate manila
container bearing the case number. Containers average 10 x 4½ x 2.
Filed with Probate Cases of Brazoria County, 1837--, C.C., office.

No. 1. AUSTIN, Stephen F., 1823-51. 215 papers in 2 containers.
Examples of these papers are: Stephen F. AUSTIN to James BARNET,
Bexar Province, Mexico, March 13, 1822, a receipt for ten doubloons,
one English guinea, and two gold pieces (value, one doubloon); Stephen
F. AUSTIN to General James WILKINSON, Mexico City, April 6, 1823, an
order of exchange for $250.00; printed acknowledgment of above order
subscribed to before Carile POLLOCK, notary, endorsed by Ja(mes)
WILKINSON, addressed to Joseph H. HAWKINS (Austin's fiscal agent),
New Orleans, July 5, 1823.

No. 1½. WILLS, William, 1836. 2 papers in 1 container.
Two notices of probate, November 12, 1836.

No. 2. ADAMS, Francis, 1787-1837. 65 papers in 1 container.
Receipts for accounts settled, land grants and deeds, claims against
estate, notices of probate, inventories, letters testamentary, and
other matters relating to the administration of the estate. Examples
of these papers are: Coahuila and Texas to Francis ADAMS, land grant;
Stephen F. AUSTIN to Francis ADAMS, receipt for $50.00 as payment for
title; Estavan MIRO to Pierre DUPUY, New Orleans, February 28, 1787,
passport.

No. 4. ANDERSON, Ephriam, 1820-37. 75 papers in 1 container.
Packet of personal letters, land grant from Coahila and Texas, receipts, vouchers, inventories, letters testamentary, and other
matters relating to estate.

No. 8. ANTHONY, D. W., 1833-1837. 21 papers in 1 container.
Inventories, receipts, claims, letters testamentary, and other matters relating to estate.

No. 13. ARNOLD, William, 1833-41. 11 papers in 1 container.
Inventories, appraisals, claims, receipts, letters testamentary, and
other matters relating to estate.

Estates

No. 14. AUSTIN, john, 1831-41. 75 papers in 1 container.
Inventories, claims, appraisals, receipts, vouchers, and other matters
relating to estate. Included is a receipt from William Barrett TRAVIS.

No. 17. BAILEY, James B., 1830-52. 75 papers in 2 containers.
Inventories, appraisals, letters testamentary, last will and testament, claims, receipts, vouchers, and other matters relating to
estate.

No. 26. BELL, Josiah H., 1833-40. 6 papers in 1 container.
Last will and testament, letters testamentary, appraisals and inventories.

No. 41. BROWN, Henry, 1834-37. 41 papers in 1 container.
Will, inventories and appraisals, claims, receipts, letters testamentary,
and other matters relating to estate.

No. 42. BOWEN, Sylvester, 1834-39. 39 papers in 1 container.
Inventories, appraisals, claims, receipts, notes, letters testamentary,
and other matters relating to estates.

No. 89. COUNCEL, James S., 1832-38. 100 papers in 1 container.
Inventories, appraisals, claims, notes, contracts, land grants, letters
testamentary, and other matters relating to estate.

No. 90. COX, John S., 1834-37. 16 papers in 1 container.
Notice of probate, inventory, claims, receipts and other matters
relating to estate.

No. 130. DARST, Abram, 1834-37. 21 papers in 1 container.
Inventories, appraisals, notes, claims, one printed notice of payment
for land, (Telegraph print, Columbia), September 12, 1836, letters
testamentary, and other matters relating to estate.

No. 154. EATON, William J., 1834-50. 210 papers in 2 containers.
Will, inventories, appraisals, claims, receipts, vouchers, notes,
accounts, letters testamentary, and other matters relating to estate.

No. 162. FANNIN, James W., Jr., 1826-43. 115 papers in 1 container.
Inventories, notices of probate, claims, receipts, accounts, vouchers,
letters testamentary, and other matters relating to estate. Included
are personal letters, one of which is:

                                        Velasco 24th Januy 1836

     Mr. Edmund Andrews
          or
     Robert Mills & co

          My friend Capt Bullock is too unwell with measles to go by
     water--and proceeds by land to Copen--He has spent several hun-
     dred dollars in bringing to our aid his company-and is now with
     (out) resources

                                    32

I am nearly so--and must ask you or either of you to advance
him from twenty to fifty dollars and I will repay it when I get
back--and greatly oblige

> yr friend &c (etc.)
> J.W. Fannin Jr

No. 175. GRAHAM, John, 1834-37. 16 papers in 1 container.
Notice of probate, inventory, appraisals, claims, receipts, letters
testamentary, and other matters relating to estate.

No. 209. HENRY, Maurice, 1827-41. 15 papers in 1 container.
Notice of probate, inventory, claims, receipts, letters testamentary.

No. 210. HAWKINS, Edmund St. John, 1832-42. 75 papers in 1 container.
Claims, inventories, receipts, letters testamentary, notices of probate, and other matters relating to estate.

No. 220. HARRISON, George, 1835-39. 21 papers in 1 container.
Notice of probate, inventory, claims, receipts, letters testamentary.

No. 222½. BYROM, John S. D., 1835-46. 47 papers in 1 container.
Inventory, notice of probate, claims, receipts, letters testamentary,
and other matters relating to estate.

No. 256. HEAD, E. G., 1835-46. 135 papers in 1 container.
Will, inventories, appraisals, notices of probate, claims, accounts,
receipts, vouchers, letters testamentary, and other matters relating
to estate.

No. 274. JAMESON, Green B., 1826-39. 95 papers in 1 container.
Notice of probate, inventories, field notes, notices of survey, land
grants, claims, accounts, receipts, personal letters, letters testamentary, and other matters relating to estate. Contains verification
of Jameson's death at the Alamo, March 6, 1836, as follows:

> I certify that Green B. JAMESON served in the Army of
> Texas from the 3rd October 1835 to Sixth of March 1836 at
> which time he was killed in the Alamo
>
> Houston 6th June 1837
> Certified by Colonel E. Burleson   (signed) Wm. H. Patton

No. 332. MAY, Samuel, 1830-37. 32 papers in 1 container.
Notice of probate, inventory, claims, receipts, letters testamentary,
one land certificate signed by Green DeWITT, April 20, 1830, also
certificate of citizenship signed by Green DeWITT.

No. 334. MILLICAN, Andrew, 1833-42. 50 papers in 1 container.
Notice of probate, inventory, claims, receipts, letters testamentary.

No. 343. MARSHALL, Isaac, 1833. 2 papers in 1 container.
Two letters of administration, June 29, 1833.

No. 346. MARTIN, Robert, 1832-37. 50 papers in 1 container.
Notice of probate, inventory, appraisal, claims, receipts, letters
testamentary, and will.

No. 349. McCORMICK, David, 1835-53. 34 papers in 1 container.
Letters testamentary, inventories, vouchers and receipts.

No. 362. MURPHY, Sylvester, 1831-37. 100 papers in 1 container.
Notice of probate, inventories, appraisals, claims, receipts, letters
testamentary, and other matters relating to estates.

No. 376. PARKINS, Samuel, 1834. 1 paper in 1 container.
Letter of administration, March 26, 1837.

No. 377. PRICE, John, 1832-33. 14 papers in 1 container.
Notice of probate, letters testamentary, inventory and appraisal.
Price, Commander of the Sloop Minerva, died of yellow fever at
Brazoria, November 17, 1832.

No. 380. PORTER, John M., 1832-39. 85 papers in 1 container.
Instruments in this container should have been filed with papers of
B. A. PORTER as they relate to that estate instead of to John M.
PORTER, who was administrator for B. A. PORTER.

No. 381. PERRY, James F., Sr., 1833. 8 papers in 1 container.
Notice of probate, letters of administration, accounts, Notification
from clerk of St. Francis County, Missouri, that James F. PERRY, Sr.
was late a resident of that county.

No. 399. PORTER, B. A., 1834. 7 papers in 1 container.
Notices of probate, letters testamentary, and appraisal.

No. 406. RICHESON, Edwin, 1833-37. 85 papers in 1 container.
Inventories, notices of probate, notices of creditors, accounts,
vouchers, claims, letters testamentary, and other matters relating
to estate.

No. 407. RANDON, John, 1832-35. 39 papers in 1 container.
Notice of probate, inventory, claims, receipts, and letters testamentary.

No. 417. REYNOLDS, Albert G., 1832-58. 115 papers in 1 container.
Inventories, appraisals, accounts, letters testamentary, notice of
probate, notices of final settlement. Included is a baptismal
certificate, March 26, 1832, signed by Father Michael MULDOON.

No. 428. ROBERTSON, Edward, 1830-41. 135 papers in 1 container.
Two packets of accounts due estate, one packet of claims, one packet
of statements by William T. AUSTIN regarding estate, one packet of
vouchers, one packet of papers in the case of Charlotte ROBERTSON,
alias JACKSON, vs. William T. AUSTIN and Asa BRIGHAM, 39 loose papers
including claims, notices of probate, inventories, letters testamentary.
Included is a power of attorney from Charlotte ROBERTSON to William D.

WALLACH, of Matagorda, to settle all matters relating to estate, given at Washington, D. C., January 14, 1841, subscribed to before Henry NAYLOR, notary, whose authority is certified by the Department of State, by John FORSYTH, January 15, 1840.

No. 438. SLEDGE, Samuel, 1833-38. 18 papers in 1 container.
Notice of probate, inventory, claims, receipts, and letters testamentary.

No. 440. STROTHER (STRODER), Edmund, 1833-51. 14 papers in 1 container.
Notice of probate, inventory, letters testamentary, and notices of final settlement.

No. 447. PICKETT, John J., 1833-37. 90 papers in 1 container.
Notice of probate, inventories, appraisals, claims, receipts, accounts, vouchers, letters testamentary, and other matters relating to estate.

No. 456. SMITH, George, 1834-35. 5 papers in 1 container.
Inventory, claims, and letters testamentary.

No. 457. SAMPIER, Joseph, 1833-37. 3 papers in 1 container.
Notice of probate, inventory, and letter of administration.

No. 458. SLAYTON, Robert G., 1836-41. 3 papers in 1 container.
Notice of probate, letters testamentary, and notice of final settlement.

No. 464. STROWDER (STROTHER,STRODER), Jesse, 1836-47. 16 papers in 1 container.
Notice of probate, inventory, letters testamentary, appraisals. A land grant of one third league of land to Robert SCOBY, relinquished to the heirs of Jesse STROTHER, Austin, Texas, December 16, 1847, signed by Governor J. Pickney HENDERSON.

No. 472. STRATTON, Horace B., 1835-51. 5 papers in 1 container.
Notice of probate, inventory, letters of administration, and notice of final settlement.

No 490. SCOTT, Captain William P., 1835-42. 175 papers in 1 container.
Notice of probate, claims, accounts, vouchers, letters testamentary, appraisals, private letters, survey field notes, and other matters relating to estate.

No. 492. SAWYER, Samuel, 1831-56. 115 papers in 1 container.
Notices of probate, letters testamentary, inventories, appraisals, accounts, claims, receipts, and other matters relating to estate.

No. 504. WILSON, Thomas, 1835-48. 27 papers in 1 container.
Inventory, appraisal, notice of probate, will, accounts and vouchers.

No. 506. WOODSON, James M., 1834-38. 10 papers in 1 container.

Estates

Notice of probate, letters testamentary, inventory, notice of final settlement.

No. 531   WALLIS, John G.   (John Y. WALLACE), 1835037.   25 papers in
           1 container.
Inventories, appraisals, last will and testament (signed John Y. WALLACE), accounts, and vouchers.

No. 547.   TURNER, James, 1833-50.   35 papers in 1 container.
Notice of probate, letters testamentary, inventories, claims, receipts, and notices of final settlement.

No. 555.   VINCE, Jesse, 1827-37.   27 papers in 1 container.
Notice of probate accounts and appraisals, notice of final settlement, letters testamentary.

No. 612.   LINDSEY, Lewis, 1831-69.   23 papers in 1 container.
Notice of probate, inventory, claims, receipts, letters testamentary, and notice of final settlement.

No. 649.   TRAVIS, William Barrett, 1838-39.   4 papers in 1 container.
Notices of probate.

No. 682.   WESTALL, James M., 1825-52.   225 papers in 2 containers.
Notice of probate, will, inventories, claims, receipts, accounts, notices to creditors, vouchers, notes, letters testamentary, and other matters relating to estate.

        The following list of estates gives reference to case number.

Estate

ADAMS, Francis	2	HEAD, E. G.	256
ANDERSON, Ephriam	4	HENRY, Maurice	209
ANTHONY, D. W.	8	JAMESON, Green B.	274
ARNOLD, William	13	LINDSEY, Lewis	612
AUSTIN, John	14	McCORMICK, David	349
AUSTIN, Stephen F.	1	MARSHALL, Isaac	343
BAILEY, James B.	17	MARTIN, Robert	346
BELL, Josiah H.	26	MAY, Samuel	332
BOWEN, Sylvester	42	MILLICAN, Andrew	334
BROWN, Henry	41	MURPHY, Sylvester	362
BYROM, John S. D.	222½	PARKINS, Samuel	376
COUNCEL, James S.	89	PERRY, James F., Sr.	381
COX, John S.	90	PICKETT, John J.	447
DARST, Abram	130	PORTER, B. A.	399
EATON, William J.	154	PORTER, John M.	380
FANNIN, James W., Jr.	162	PRICE, John	377
GRAHAM, John	175	RANDON, John	407
HARRISON, George	220	REYNOLDS, Albert G.	417
HAWKINS, Edmund St. John	210	RICHESON, Edwin	406

ROBERTSON, Edward	428	TRAVIS, William Barrett	649
SAMPIER, Joseph	457	TURNER, James	547
SAWYER, Samuel	492	VINCE, Jesse	555
SCOTT, Captain Wm. P.	490	WALLIS, John G.	
SLAYTON, Robert G.	458	(WALLACE, John Y.)	531
SLEDGE, Samuel	438	WESTALL, James M.	682
SMITH, George	456	WILLS, William	1½
STRATTON, Horace B.	472	WILSON, Thomas	504
STROTHER (STRODER),		WOODSON, James M.	506
Edmund	440		
STROWDER (STROTHER, STRODER)			
Jesse	464		

5.   ESTATE OF DOCTOR JAMES (DIEGO) GRANT, 1833-36.   87
          instruments in 1 packet.
Original papers relating to the estate of and to accounts held by
Dr. Grant in Texas, Mexico, the United States, and England.   The
correspondence includes inquiries to and from Mexican officers at
Monclova, Monterrey, Bexar, and Mexico City.   Included are inventor-
ies of property, papers relating to the Hacienda de los Hornos, ac-
counts due and against Dr. Grant, a copy of his will, and orders in
settlement of accounts.   The signature of Dr. Grant appears both as
James and Diego, taking the Spanish equivalent whenever addressing
Mexican authorities.   These papers are given individual treatment
in this Inventory because of the importance of the transactions of
Dr. Grant and because they are not filed with other probate papers.
Wrapped and marked Estate of Dr. James (Diego) GRANT, filed in file
box marked Old Papers, No. 1.   No arr.   No index.   10½ x 4 x 4½.
C. C., office.

As an example of the papers found, one instrument in Spanish
with an English translation follows:

Sello Tercero
Para el Bienio de 1834 y 1835
Dos Reales
     Por el presente me obligo en toda forma de derecho a entre-
gar en la Hacienda de los Hornos a los Sors.   Guarlay y Jewett
de comercio Matamoros en la proxima cosecha la cantidad de trigo
que sea suficiente para cubrir el importe de las cantidades que
resulten en mi contra y la de Hugo Grant por mi cuenta corriente
y costos de flete de maquinas verificada que sea la liquidacion
correspondiente que se practicara entre mi encargado D. Daniel
J. Tolar y D. Diego Jewett cualesquiera otro agente de la casa
dicha.   El espresado trigo sera entregado de toda preforencia
hasta cubrir la suma que resulto en mi contra, y se me abonar
(a) al precio liquido con solo la deducion de fletes y demas
gastos a que se expenda en Matamoros.   Y como para asegurar el
pago de dichas cantidades hipoteco formalmente la cosecha de
trigo de los Hornos actualmente en las semesteras, quedan por
lo mismo libres de todo gravamen y responsabilidad las maquinas

y demas bienes del otorgante y Hugo Grant. Y para que todo lo
contenido en este documento tenga el mas ecsacto cumplimiento en
todas sus partes firmo conmigo las de un tenor el Sor. Jewett y
los testigos Ciudadanos Juan Jose Delgado, Leon R. Almy, y Jose
Maria Mier en Monclova a dos de avril de mil ocho cientos treinta
y cinco anos.

(firmas)

Diego Grant   Diego Jewett
    Juan Jose Delgado   Leon R. Almy   Jose Ma. Mier
(es copia)

Third Seal
for the Biennium of 1834 and 1835
Two Reales

By the present (instrument) I oblige myself in every form
of law to deliver at the next harvest on the Hornos Hacienda,
to Messrs. Guarlay and Jewett of a Matamoros business (firm)
a sufficient quantity of wheat to cover the duty and freight cost
of machines against my account and Hugo Grant's, as soon as they
are liquidated by my agent Dan J. Tolar through Diego Jewett and
any other agent of said house. The above mentioned wheat will
be delivered with all preference until the amount resulting
against me is covered and I am to be refunded according to the
price of liquidation less only the deduction of freight and
the other expenses incurred in Matamoros. And since to insure
the payment of said amount I formally mortgage the wheat crop
of Hornos, now being planted, the machines and other goods of the
grantor and Hugo Grant are free of all liability. And in order
that all contained in this document may have the most exact
fulfilment in all its parts, Mr. Jewett and witnesses, citizens
Juan Jose Delgado, Leon R. Almy, and Jose Maria Mier, have
signed to the same effect with me in Monclova the second of
April, 1835.

(signatures)

Diego Grant   Diego Jewett
    Juan Jose Delgado   Leon R. Almy   Jose Ma. Mier
(this is a copy)

IV. COURT RECORDS

6. DOCKET FOR THE PRECINCT OF VICTORIA, MUNICIPALITY OF
     AUSTIN, 1832-33. 1 vol.

Docket of cases tried before Asa BRIGHAM, comisario of the Precinct
of Victoria, Municipality of Austin, from February 1, 1832, to
January 1, 1833. Shows name of plaintiff, name of defendant, number
of case, recapitulation of fees assessed in case, brief of proceedings,
orders of court, and date of orders. Arr. chron. by date of trial.

38

Alph. index by name of plaintiff with reference to page no. 101 pp 14 x 8 x 3/4. D. C., office.

The following is the full text of a criminal case (pp. 58-59, 68):

Personally come and appeared before me Asa BRIGHAM Comisario, J. PIEDRAS and entered Complaint against a negroe man named William CHEPHAS--said PIEDRAS stated that about fifty dollars had been stolen from him, from on board the Schooner Comet, and he had every reason to believe that the said William was the thief, and wished him apprehended.

Brazoria Sept 8th 1832

Asa Brigham
Comisario

State of Coahuila & Texas
vs
William Chephas

To Edwin RICHESON You are hereby required to apprehend and take into custody a negro man called William CHEPHAS to answer the complaint of J. PIEDRAS and bring him forthwith before me. In this you will fail not and in case you may want assistance to put this order into execution you may require the aid of any number of good Citizens of this Precinct that might be necessary Given under my hand this 8th of Sept 1832.

Asa Brigham
Comisario

State of Coahuila & Texas
vs
William Chephas

The prisoner in this case being brought into court by the proper Officer, the Comisario appointed a Jury of three Viz. A. CALVIT, John W. CLOUD and S. G. McNEEL three good Citizens of this Precinct who after hearing all the Testimony do say on their oaths that in their opinion the prisoner was guilty of the Charge, the Comisario therefore ordered him held by the proper officer and required that the aforesaid jury should see that proper means was used to obtain the money stolen, which was promptly attended to and prisoner was returned to the Comisario together with Twenty six dollars thirty seven cents of the money stolen, the Comisario considered it necessary that two persons should be added to the former jury, viz J. H. BELL and C. G. COX two good citizens of the precinct who being placed on their oaths, do say as follows,

We the Jury find the prisoner guilty as in manner and form Indicated and also say that he is personally accountable for all expenses and defiensency of amt. Stolen. and that the Comisario has the right of disposing of said defendant until such costs and charges are paid. A. CALVIT, J. H. BELL, S. G.

Court Records

McNEEL, C. G. COX & J. W. CLOUD Paid over the Col. PIEDRAS $26.37
                                        Asa Brigham
Brazoria 8th Sept 1832   Comisario

State of Coahuila & Texas   To Edwin Richeson
            Vs   You are hereby authorized
William Chephas   to advertise and sell at
                                        Public Auction, the time
                                        of the Prisoner William
CHEPHAS a man of couler (who calls himself free) as will make
the sum of twenty four dollars sixty two cents. In this you
will fail not, and make return to me of your procedings on the
13th day of the present month. Given under my hand this 9th
day of Sept 1832

                                        Asa Brigham
                                        Comisario
Executed the above order by selling at Public sale the time
of the said William CHEPHAS, from this date to the last day
of December next, at the rate of seven dollars per month to
Edmund ANDREWS

Brazoria Sept 13, 1832   Asa Brigham   Edwin Richeson
                               Comisario
Redc of E. Andrews $7.00   (Notation on side of page)

State of Coahuila and Texas
vs
William Chephas

Mr. Brigham
        Dear Sir ---
            They have come and taken William which I
hired of you from me and this is to serve as information that
I no longer hold myself as responsible for the delivery of him
nor for the payment of the note. I wish to see you on the
subject.
                                        Yours
Oct 19th 1832   Edmund Andrews

    On receiving this note I made immediate enquiry and was
informed that Thomas BRADLY then acting as Sheriff had taken
said William--on inquiring of said BRADLY by what authority
he took the negroe he replied that John AUSTIN (then acting
as Second Constitutional Alcalde) has given him the order

Brazoria Oct 20th 1832

The following direct index by name of plaintiff to page number
in the Docket for the Precinct of Victoria, Municipality of Austin,
has been copied from the original index in the volume.

------(Plaintiff vs. Defendant)

Court Records

Court Records

(Plaintiff vs. Defendant)

The following reverse index by name of defendant to page number in Docket for the Precinct of Victoria, Municipality of Austin, has been prepared by the Historical Records Survey.

Court Records

(Defendant vs. Plaintiff)

Court Records

(Defendant vs. Plaintiff)

7.   FILE DOCKET, 1834-35. 1 vol.
Docket of cases filed in the Jurisdiction of Brazoria. This docket served the purpose of a file docket and fee book. The cases are arranged without number or date. The only notation by case is the amount of fees for docketing. This book was used as a fee book by the county clerk, 1844-47. Forty pages are devoted to cases filed in the Jurisdiction of Brazoria. Arrangement appears to be by order of filing. The cases appear in the same order as the docket containing the proceedings of the cases, Docket, Jurisdiction of Brazoria, 8. No index. 120 pp. 18 x 6 x 1. C. C., office.

8.   DOCKET, JURISDICTION OF BRAZORIA, 1834-35. 1 vol.
Docket of the alcalde court of the Jurisdiction of Brazoria, showing the cases tried by or brought before Alcalde Edwin WALLER. This docket is similar to a modern justice of peace docket, showing name of plaintiff, name of defendant, names of attorneys, recapitulation of fees, brief of proceedings in case, date of execution, date execution returnable, and other notations. The usual amounts of fees charged in the cases were: for filing paper 30¢, issuing notice 35½¢, issuing alias 35¢, filing petition 50¢, issuing order 50¢, issuing certificate 50%, recording judgment 75¢, issuing order of judgment 75¢, serving executions from 62½¢ to $8.00. Arr. numer. by case no. No index. 200 pp. (166 used) 10 x 8 x 1½. C. C., office.

The following are the entries by case number, which corresponds to page number in volume.

Court Records

No. 1. Edmund St. John HAWKINS vs. Peter M. HEWS. Notice of suit issued February 6, 1834.

No. 2. J. A. H. CLEVELAND vs. William T. AUSTIN. New trial granted in action on account for $60.00, February 6, 1834.

No. 3. P. R. and Ann D. W. APLANE vs. three creditors (not named). Notice of suit issued February 12, 1834.

No. 4. HOWTH and STEVINSON vs. Napoleon D. WILLIAMS. Notice of continuation issued February 12, 1834.

No. 5. William H. PATTON vs. Pleasant BELL. Notice of suit issued February 5, 1834. Action on note for $26.45 submitted to arbitrators Elijah CAPLE and Jacob BETTS. Judgment in favor of plaintiff.

No. 6. William H. PATTON, administrator for Isaac MARSHALL, vs. Zeno PHILLIPS. Action on note for $81.50 submitted to arbitrators W. H. SETTLE and Edmund DANIELS. Judgment in favor of plaintiff, February 6, 1834.

No. 7. William H. PATTON, administrator for Isaac MARSHALL, vs. George TENNEL. Notice of suit issued February 6, 1834.

No. 8. William H. PATTON, administrator for Isaac MARSHALL, vs. William J. RUSSELL, submitted to arbitrators Jacob BETTS and Elijah CAPLE, judgment in favor of plaintiff for amount of note, $22.25.

No. 9. William H. PATTON, administrator for Isaac MARSHALL, vs. William J. RUSSELL. Judgment against defendant for $11.50 and costs.

No. 10. Susan BREEDLOVE vs. John THOMAS. Notice of suit issued on account of $5.00, February 6, 1834.

No. 11. E. JEFFERY vs. D. W. ANTHONY, T. F. L. PARROTT, and E. St. John HAWKINS. Action submitted to arbitrators John W. CLOUD and Edmund DANIELS. Judgment in favor of plaintiff, March 6, 1834.

No. 12. E. JEFFERY vs. William FREAM, William DAILEY, and E. St. John HAWKINS. Action on note for $23.34 submitted to arbitrators William H. LITTLE and Edmund DANIELS. Judgment in favor of plaintiff, March 6, 1834.

No. 13. J. T. HARRELL vs. William T. AUSTIN. Notice of suit issued. Action on note for $11.00 dismissed by plaintiff, March 6, 1834.

No. 14. Henry SMITH, executor for J. B. BAILEY, vs. Sylvester BOWEN, and Joseph POLLEY. Judgment in favor of defendant for $27.50, March 6, 1834.

No. 15. Henry SMITH, executor for J. B. BAILEY, vs. (not named).

Action in suit for $152.50. Certificate granted and notice waived. Parties to appear April 28, 1834.

No. 16. Henry SMITH, executor for J. B. BAILEY, vs. Elijah CAPLE and Sylvester BOWEN. Action submitted to arbitrators William H. LITTLE and Edmund DANIELS. Judgment against defendant for $16.25, March 6, 1834.

No. 17. Henry SMITH, executor for J. B. BAILEY, vs. William J. RUSSELL and Sylvester BOWEN. Action submitted to arbitrators Allen LARRISON and Elijah CAPLE. Compromise, defendant receiving $7.25 from plaintiff, March 6, 1834.

No. 18. Henry SMITH, executor for J. B. BAILEY, vs. David SHELBY and Gerren HINDS. Defendant appeared and settled account, February 22, 1834.

No. 19. Henry SMITH, executor for J. B. BAILEY, vs. Peyton R. SPLANE, William T. AUSTIN, and Elizabeth LIPPENCOTT, representatives of John AUSTIN. Submitted to arbitrators William H. LITTLE and Edmund DANIELS. Judgment against defendant for $57.25, March 4, 1834.

No. 20. Edwin WALLER vs. John THOMAS. Notice to appear for settlement of note for $70.00, February 24, 1834.

No. 21. William STAFFORD vs. Jacob BETTS. Notice issued to make amicable settlement for $150.00 note, February 7, 1834. Parties failed to appear; alias issued March 12, 1834.

No. 22. Edwin WALLER vs. Robert D. MOORE, W. E. HOWTH, and F. I. CALVIT. Notice issued, February 7, 1834, for parties to appear to effect amicable settlement, February 24, 1834.

No. 23. Edwin WALLER vs. Milton ANDERSON, F. I. CALVIT, and Peyton R. SPLANE. Notice issued on joint note for $462.50, March 10, 1834.

No. 24. Henry SMITH, executor for J. B. BAILEY, vs. Valentine BENNETT and Peyton R. SPLANE. Submitted to arbitrators William H. LITTLE and Edmund DANIELS. Judgment in favor of plaintiff for $64.25 and interest.

No. 25. Henry SMITH, executor for J. B. BAILEY, vs. William H. LEE and Joseph POLLEY. Submitted to arbitrators William H. LITTLE and Edmund BROWN. Judgment in favor of plaintiff for $17.65 and interest, March 6, 1834.

No. 26. Samuel HOIT vs. Solomon WILLIAMS. Defendant sent written authority to have alcalde enter judgment against him, February 8, 1834. Alias issued January 26, 1835.

No. 27. A. G. and R. MILLS vs. James MOORE and Joseph MIMS.

Submitted to arbitrators. Judgment in favor of plaintiff for $44.01 and interest; execution issued March 17, 1834.

No. 28. T. F. L. PARROTT vs. L. C. MANSON. Attorney for defendant agreed that judgment be rendered for $42.50 and interest. Execution issued April 9, 1834. New execution issued January 30, 1835.

No. 29. E. ANDERSON vs. Caleb KEMP. Submitted to arbitrators. Judgment in favor of plaintiff for $25.00 and interest. Execution issued April 23, 1834.

No. 30. Jonathan C. PEYTON vs. Alvan WETHERBAY. Judgment by court against defendant for $9.69, March 6, 1834.

No. 31. J. T. TINSLEY vs. William B. and John SWEENEY and David McCORMICK. Brief of case submitted to court. Judgment in favor of plaintiff for $849.43 3/4 and interest. Execution issued September 11, 1834. New execution issued by W. H. SLEDGE, secretary, June 30, 1835. A notation states that satisfaction was received of A. G. and R. MILLS, signed by John A. WHARTON.

No. 32. George ROBINSON vs. Ephriam ANDERSON. Defendant came into court and confessed judgment February 20, 1834. Execution issued March 17, 1834.

No. 33. Succession of M. HENRY vs. William B. SWEENEY. Submitted to court. Judgment issued in favor of plaintiff for $600.00 and interest. Certificate of record issued January 24, 1834. John A. WHARTON, attorney for plaintiff, certified that satisfaction was had from A. G. and R. MILLS.

No. 34. HOWTH and STEVINSON vs. Joseph REES, executor for Christopher G. COX, and Charles D. SAYRE. Submitted to arbitrators William T. AUSTIN and Thomas R. ERWIN. Judgment in favor of plaintiff for $45.00 and interest, March 6, 1834. Execution issued March 17, 1834.

No. 35. HOWTH and STEVINSON vs. Joseph REES. Default judgment for $23.00 and interest. Execution issued September 23, 1834.

No. 36. George B. McKINSTRY, holder of note to McKINSTRY and AUSTIN, vs. Samuel YOUNG. Defendant appeared and confessed judgment for $299.48 and interest. Notation shows credit for $138.00 on account by C. B. STEWART, administrator for Samuel YOUNG, March 20, 1837.

No. 37. J. S. D. BYROM, holder of note to McKINSTRY and AUSTIN, vs. Samuel YOUNG. Defendant appeared and confessed judgment for $325.15 and interest, March 24, 1834. Notation states YOUNG paid $210.30. $104.50 was allowed BYROM'S order, and C. B. STEWART paid $98.50 cash.

No. 38. HOWTH and STEVINSON vs. Milton HICKS. Submitted to arbitrators William T. AUSTIN and Thomas R. ERWIN. Judgment in favor of plaintiff for $81.00 and interest. Execution issued March 17, 1834.

No. 39. HOWTH and STEVINSON vs. Thomas CAYCE. Submitted to arbitrators William T. AUSTIN and Thomas R. ERWIN. Judgment in favor of defendant for $46.00 and interest. Execution issued March 8, 1834.

No. 40. HOWTH and STEVINSON vs. John D. NEWELL. Case before Edwin WALLER, alcalde, not tried; plaintiff assumed costs.

No. 41. HOWTH and STEVINSON vs. HALEY and CARSON. Submitted to arbitrators William T. AUSTIN and Thomas R. ERWIN. Judgment in favor of plaintiff for $100.33 and interest. Execution issued March 17, 1834. Execution renewed for 60 days, September, 1834. Alias issued April 5, 1835.

No. 42. HOWTH and STEVINSON vs. William H. CARSON. Submitted to arbitrators William T. AUSTIN and Thomas R. ERWIN. Judgment in favor of plaintiff for $30.00 and interest. Execution issued March 17, 1834. Execution renewed for 60 days. Alias issued April 5, 1835.

No. 43. HOWTH and STEVINSON vs. Sylvester BOWEN. Submitted to arbitrators William T. AUSTIN and Thomas R. ERWIN. Judgment in favor of plaintiff for $22.06 and interest. Execution issued September 23, 1834. Execution renewed January 30, 1835.

No. 44. HOWTH and STEVINSON vs. Thomas M. BLAKE. Case called for action on note for $58.00, February 12, 1834, but notice had not been served.

No. 45. Jonathan C. PEYTON, administrator for George SMITH, vs. Phineas SMITH and Asa BRIGHAM. Notice issued February 25, 1834; returnable March 14, 1834. Petition filed April 8, 1834. New notice issued March 14, 1835.

No. 46. Wyly MARTIN vs. John A. WHARTON, agent and curator for John M. PORTER and Pamilia PORTER, administrators for B. A. PORTER, and George TENNEL. Judgment in favor of plaintiff for $281.25 and interest. Execution issued September 11, 1834. New execution issued by W. H. SLEDGE, secretary, January 30, 1835.

No. 47. George HUFF, administrator for S. SAWYER, vs. Samuel DAMON. Submitted to arbitrators Charles D. SAYRE and Edmund ANDREWS. Judgment in favor of plaintiff for $40.44 and interest. R. HODGE agreed to pay cost if Samuel DAMON did not satisfy judgment by July 1, 1834. Arrangement agreed to by John A. WHARTON, for plaintiff, and Samuel DAMON. Signed by R. HODGE, February 25, 1834.

No. 48. William T. AUSTIN vs. Francis MOORE. Defendant appeared and confessed judgment for $35.00 and interest, February 24, 1834. Attached to page are two papers: William T. AUSTIN instructs Edwin WALLER, alcalde, to pay to J. McNEEL judgment on docket against F. MOORE, June 14, 1834; William T. AUSTIN gives receipt to F. MOORE for $9.50 on judgment.

No. 49. William T. AUSTIN vs. William J. RUSSELL, J. G. McNEEL, administrator for James WESTALL and Charles A. BETNER. Notice issued February 15, 1834; new notice issued March 19, 1834.

No. 50. William T. AUSTIN vs. William J. RUSSELL. Defendant appeared and confessed judgment for $200.00 and interest, February 15, 1834. Notation states that entire sum was paid to Edwin WALLER, alcalde.

No. 51. Ira INGRAM vs. C. G. COX and Joseph REES. Submitted to arbitrators Robert HODGE and Elijah CAPLE. Judgment in favor of plaintiff for $26.50 and interest. Execution issued October 22, 1834; new execution issued January 20, 1835, by W. H. SLEDGE, secretary.

No. 52. E. R. WIGHTMAN vs. William T. AUSTIN and Elizabeth E. PARROTT, administrator for John AUSTIN. Submitted to arbitrators John CHAFFIN and Elijah CAPLE. Judgment against plaintiff, and costs assessed plaintiff, March 24, 1834.

No. 53. E. R. WIGHTMAN vs. Thomas B. BELL. Notice issued February 15, 1834; continued at March term, by common consent, until May 17, 1834.

No 54. S. F. AUSTIN vs. P. R. SPLANE. Continuance granted defendant. Notice issued February 15, 1834.

No. 55. William H. PATTON, administrator for Isaac MARSHALL, vs. John SWEENEY. Submitted to arbitrators Elijah CAPLE and Jacob BETTS. Judgment in favor of defendant for $29.80 and interest. Execution issued April 4, 1834.

No. 56. William H. PATTON, administrator for Isaac MARSHALL, vs. Sally KANADAY. Notice issued February 15, 1834. Continuance granted defendant.

No. 57. E. R. WIGHTMAN vs. Joseph REES, executor for C. G. COX. Notice issued February 15, 1834. Continuance granted defendant.

No. 58. Catharine CARSON vs. Thomas CAYCE. Notice issued February 17, 1834. Defendant appeared and paid debt, $15.25.

No. 59. John CHAFFIN vs. Thomas CAYCE. Case dismissed at cost to plaintiff. Notice issued February 17, 1834.

No. 60. Edmund JEFFERY vs. John THOMAS. Suit dismissed by plain-

Court Records

tiff, who assumed costs. Notice issued February 17, 1834.

No. 61. A. G. and R. MILLS vs. Samuel YOUNG. Submitted to arbitrators William H. JACK and William H. LITTLE. Judgment in favor of plaintiff for $17.80 and interest. Judgment paid by John CHAFFIN, October 1, 1834.

No. 62. LYONS and COMPANY by A. G. and R. MILLS vs. William HARRIS. Submitted to arbitrators Elijah CAPLE and Shubael MARSH. Judgment in favor of plaintiff for $37.50 and interest. Execution issued April 19, 1834; renewed September 8, 1834; new execution issued by W. H. SLEDGE, secretary.

No. 63. A. G. and R. MILLS vs. William HARRIS. Submitted to arbitrators Shubael MARSH and Elijah CAPLE. Judgment in favor of plaintiff for $41.76 and interest. Execution issued April 19, 1834; renewed September 8, 1834; new execution issued January 30, 1835, by W. H. SLEDGE, secretary.

No. 64. Margaret JAMESON, administrator for Isaac JAMESON, vs. P. R. SPLANE. Judgment by court in favor of plaintiff for $286.50 and interest. Execution issued February 23, 1835, by W. H. SLEDGE, secretary.

No. 65. Edmund DANIELS vs. Thomas CAYCE. Defendant appeared and paid $43.00, amount of claim. Notice issued, February 24, 1834.

No. 66. Edmund DANIELS vs. Joseph REES. Judgment against defendant for $4.50; paid to Edwin WALLER, alcalde, and received by Edmund DANIELS. Notice issued February 18, 1834.

No. 67. T. F. L. PARROTT vs. A. WILLIAMS. Submitted to arbitrators William B. TRAVIS and H. H. LEAGUE. The difference between the two notes submitted in the case, $12.50, was awarded defendant. Execution issued March 17, 1834; returned satisfied April 1, 1834.

No. 68. A. G. and R. MILLS vs. Robert D. MOORE. Defendant appeared and confessed judgment for $179.64 and interest. New execution issued March 16, 1835.

No. 69. T. F. L. PARROTT vs. J. G. McNEEL, administrator for James M. WESTALL. Case continued by common consent. Notice issued February 20, 1834.

No. 70. T. F. L. PARROTT vs Ephriam ANDERSON and Milton ANDERSON. Defendant appeared and confessed judgment for $4.50. Notice issued February 20, 1834.

No. 71. James YOUNG vs. R. H. W. REEL. Judgment by default for $50.00. Execution issued September 29, 1834; new execution issued February 2, 1835.

No. 72. HOWTH and WILLIAMS vs. Robert Dillon MOORE. Defendant appeared without process, and confessed judgment for $211.82 and interest, February 21, 1834. New execution issued March 16, 1835.

No. 72½. McNEEL and WOODSON vs. Robert D. MOORE. Defendant appeared without process, and confessed judgment for $172.09 and interest, February 22, 1834. New execution issued March 16, 1835.

No. 73. Edmund JEFFERY vs. Ephriam ANDERSON and Milton ANDERSON. Submitted to arbitrators Robert STEVENSON and Charles A. BETNER. Judgment in favor of plaintiff for $20.00 and interest, March 20, 1834.

No. 74. Edmund JEFFERY vs. G. M. COLLINSWORTH, agent for William H. RUTHERFORD and COMPANY. Submitted to arbitrators R. H. W. REEL and William DAILEY. Judgment in favor of plaintiff for $35.75 and interest.

No. 75. George B. McKINSTRY vs. William H. JACK, curator and defender of Benjamin F. SMITH. Certificate granted February 25, 1834; continued until March term, 1834.

No. 76. Robert VINCE vs. P. R. BARTLESON. Line drawn across names of parties. Notice issued February 24, 1834.

No. 77. James M. WESTALL vs. Asa MITCHELL. Submitted to arbitrators Charles B. STEWART and J. S. D. BYROM. Judgment in favor of defendant for court costs since arbitrators deemed notes in case still property of J. AUSTIN or McKINSTRY and AUSTIN.

No. 78. Robert VINCE vs. P. R. BARTLESON, I. G. WRIGHT. Attorney for defendant confessed judgment for $66.67 and interest, February 25, 1834.

No. 79. Shubael MARSH for himself and the heirs of Obidiah PITTS vs. Henry SMITH, testamentary executor for Obidiah PITTS. Plaintiff alleged that the will of Obidiah PITTS was void because there were not as many witnesses to it as the law required, and because PITTS and Polly ABERNATHY were never legally married. The facts showed that the will was made before a notary in the presence of two witnesses, one of which was incompetent. The law required three witnesses if a will was made before a notary, or five witnesses if no notary was available. Although the will stated that only two witnesses were available at the house, it was ruled that it did not follow that no more could have been obtained. The court held the will void, and ordered the estate of Obidiah PITTS administered as the law required.

No. 80. The People of the Jurisdiction of BRAZORIA vs. Ruben P. T. STONE. Notice was issued to summon 48 men, from which 12 were to be selected to try defendant. Summons were issued for 14 witnesses, and case was submitted to 12 freemen. Defendant was found guilty, and sentenced to have 39 lashes applied to his bare back, the letter M branded in his hand, and to leave the colony within ten days or be considered an outlaw, April, 1834.

No. 81.   A. G. and R. MILLS vs. Henry WILLIAMS and Solomon WILLIAMS. No other entries. Notice issued March 3, 1834; returnable March 24, 1834.

No. 82.   Edmund St. John HAWKINS vs. Charles CAVENAH. Plaintiff appeared and dismissed action, assuming costs, March 3, 1834.

No. 83.   Jacob SHANNON vs. H. H. LEAGUE and Peter R. BARTLESON. Submitted to arbitrators Gowin HARRIS and Thomas CHADOWIN. Judgment against defendants, court costs to be assessed against defendants, March 5, 1834.

No. 84.   H. H. LEAGUE vs. Samuel WILDY. Submitted to arbitrators Gowin HARRIS and Benjamin F. SMITH. Judgment against plaintiff, court costs to be assessed against plaintiff.

No. 85.   John A. WHARTON, for R. P. T. STONE, vs. S. VANDIVERS and O. H. SPENCER as garnisher. SPENCER appeared and confessed judgment for $175.00 to cover demand of plaintiff anc court costs, March 8, 1834.

No. 86.   Succession of John McCROSKEY vs. Joseph REES, curator for C. G. COX, deceased. Judgment in favor of plaintiff for $689.56 and interest on $897,38 from date, and interest on $796.56 from March 12, 1834. Execution issued March 12, 1834; renewed September 8, 1834. Notation states that satisfaction was entered on execution. Date of judgment destroyed.

No. 87.   William H. CARSON vs. Peter POWELL. Judgment in favor of plaintiff. Orders issued to J. D. NEWELL to answer questions in case. NEWELL stated that he was indebted to POWELL for $10.00. Judge order this $10.00 paid to William H. CARSON to satisfy judgment, March 12, 1834.

No. 88.   HALEY and CARSON vs. James TINSLEY. Submitted to arbitrators R. H. W. REEL and Robert COLDRON. Judgment in favor of plaintiff for $9.81.

No. 89.   John TALBOT vs. William HARRIS. No other entries. Notice issued March 12, returnable March 24, 1834.

No. 90.   Henry S. BROWN vs. Margaret JAMESON. Submitted to arbitrators George HUFF and H. STRATTON. Judgment in favor of plaintiff for $84.00 and interest. Execution issued October 22, 1834; new execution issued by W. H. SLEDGE, January 30, 1835.

No. 91. John JAMES, administrator of E. D. SHOON, vs. Zeno PHILLIPS. Certificate granted at March term.

No. 92. Edmund JEFFERY, holder of note payable to J. S. D. BYROM, vs. M. W. SMITH. Judgment in favor of plaintiff for $200.00 and interest. Execution issued September 8, 1834; new execution issued by W. H. SLEDGE, date torn.

No. 93. Edmund JEFFERY vs. M. W. SMITH. Submitted to arbitrators A. G. MILLS and G. B. JAMESON. Judgment in favor of plaintiff for $39.50 and interest. Execution issued April 16, 1834; new execution issued by W. H. SLEDGE, January 30, 1835.

No. 94. E. W. GREGORY vs. William T. AUSTIN, surviving partner of REYNOLDS and AUSTIN. Defendant appeared and confessed judgment for $2,524.10 and interest, March 18, 1834.

No. 95. S. F. AUSTIN, executor for James F. PERRY, vs. Francis MOORE. No other entries. Notice issued March 18, 1834, returnable March 25, 1834.

No. 96. Patrick GREEN vs. Mrs. M. JAMESON. Judgment in favor of plaintiff for $10.12½. Execution issued October 22, 1834.

No. 97. Edmund JEFFERY vs. Peyton R. SPLANE. Submitted to arbitrators R. H. W. REEL and H. B. STRATTON. Judgment in favor of plaintiff for $60.00 for rent, $28.42 on note, March 26, 1834. New execution issued January 31, 1835. Warren D. C. HALL became security on judgment, March 28, 1834.

No. 98. Sylvester BOWEN vs. Peyton R. SPLANE. Notice issued March 18, 1834.

No. 99. Jesse THOMPSON vs. Peyton R. SPLANE. Notice issued March 18, 1834.

No. 100. Administrators of John AUSTIN vs. Solomon WILLIAMS. Continuance granted defendant. Notice issued March 28.

No. 101. Polly (Mary) BAILEY, administrator of Smith BAILEY, vs. William J. RUSSELL. Submitted to arbitrators A. ROBERTSON and John CHAFFIN. Judgment in favor of plaintiff for $46.52 and interest. Execution issued September 22, 1834. Injunction awarded to stay defendant, September 25, 1834. On trial of injunction, defendant was granted $23.50. Signed by S. DINSMORE, primary judge, April 28, 1835.

No. 102. Mary BAILEY, administrator of Smith BAILEY, vs. William J. RUSSELL. Notice issued March 19, 1834, alias issued, April 19, 1834, acknowledged by defendant, summons issued March 16, 1835.

No. 103. G. B. COTTEN vs. John A. WHARTON, curator and defender of O. H. ALLEN. No other entries. Notice issued March 20, 1834.

No. 104. HOWTH and WILLIAMS vs. W. B. SWEENEY. Submitted to arbitrators E. DANIELS and John FOSTER. Judgment in favor of plaintiff for $73.75 and interest. Execution issued April 16, 1834; renewed September 8, 1834; new execution issued by W. H. SLEDGE, secretary, January 30, 1835.

No. 105 Henry KLONNE vs Jesse THOMPSON, William H PATTON, and A. W. PATTON. Certificate granted by defendant. Notice issued March 18, 1834.

No. 106. HOWTH and WILLIAMS vs. R. H. W. REEL. Submitted to arbitrators Asa BRIGHAM and Ephriam ANDERSON. Judgment in favor of plaintiff for $30.12 and interest. Execution issued April (torn) 1834, renewed September 8, 1834; new execution issued by W. H. SLEDGE, secretary, January 30, 1835.

No. 107. George B. McKINSTRY vs. Nancy BAILEY. Submitted to arbitrators T. F. L. PARROTT and A. G. MILLS. Judgment in favor of plaintiff for $60.00 and interest. Execution issued October (torn) 1834; new execution issued March 16, 1835.

No. 108. E. JEFFERY vs. R. H. W. REEL. Submitted to arbitrators T. F. L. PARROTT and A. G. MILLS. Judgment in favor of plaintiff for $14.40 and interest. Execution issued April 16, 1834; renewed September 8, 1834; new execution issued by W. H. SLEDGE, secretary, endorsed by Silas DINSMORE, primary judge, January 30, 1835.

No. 109. Samuel YOUNG vs. L. C. MANSON. Submitted to arbitrators David RANDON and Francis MOORE. Judgment in favor of plaintiff for $15.30 and interest. Execution issued April 19, 1834. Statement by William H. JACK that execution and amount had been certified.

No. 110. T. F. L. PARROTT vs. W. D. C. HALL. Attorney for defendant appeared and confessed judgment for $73.75 and interest. Execution issued October 22, 1834, new execution issued January 30, 1835.

No. 111. T. F. L. PARROTT vs. J. A. H. CLEVELAND. Defendant appeared and confessed judgment for $10.25. Execution issued October 22, 1834, new execution issued by W. H. SLEDGE, secretary, January 30, 1835.

No. 112. T. F. L. PARROTT vs. Sylvester BOWEN. Submitted to arbitrators J. S. D. BYROM and Ephriam ANDERSON. Judgment in favor of plaintiff for $13.50 and interest. Execution issued October 22, 1834, new execution issued by W. H. SLEDGE, secretary, January 30, 1835.

No. 113. S. FULLER vs. William E. HOWTH, Augustus WILLIAMS, and A. G. and R. MILLS. No defense was offered; judgment in favor of plaintiff for $783.86 and interest, April 23, 1834. Copy certified by superior district judge, January 24, 1835.

No. 114. E. JEFFERY, holder of note payable to J. S. D. BYROM, vs. Louis C. MANSON. Case continued until April 12, 1834, when attorney for plaintiff appeared and confessed judgment for $80.00 and interest. Execution issued April 19, renewed September 8, 1834; new execution issued by W. H. SLEDGE, secretary, for Silas DINSMORE, primary judge, May 25, 1835.

No. 115. E. JEFFERY vs. William T. AUSTIN. Defendant appeared and confessed judgment for $13.78 and interest. Execution issued, April 16, 1834; new execution issued by W. H. SLEDGE, secretary, January 30, 1835.

No. 116. T. F. L. PARROTT vs. Margaret JAMESON. Defendant appeared and confessed judgment for $38.00 and interest. Plaintiff granted stay of execution for 90 days. Execution issued October 22, 1834; new execution issude by W. H. SLEDGE, secretary, January 30, 1835.

No 117. T. F. L. PARROTT vs. W. H. HENDRICK. Submitted to arbitrators Asa BRIGHAM and William BAIRD. Judgment in favor of plaintiff for $45.75 and interest. Plaintiff granted stay of execution until May 28. New execution issued March 16, 1835.

No. 118. T. F. L. PARROTT vs. Phineas SMITH. Submitted to arbitrators Charles D. SAYRE and Francis MOORE. Judgment in favor of plaintiff for $36.75 and interest. Execution issued October 22, 1834; new execution issued by W. H. SLEDGE, secretary, January 30, 1835.

No. 119. Joseph H. POLLEY vs. William B. SWEENEY and John D. NEWELL. Notice issued, March 22, 1834; notice returned March term, 1834.

No. 120, 121. Charlotte ROBERTSON, alias JACKSON, vs. Asa BRIGHAM and William T. AUSTIN, administrators for Edward ROBERTSON. Case came to trial March 12, 1834. Court ruled in favor of plaintiff, since examination of testimony and the law indicated that plaintiff's claims were correct, on account of a marriage contract. Judgment in favor of plaintiff for $2,300.00 and interest from June 26, 1832. Judgment against defendants: William T. AUSTIN, $887.22 for money collected from succession of Edward ROBERTSON; against Asa BRIGHAM sufficient to make full amount of judgment and costs. Order of payment issued to William T. AUSTIN, March 28, 1834. Execution issued by W. P. SCOTS, April 25, 1834.

No. 122. Edwin WALLER, abrogation of court procedure, March, 1834.

Court Records

Full Text:

At the March term of the Alcaldes Court for the Jurisdiction of Brazoria--The following order was entered by the
court after consultation of all the causes at the bars: It
was ordered that the old order of this Court be abrogated
and that the code of practice for the State of Louisiana be
adopted as the rules of this Court so far as they are applicable and in conformity with the existing laws of this
State. And it was ordered that the same be adopted and conformed to as the rules of this Court from this time forward.
I certify to the above

                              Edwin Waller
                              Alcalde

No. 123. Asa BRIGHAM vs. HOWTH and WILLIAMS. Defendants appeared
and confessed judgment for $80.39 and interest. Execution issued
October 8, 1834; new execution issued January 24, 1835.

No. 124. Nancy BAILEY vs. E. ANDERSON, administrator of J. S.
COUNCEL. Notice issued March 25, 1834; continued until April 12;
continued until April 18.

No. 125. Nancy BAILEY vs Joseph REES, administrator of C. G. COX.
Notice issued March 25, 1834.

No. 126. Nancy BAILEY vs. T.F.L. PARROTT. Notice issued March 25,
1834.

No. 127. H. H. LEAGUE, agent for Robert H. BOYCE and COMPANY, vs.
Samuel WILDY. After hearing testimony and examining law, court
ruled that original plaintiff was entitled to $557.89; defendant
entitled to $604.09, leaving balance of original judgment $46.20;
cost to be assessed against original plaintiff.

No. 128. William STAFFORD vs. Jacob BETTS. Submitted to arbitrators E. ANDREWS and E. ANDERSON. Compromise could not be reached;
suit continued to April 28, 1834.

No. 129. C. B. STEWART vs. J. A. H. CLEVELAND. Submitted to
arbitrators William J. RUSSELL and Henry AUSTIN. Judgment in
favor of plaintiff for $17.00, costs to be assessed against plain-
tiff. Execution issued October 22, 1834; new execution issued by
W. H. SLEDGE, secretary, for Silas DINSMORE, primary judge, January
28, 1835.

No. 130. C. B. STEWART vs. L. C. MANSON. Attorney for defendant
appeared and confessed judgment for $14.63 and interest. Execution
issued September 4, 1834, new execution issued by W. H. SLEDGE,
secretary, for Silas DINSMORE, primary judge, January 28, 1835.

No. 131. Joseph BROWN vs. Elizabeth POWELL. Submitted to arbitrators A. W. BREEDLOVE and R. L. REEDING. Judgment in favor of plaintiff for $43.00 and interests Execution issued October 22, 1834; new execution by W. H. SLEDGE, secretary, for Silas DINSMORE, primary judge, January 28, 1835.

No. 132. George HUFF, surviving partner of Lewis S. VIDIR, vs. Elizabeth POWELL. Submitted to arbitrators H. STRATTON and Stephen RICHESON. Judgment in favor of plaintiff for $15.38. Execution issued October 22, 1834; new execution issued by W. H. SLEDGE, secretary, for Silas DINSMORE, primary judge, January 28, 1835.

No. 133. John O'NEAL, for Enoch HARRIS, vs. G. B. COTTEN. Submitted to arbitrators G. M. COLLINSWORTH and Asa BRIGHAM. Judgment in favor of plaintiff for $10.00 and interest.

No. 134. Charles B. STEWART vs. James P. CALDWELL. Defendant sent written confession of judgment for $58.35, March 26, 1834. Original note attached to page.

No. 135. Thomas F. McKINNEY vs. Wm. H. JACK, curator and defender of HOOD and MILTON, Charles D. SAYRE, garnisher. Submitted to arbitrators Gowin HARRIS and Edmund ANDREWS. Agreement could not be reached; case submitted to court. Judgment against plaintiff, who had not been able to substantiate his claims; costs assessed against plaintiff, April 12, 1834.

No. 136. John J. GAY vs. Thomas R. ERWIN. Notice issued, March 29, 1834; case continued until April 26, 1834. Judgment against defendant for $8.00, April 26, 1834. Execution issued October 22, 1834.

No. 137. HOWTH and WILLIAMS, holder of note made payable to John AUSTIN, vs. William FREAM and William DAILEY. Submitted to arbitrators Sylvester BOWEN and Francis MOORE. Judgment in favor of plaintiff for $23.00 and interest. Execution issued April 16, 1834, alias issued April 5, 1835.

No. 138. Ephriam ANDERSON, administrator for succession of J. S. COUNCEL vs. John A. WHARTON, curator O. H. ALLEN. No other entries.

No. 139. Shubael MARSH vs. William H. PATTON. Submitted to arbitrators George M. COLLINSWORTH and Asa BRIGHAM. Judgment in favor of plaintiff for $17.00. Notation states that above amount was paid; receipt for amount by William H. JACK, April 19, 1834.

No. 140. A. W. BREEDLOVE vs. John A. WHARTON, curator and defender of O. H. ALLEN. No other entries. Summons issued March 16, 1835.

No. 141. HALEY and CARSON vs. John A. WHARTON, curator and defender of O. H. ALLEN. No other entries.

No. 142. Sylvester BOWEN vs. John A. WHARTON, curator and defender of O. H. ALLEN. No other entries.

No. 143. L. H. PETERS vs. Thomas R. ERWIN. Never tried, as case crossed off.

No. 144. L. H. PETERS vs. J. B. COWAN. Notice issued April 4, 1834.

No. 145. L. H. PETERS vs. Thomas R. ERWIN. Submitted to arbitrators Horace STRATTON and Sylvester BOWEN. Judgment in favor of plaintiff for $18.18 and interest. Execution issued October 22, 1834.

No. 146. L. H. PETERS vs. Abraham JUNKER. Defendant appeared and confessed judgment for $3.80. Execution October 22, 1834; alias issued April 5, 1835.

No. 147. Thomas A. BORDEN vs. William J. RUSSELL, administrator for Francis HAMILTON. Notice issued April 4, 1834.

No. 148. Thomas R. ERWIN vs. Thomas JAMESON. Notice issued April 9, 1834.

No. 149. Thomas R. ERWIN vs. Benjamin TENNEL, administrator for Robert MARTIN. Notice issued April 9, 1834; defendant out of jurisdiction.

No. 150. HALEY and CARSON vs. Benjamin TENNEL. Notice issued April 9, 1834; defendant out of jurisdiction.

No. 151. Joseph POWELL vs. Joseph S. MARTIN. Notice issued April 9, 1834

No. 152. Edmund ANDREWS vs. HOWTH and WILLIAMS. Defendant appeared and confessed judgment for $97.80 and interest. Execution issued September 22, 1834; new execution issued by W. H. SLEDGE, secretary, January 28, 1835.

No. 153. Peter M. HEWS, holder of note payable to J. C. PEYTON, vs. William H. PATTON, administrator for Isaac MARSHALL. Attorney for defendant appeared and confessed judgment for $8.81. Execution issued October 22, 1834.

No. 154. William H. JACK vs. George HUFF, administrator of Samuel SAWYER. Notice issued April 10, 1834. No other entries.

No. 155. H. S. and N. BROWN vs. A. SNIDER. Notice issued April 10, 1834. No other entries.

No. 156. Henry S. and N. BROWN vs. George McKINSTRY. Defendant appeared and confessed judgment for demand of plaintiff. Notation states that $1,862.00 was received by LEAGUE and AINSWORTH.

Court Records

No. 157. H. S. and N. BROWN vs. Charles H. BENNETT. Notice issued April 10, 1834. No other entries.

No. 158. H. S. and N. BROWN vs. T. F. L. PARROTT, administrator of D. W. ANTHONY, deceased. Notice issued April 10, 1834. No other entries.

No. 159. Henry S. and N. BROWN vs. C. G. COX. Notice issued April 11, 1834. No other entries.

No. 160. H. S. and N. BROWN vs. W. D. C. HALL, administrator of Samuel PARKINS. Notice issued April 11, 1834; continued to April 26, 1834.

No. 161. William S. BROWN vs. Thomas S. MARTIN. Notice issued April 11, 1834. No other entries.

No. 162. A. G. and R. MILLS vs. William J. RUSSELL. Notice issued April 12, 1834. No other entries.

No. 163. William THOMPSON, for Sidney PHILLIPS, vs. Henry KLONNE. Notice issued April 12, 1834; suit settled; full amount paid by H. H. LEAGUE.

No. 164. H. S. and N. BROWN vs. Oliver H. ALLEN. No other entries.

No. 165. Arche HODGE vs. Henry AUSTIN. Submitted to arbitrators T. F. L. PARROTT and William DAILEY. Judgment in favor or plaintiff for $5.00   Notation states that judgment was paid to Captain H. (torn).

No. 166. McKINNEY, GROCE, and COMPANY vs. Joseph S. MARTIN. Judgment in favor of plaintiff for $49.62½, March 30, 1834.

The following index, direct by name of plaintiff and reverse by name of defendant, to the Docket, Jurisdiction of Brazoria, with reference to case number, has been prepared by the Historical Records Survey.

Direct

(Plaintiff vs. Defendant)

Court Records

(Plaintiff vs. Defendant)

Court Records

(Plaintiff vs. Defendant)

Court Records

(Plaintiff vs. Defendant)

Court Records

(Plaintiff vs. Defendant)

(Plaintiff bs. Defendant)

Court Records

(Plaintiff vs. Defendant)

Reverse

(Defendant vs. Plaintiff)

Court Records

(Defendant vs. Plaintiff)

Court Records

(Defendant vs. Plaintiff)

Court Records

(Defendant vs. Plaintiff)

Court Records

(Defendant vs. Plaintiff)

Court Records

(Defendant vs. Plaintiff)

Court Records

(Defendant vs. Plaintiff)

WHARTON, John A., curator for
O.H. ALLEN, vs. Ephriam ANDERSON,
adm. for succession of
J.S. COUNCEL   138
WHARTON, John A., curator for
O.H. ALLEN, vs. Sylvester
BOWEN   142
WHARTON, John A., curator of
O.H. ALLEN, vs. A. W.
BREEDLOVE   140
WHARTON, John A., curator and
defender of O.H. ALLEN, vs.
G.B. COTTEN   103
WHARTON, John A., curator for
O.H. ALLEN, vs. HALEY and
CARSON   141
WHARTON, John A., agt. and
curator for John M. and
Pamilia PORTER, adms. for
B.A. PORTER, and George
TENNELL vs. Wyly MARTIN   46
WILDY, Samuel vs. H.H. LEAGUE   84
WILDY, Samuel vs. H.H. LEAGUE,
agt. for Robert H. BOYCE
and COMPANY   127
WILLIAMS, A. vs. T.F.L.
PARROTT   67

WILLIAMS, Augustus, Wm.
E. HOWTH, A.G. and R.
MILLS vs. S. FULLER   113
WILLIAMS, Henry and Solomon,
vs. A.G. and R. MILLS   81
WILLIAMS and HOWTH vs.
Edmund ANDREWS   152
WILLIAMS and HOWTH vs.
Asa BRIGHAM   123
WILLIAMS, Napoleon D. vs.
HOWTH and STEVINSON   4
WILLIAMS, Solomon vs.
adms. of John AUSTIN   100
WILLIAMS, Solomon vs. S.HOIT   26
WRIGHT, I.G., and P.R. BARTLESON
vs. Robert VINCE   78
YOUNG, Samuel vs. J.S.D.
BYROM, holder of note to
McKINSTRY and AUSTIN   37
YOUNG, Samuel vs.
George B. McKINSTRY   36
YOUNG, Samuel vs.
A.G. and R. MILLS   61

9. A GENERAL DOCKET OF ALL THE SUITS INSTITUTED BEFORE THE
PRIMARY COURT OF JURISDICTION OF COLUMBIA SINCE ITS
ORGANIZATION, 1835.
1 vol.

General docket of the cases instituted in the primary court of the
Jurisdiction of Columbia, showing the name of plaintiff, name of
defendant, number of case, date of notice, recapitulation of fees.
A few show notations of final settlement. Arr. chron. by date of
filing. Partial alph. index, E-Z, with direct reference by name
of plaintiff to case number. 268 pp. 10 x 8 x 2. C.C., office.

The following index, direct by name of plaintiff and reverse
by name of defendant, with reference to page number, has been prepared by the Historical Records Survey

Direct

(Plaintiff vs. Defendant)

ANDERSON, Ephriam vs.
Thomas B. BELL   52

ANDERSON, E. vs. J. W.
CLOUD   51

Court Records

(Plaintiff vs. Defendant)

Court Records

(Plaintiff vs. Defendant)

Court Records

(Plaintiff vs. Defendant)

Court Records

(Plaintiff vs. Defendant)

Court Records

(Plaintiff vs. Defendant)

Court Records

(Plaintiff vs. Defendant)

Court Records

(Plaintiff vs. Defendant)

Court Records

(Plaintiff vs. Defendant)

TAYLOR, Jesse vs. W. B.
     SWEENEY   42
TAYLOR, John B. vs. R. H. W.
     REEL   118
TAYLOR, Samuel vs. Henry
     AUSTIN   21
TAYLOR, S. vs. P. R. SPLANE   84
THOMPSON, Jesse for T. McCLELLAN
     vs. S. SMITHERS   37
TINSLEY, A.B. vs. John D.
     NEWELL   54
TONE, Thomas vs. W.B. SWEENEY 227
VELASCO ASSOCIATION vs. B.T.
     ARCHER and Daniel T.
     DONALSON   217, 222
VELASCO ASSOCIATION vs.
     J. BROWN   216, 221
VELASCO ASSOCIATION vs. B.A.
     PORTER and Asa MITCHELL
                                  217, 222
VERNON, Alexander vs.
     Anderson ESTES   226
WAKEFIELD N., vs. T.R. ERWIN   44
WALKER, Joseph vs.
     succession of A. MILLICAN   124
WALLER, E. vs.
     succession of Milton
     ANDERSON   122
WALLER, E. vs. A.W. BREEDLOVE 166
WALLER, E. vs. W.D.C. HALL   232
WALLER, E. vs. Joseph MIMS   166
WALLER, E. vs. R. D. MOORE   115
WALLER, E. vs. P. R. SPLANE   116
WALLER, E. vs. J. THOMAS   108
WESTALL, Andrew vs. W.D.C.
     HALL   36
WESTALL, Andrew vs. E. WALLER 211
WESTALL, James M., deceased, by
     Edward L. PETTUS vs.
     Elizabeth MARTIN, alias
     POWELL   164
WESTALL, J.M., succession of vs.
     Elizabeth POWELL   165
WHARTON, J.A. vs. P.R.SPLANE   119
WHARTON, W.H. vs. R.D.MOORE   150
WHITE, Walter C. vs.
     succession of J. AUSTIN   81
WHITE, W.C. vs. W.T. AUSTIN   42
WHITE, W.C., J.H. BELL, T.F.
     McKINNEY, W.H. PATTON, and

S.M. WILLIAMS vs.
     S. SMITHERS   71
WHITESIDES, James vs.
     Davis TALLEY   78
WHITING, Samuel
     vs. James A.E. PHELPS
                                  205, 226
WIGHTMAN, E.R. vs. J. REES 55
WILLIAMS and HOWTH vs.
     John CAMPBELL   178
WILLIAMS and HOWTH vs.
     E. DEAL   44
WILLIAMS and HOWTH vs.
     E. JEFFERY   48
WILLIAMS and HOWTH vs.
     Anson JONES   43
WILLIAMS and HOWTH vs.
     Benjamin McKINNEY   48
WILLIAMS and HOWTH vs.
     T.F.L. PARROTT   86
WILLIAMS and HOWTH vs.
     P.R. SPLANE   47
WILLIAMS and HOWTH vs.
     Benjamin TENNEL   95
WILLIAMS and McKINNEY vs.
     S. BOWEN   146, 202
WILLIAMS and McKINNEY vs.
     HOWTH and WILLIAMS   121
WILLIAMS, R. H. vs.
     W. B. SWEENEY   27
WILLIAMS, R.H. vs.
     A. WILLIAMS   143
WILLIAMS, S.M., J.H. BELL,
     T.F. McKINNEY, W.H.
     PATTON, and W.C. WHITE vs.
     S. SMITHERS   71
WILSON, James vs. T.
     SPLANE   69
WILSON, Wm. vs. Edwin
     WALLER   104
WINSTON, Anthony vs.
     R. H. WILLIAMS   112
WOODRUFF, John vs.
     Andrew ROBINSON   75
WOODSON and McNEEL vs.
     T. R. ERWIN   97
WRAY, Edward vs. Thomas
     SPLANE   68
YOUNG, Samuel vs. A.
     BRIGHAM   138

Court Records

(Plaintiff vs. Defendant)

YOUNG, Samuel vs.
  John CAMPBELL   66

YOUNG, Samuel, succession
  of vs. R.F. NUGENT   167

Reverse

(Defendant vs. Plaintiff)

AINSWORTH, A.C. vs. W. T.
  AUSTIN   111
AINSWORTH, A.C. vs. J. H.
  BELL   228
AINSWORTH, A.C. vs. W. H.
  JACK   11
AINSWORTH, A.C. vs. P.SMITH   231
ALEXANDER, C.R. vs. Joseph
  REES   204
ALSBURY, L. vs. A. JONES   186
ALSBURY, Thos. J. vs.
  Robert COCHRANE   6
ALSBURY, T.J., and W. GIBSON
  vs. Robt. COCHRANE   5
ANDERSON, E. vs. Jeremiah
  BROWN   197
ANDERSON, E. vs. A. JONES   182
ANDERSON, Milton, succession
  of vs. E. WALLER   122
ANDREWS, E. vs. W.T. AUSTIN   229
ANTHONY, D.W., succession of
  vs. RUTHERFORD and CO.   120
ARCHER, Branch T. vs.
  Asa MITCHELL   207
ARCHER, B.T., and
  Daniel T. DONALSON vs.
  VELASCO ASSOCIATION   217, 222
AUSTIN, Henry, vs. succession
  of D.W. ANTHONY   156
AUSTIN, H. vs. W.T. AUSTIN   93
AUSTIN, H. vs. W.D.C. HALL   112
AUSTIN, H. vs. C.R. PATTON   123
AUSTIN, H. vs. Samuel TAYLOR   21
AUSTIN, H., and W. ROBERTS
  vs. K.C. CUNNINGHAM   223
AUSTIN, J., succession of vs.
  A.W. BREEDLOVE   131
AUSTIN, J., succession of vs.
  Walter WHITE   81
AUSTIN and REYNOLDS vs. succes-
  ion of D.W. ANTHONY   161
AUSTIN and REYNOLDS vs. succes-
  sion of M. HENRY   175

AUSTIN, W.T. vs. C. H.
  BENNETT   37
AUSTIN, W.T. vs. C.G. COX   195
AUSTIN, W.T. vs. T.R.
  ERWIN for B.F. CAGE   195
AUSTIN, W.T. vs. Thomas
  GAY   201
AUSTIN, W.T. vs. succession
  of M. HENRY   196
AUSTIN, W.T. vs. W.E.
  HOWTH   77, 90
AUSTIN, W.T. vs.
  Margaret JAMESON   46
AUSTIN, W.T. vs. A. JONES   194
AUSTIN, W.T. vs. W.E.
  MATHER for Mr. PANTALIAN
                                   194
AUSTIN, W. T. vs.
  T. F. L. PARROTT   196
AUSTIN, W.T. vs. L.H.
  PETERS   7
AUSTIN, W.T. vs.
  Walter C. WHITE   42
BAILEY, J.B., succession of
  vs. BRIGHAM and
  RICHARDSON   54
BAILEY and SMITH vs.
  J. CHAFFIN   105
BAILEY, William P. vs.
  A. JONES   185
BAXTER, William, and G. W.
  WHITESIDES vs. T.
  DILLARD   173
BELL, Josiah H. vs.
  Stephen RICHARDSON   124, 144
BELL, J.H. for W. HARVEY vs.
  RICHARDSON and DAVIS   88
BELL, Pleasant vs.
  A. BRIGHAM   29
BELL, Thomas B. vs.
  E. ANDERSON   52
BENNETT, Charles H. vs.
  H.S. and N. BROWN   46

Court Records

(Defendant vs. Plaintiff)

Court Records

(Defendant vs. Plaintiff)

Court Records

(Defendant vs. Plaintiff)

Court Records

(Defendant vs. Plaintiff)

(Defendant vs. Plaintiff)

Court Records

(Defendant vs. Plaintiff)

86

Court Records

(Defendant vs. Plaintiff)

Court Records

(Defendant vs. Plaintiff)

WILLIAMS, A. vs.
   R. H. WILLIAMS   143
WILLIAMS, A., and C.B. RAINS
   vs. S.G. BREEDLOVE   116
WILLIAMS, Elliott vs.
   M.W. SMITH   133
WILLIAMS and HOWTH vs.
   McKINNEY and WILLIAMS 121
WILLIAMS, R.H. vs. L.C.
   MANSON   220
WILLIAMS, R.H. vs.
   Thomas OSBORNE   189
WILLIAMS, R.H. vs.
   Anthony WINSTON   112
WILLIAMS, S. vs.
   succession of J. AUSTIN 148
WILLIAMSON, R.M. vs.
   J.S.D. BYROM   119

WILLIAMSON, R.M. vs.
   J.F. PERRY   212
WILSON, Abraham S. vs.
   T.F.L. PARROTT   128
WILSON, R., and R.T. ERWIN
   vs. succession of J.
   AUSTIN   58
WILSON, Wm. vs. T. R.
   ERWIN   7
WOODRUFF, William vs.
   Anson JONES   10
WOODSON and McNEEL vs.
   succession of
   D.W. ANTHONY   158
WRIGHT, R.T. vs.
   W.T. AUSTIN   30

10. FILE DOCKET, JURISDICTION OF COLUMBIA, 1835. 1 vol.
Docket of cases filed in the primary court of the Jurisdiction of
Columbia, during the year 1835. A brief notation of the disposition of the case is written beside each entry. An occasional
note refers to recording of the proceedings in Book A, which is
Record (Final), 12. Arr. numer. by case no. No index. Last 53
pages of Execution Docket (District Court), 1837-41, Vol. B. 53
pp. 16 x 9 x 2. D.C., office.

The following index, direct by name of plaintiff and reverse
by name of defendant, has been prepared by the Historical Records
Survey. Reference is to case number.

Direct

(Plaintiff vs. Defendant)

ANDREWS, Edmund vs.
   Anson JONES   452
ANGIER, S.F. vs. W.D.C. HALL 352
ANGIER, S.F. vs. Gerren
   HINDS   357
ANGIER, S.F. vs. Polly
   McNEEL   356
ANGIER, S.F. vs.
   Andrew ROBINSON   353
ANGIER, S.F. vs. Edwin
   WALLER   351
ANGIER, S.F. vs.
   Andrew WESTALL   355
ANTHONY, D.W., succession of
   vs. Henry AUSTIN   304

ANTHONY, D.W., succession of
   vs. Sylvester BOWEN 316
ANTHONY, D.W., succession of
   vs. J. BROWN   307
ANTHONY, D.W., succession of
   vs. BROWN, SMITH, and
   McKINSTRY   312
ANTHONY, D.W., succession of
   vs. J.W. CALVERT   306
ANTHONY, D.W., succession of
   vs. Thomas R. ERWIN 317
ANTHONY, D.W., succession of
   vs. John FOSTER   319
ANTHONY, D.W., succession of
   vs. Margaret JAMESON 308

Court Records

(Plaintiff vs. Defendant)

ANTHONY, D.W., succession of vs. McNEEL and WOODSON	309	
ANTHONY, D.W., succession of vs. MESSRS. PATTON	318	
ANTHONY, D.W., succession of vs. David RANDON	310	
ANTHONY, D.W., succession of vs. REYNOLDS and AUSTIN	314	
ANTHONY, D.W., succession of vs. B.F. SMITH	313	
ANTHONY, D.W., succession of vs. P.R. SPLANE	311	
ANTHONY, D.W., succession of vs. Edwin WALLER	315	
AUSTIN, John, succession of vs. Thomas HALL	393	
AUSTIN, John, succession of vs. W.D.C. HALL	392	
AUSTIN, John, succession of vs. John SHARP	406	
AUSTIN, John, succession of vs. Peyton R. SPLANE	394	
AUSTIN, John, succession of vs. adm. of WESTALL	248	
AUSTIN, S.F. for James F. PERRY vs. R. HODGE	423	
AUSTIN, S.F. for James F. PERRY vs. F. MOORE	421	
AUSTIN, William T. vs. Edmund ANDREWS	454	
AUSTIN, W.T., and G.B.McKINSTRY vs. C.G. and J.S. COX	299	
BABCOCK, GARDINER, and CO. vs. A. BRIGHAM	270	
BAILEY, J.B., succession of vs. T.F.L. PARROTT	379	
BAILEY, J.B., succession of vs. Joseph H. POLLEY	405	
BAILEY, J.B., succession of vs. Robert STEVENSON	377	
BAILEY, Mary and Elizabeth vs. Henry SMITH	396	
BAIRD, Charles vs. J.C. HAWKINS	305	
BELL, Josiah H. vs. A. C. AINSWORTH, curator for James HUGHES	452	
BELL, J.H. vs. Robert H. COCHRANE	410	
BELL, J.H. vs. John SHARP	441	

BENNETT and BROWN vs. E. POWELL	387	
BENNETT, Charles H. vs. P.R. SPLANE	431, 433	
BETNER, Charles A. vs. J.A.H. CLEVELAND	376, 449	
BETNER, C.A. vs. Augustus WILLIAMS	391	
BIGGAM, Francis vs. William HARRIS	375	
BOWEN, Sylvester vs. T.F.L. PARROTT	408	
BOWEN, Sylvester vs. T.F.L. PARROTT and LADY	419	
BRADLEY, James vs. E. MATHER and M.W. SMITH	443	
BREEDLOVE, A.W. vs. John AUSTIN	259	
BREEDLOVE, A.W. and S.G. vs. John A. WHARTON	295	
BREEDLOVE, Susan G., and PETERS vs. R.H. COCHRANE	247	
BROWN and BENNETT vs. E. POWELL	387	
BROWN, H.S. and N. vs. Benjamin TENNEL	32	
BROWN, Jeremiah vs. Ephriam ANDERSON	386	
BROWN, Jeremiah vs. Sylvester BOWEN	340	
BROWN, Jeremiah vs. F.I. HOSKINS	341	
BROWN, Jeremiah vs. Joseph MIMS	343	
BROWN, Jeremiah vs. R.D. MOORE	354	
BROWN, Jeremiah vs. James A. E. PHELPS	390	
BROWN, Jeremiah vs. W.B. SWEENEY	389	
BUCKNER, W. vs. W. B. SWEENEY	404	
BURNET, D.G. vs. Robert CLOKY	457	
BYROM, John S.D. vs. P.R. SPLANE	429	
BYROM, J.S.D. vs. R.M. WILLIAMSON	235	
CAGE, B.F. by Thomas R. ERWIN vs. W.T. AUSTIN	383	

Court Records

(Plaintiff vs. Defendant)

Court Records

(Plaintiff vs. Defendant)

Court Records

(Plaintiff vs. Defendant)

Reverse

(Defendant vs. Plaintiff)

Court Records

(Defendant vs. Plaintiff)

93

Court Records

(Defendant vs. Plaintiff)

Court Records

(Defendant vs. Plaintiff)

Court Records

(Defendant vs. Plaintiff)

Court Records

(Defendant vs. Plaintiff)

11. ALCALDE COURT PAPERS, 1831-36. 148 instruments in 4 containers. Original papers filed in cases or issued by the alcalde or primary court in the Municipality of Brazoria from December 28, 1831, to November 12, 1836. The instrument usually shows the names of the parties, place and date signed, nature of the instrument, conditions and amount involved, court orders, judgments and notices with officer's returns. Most of the instruments relate to civil, criminal, or probate cases; a few to agreements between individuals. Arr. chron. by date of instrument. No index. 10½ x 4½ x 4. Location of individual papers is shown by group number:

Group I: 85 instruments, 1832-36, filed in file box marked Old Papers, No. 1, wrapped and marked Colonial Records. C.C., office.

Group II: 2 instruments, 1833, filed in file box marked Executions Issued and Returned. C.C., office.

Group III: 35 instruments, 1831-35, filed in file box marked Old Alcalde, in container marked Old Alcalde Papers. D.C., office.

Group IV: 26 instruments, 1833-35, filed in file box marked Old Alcalde, in container marked Exhibits in 15491, CONLEY vs. ABRAMS. D.C., office.

The following calendar and index have been prepared by the Historical Records Survey. The index is a list of the names of parties mentioned in the instruments; reference is to serial number supplied for the purpose of reference.

1831

No. 1. John P. DILLARD to Robert H. WILLIAMS, Austin's Colony, December 28, 1831. Contract to purchase three slaves for $1500.00. Group III.

1832

No. 2. John BROWN, February 27, 1832. Affidavit subscribed to before Alcalde Henry SMITH that itemized account of Sylvester MURPHY was a true account of the indebtedness, $170.91. Debt contracted on July 31, 1831. Group III.

No. 3. Abner HARRIS, Bolivar, to William H. LEE, Brazoria, March 1, 1832. Transfer of blacksmith tools upon payment of $18.00. Group I.

No. 4. Solomon WILLIAMS to George B. McKINSTRY and John AUSTIN, Brazoria, March 4, 1832. Mortgage for $400.00 on one negro girl, SABETHA. Group I.

No. 5. William McKNIGHT, Bordentown, New Jersey, to John H. BOSTWICK, Brazoria, April 5, 1832. Power of attorney to settle accounts with Charles H. BENNETT, Brazoria, and with Nicholas D. BOND in regard to the cargo of the Schooner NORTH AMERICA, and other accounts due McKNIGHT in Mexico. Printed form. Faded. Group I.

No. 6. William HARRIS to Henry KLONNE, April 15, 1832. Promissory note for $168.00. Group III.

No. 7. Sylvester MURPHY, July 21, 1832. Probate papers. Group III.

No. 8. Sylvester MURPHY, deceased, July 24, 1832. Inventory of property made by Wyly MARTIN and others, subscribed to before Alcalde John AUSTIN, value $16,254.50. Group III.

No. 9. George B. McKINSTRY and William T. AUSTIN, August 27, 1832. Authorization to seize effects of Sylvester MURPHY, as per inventory attached, to satisfy claims issued by John AUSTIN. Group III.

No. 10. Phineas SMITH and Asa BRIGHAM, December 2, 1832. Notice to appear and effect amicable settlement with George W. SMITH through Jonathan C. PEYTON, issued by Alcalde Henry SMITH. Group I.

No. 11. Sylvester MURPHY, 1832. Itemized list of purchases by estate of MURPHY, for goods bought in 1832 from A.G. and R. MILLS, total amount $1,826.81. Group III.

1833

No. 12. Sylvester MURPHY, January 1, 1833. Bill of goods purchased by estate of MURPHY from A.G. and R. MILLS, $11.60. Group III.

No. 13. George ELLIOTT, February 8, 1833. Mortgage and judgment in favor of H.W. MUNSON and David RANDON, for $236.56, issued by Alcalde Henry SMITH. Group I.

No. 14. William PARKS, San Felipe de Austin, February 12, 1833. Complete inventory of articles taken from John McCROSKEY, amounting to $1,456.97. Nathaniel CABORN swore that he saw PARKS take the property from the house of McCROSKEY, that PARKS reminded him that the property belonged to McCROSKEY, that the property was carried away by wagon by PARKS, and that CABORN accompanied PARKS for some distance along the road to San Felipe. Group I.

No. 15. McKINSTRY and AUSTIN to Samuel YOUNG, March 2, 1833. Recepit for $25.00. Group I.

No. 16. D.H. HUNTER and WIFE vs. administrators of Samuel MURPHY, March 14, 1833. Petition. Group IV.

No. 17. REYNOLDS and AUSTIN, February to April, 1833. Account with E.W. GREGORY, New Orleans, with list of articles purchased. Group I.

No. 18. A.G. and R. MILLS vs. P.R. and Ann SPLANE, April 7, 1833. Account presented in suit brought. Group III.

No. 19. William McKNIGHT, Bordentown, New Jersey, to Charles D. SAYRE, Brazoria, Province of Texas, April 11, 1833. Power of attorney to collect debts due in the province. Group I.

No. 20. McKINSTRY and AUSTIN to Samuel YOUNG, April 22, 1833. Receipt for $40.00. Group I.

No. 21. Wyly MARTIN vs. estate of John AUSTIN, May 7, 1833. Petition for and order of payment. Group IV.

No. 22. J. BROWN to J.S.D. BYROM, July 1, 1833. Promissory note for $176.84. Group III.

No. 23. Henry SMITH to sheriff, July 1, 1833. Notice to AUSTIN and McKINSTRY to appear in action brought by J.S.D. BYROM on claim for $242.37. Group III.

No. 24. Allen LARRISON to Alcalde Henry SMITH, July 3, 1833. Petition for guardianship in which LARRISON states that he is a mill and gin wright, that one Jesse WILLIAMS, aged about sixteen, has applied to become an apprentice under him. The alcalde granted LARRISON permission to become guardian for WILLIAMS for four years. Group I.

No. 25. George D. SHAW, curator for William PARKS, July 11, 1833. Notice to appear to answer to cause brought by Sally McCROSKEY and William D. LACY, amount $1,606,43 3/4, issued by Henry SMITH. Group I.

No. 26. George D. SHAW, July 11, 1833. Designation as curator for William PARKS, and order to answer petition of Sally McCROSKEY, issued by William SMITH. Group I.

No. 27. William HARRIS, Chocolate Bayou, to Henry SMITH, Brazoria, July 12, 1833. Group III. Full text:

> dear sir
>   These authorize Mr. F. MOORE to arrange the business with you relative to a note against me in favor of Mr. KLONNE I wish I have what time the law will allow me.
>
> Henry Smith, Esq.
>
> Yours respectfully
> William Harris

No. 28. Charlotte ROBERTSON vs. Asa BRIGHAM, administrator of estate of Edward ROBERTSON, July 15, 1833. Petition, citation for compromise, certificate, and citation to answer demands. Group IV.

No. 29. D.W. ANTHONY, July 20, 1833. Appointment as curator for William PARKS in place of George D. SHAW, who was absent, issued by Alcalde Henry SMITH. ANTHONY acknowledged the appointment on the same day. Group I.

No. 30. Samuel SAWYER vs. George B. McKINSTRY, July 27, 1833. Brazoria. Note on judgment for $9,755.75. Group IV.

No. 31. S. Rhodes FISHER vs. Seth INGRAM, Department of Bexar, Jurisdiction of Austin. Execution in favor of plaintiff for $383.43 with interest from September 25, 1830, amounting to $30.68½. Executed by B.F. CAGE for G.M. COLLINSWORTH, sheriff, August 5, 1833, on one-half league of land on NE of San Bernard River. Group II.

No. 32. A.G. and R. MILLS vs. administrators of Sylvester MURPHY, September 6, 1833. Petition for order of payment. Group IV.

No. 33. A. G. and R. MILLS vs. representatives of Sylvester MURPHY, September 6, 1833. Petition for inventory of estate. Group IV.

No. 34. Charles H. BENNETT vs. W. D. C. HALL, September 7, 1833. Petition issued. Group IV.

No. 35. Administrators of John AUSTIN vs. Louis C. MANSON, September 7, 1833. Mandate executed. Group IV.

No. 36. J. S. D. BYROM vs. Jeremiah BROWN, September 8, 1833. Notice to appear to answer cause on note for $176.84, issued by Alcalde Henry SMITH. Group III.

No. 37. Robert D. MOORE vs. M. W. SMITH, September 8, 1833. Petition on contract and note, $150.00. Group III.

No. 38. Robert D. MOORE vs. M. W. SMITH, September 8, 1833. Notice to attach goods and effects of M. W. SMITH sufficient to pay $150.00 with costs, issued by Alcalde Henry SMITH. Group III.

No. 39. L. LESASSIER, F.W. JOHNSON, Samuel M. WILLIAMS, Stephen F. AUSTIN, and Oliver JONES, San Felipe de Austin, September 11, 1833. Petition to stay sale of printing press, type, and fixtures belonging to estate of David W. ANTHONY, subscribed to before John P. COLES, regidor acting as alcalde, witnessed by William H. JACK and R. VAUGHAN. Group IV.

No. 40. R. M. WILLIAMSON, Brazoria, September 15, 1833. Injunction granted against T. F. L. PARROTT to prevent him from selling a printing press and other property belonging to estate of David W. ANTHONY. WILLIAMSON acting for Luke LESASSIER, Francis W. JOHNSON, Stephen F. AUSTIN, Oliver JONES, and Samuel WILLIAMS. Group IV.

No. 41. D. H. HUNTER and Ann, his wife, vs. representatives of

Sylvester MURPHY, September 18, 1833. Notice for amicable settlement, executed on W. T. AUSTIN by G. M. COLLINSWORTH. Group IV.

No. 42. WILLIAMS and HALEY vs. L. C. MANSON, September 23, 1833. Injunction executed. Group IV.

No. 43. Joseph McGEE vs. Daniel MILLIGAN, September 23, 1833. Group III. Full text:

> District of Brazoria to Citizen, Henry SMITH Constitutional Alcalde, for said Jurisdiction Joseph McGEE, a resident of his jurisdiction represents to your Honor that on or about the 18th of the present month, in said jurisdiction the said MILLIGAN made an assault upon the body of the said McGEE and with malice upressence and without having the fear of the law before his eyes beat bruised whipped and greatly abused the said McGEE to his great damage of five hundred dollars and to the great injury to the peace and harmony of this community--Therefore he prays your honor to issue your writ and caused the said MILLIGAN to appear before you at your office on some covenant day to answer to the above, charge and do such other justice as to you may seem equitable. This said McGEE personally appeared before me and made oath that the matter and things set forth in his petition were just and true as therein adjudged and set forth this 23 Sept 1833.
>
> Henry Smith
> Alcalde

No. 44. Joseph McGEE vs. Daniel MILLIGAN, September 30, 1833. Henry SMITH to sheriff to summon Daniel MILLIGAN to answer charges set forth in statement filed September 23, 1833. Group III.

No. 45. R. D. MOORE vs. M. W. SMITH, October 3, 1833. Defendant pleaded that the facts as presented were not true, and prayed to be released from attachment. Group III.

No. 46. Warren D. C. HALL, October 5, 1833. Notice to appear to answer cause brought by Charles H. BENNETT on note for $125.00, issued by Alcalde Henry SMITH. Group III.

No. 47. Seth INGRAM, Robert H. WILLIAMS, W. L. CAZNEAU, and L. RAMSEY, October 7, 1833. Appraisements of land involved in execution in favor of S. Rhodes FISHER. Appraised by WILLIAMS and INGRAM at $1.00 per acre; appraised under affidavit by CAZNEAU at 20¢, and by RAMSEY at 30¢. Sworn to before Samuel HOIT, commissioner. Group II.

No. 48. Louis C. MANSON, October 8, 1833. Notice to appear to answer to cause brought by T. F. L. PARROTT on bill for $188.25. Group II.

No. 49 A. W. BREEDLOVE and G.B. COTTEN, October 14, 1833. Notice to appear to testify in suit brought by T. F. L. PARROTT, administrator of D. W. ANTHONY, issued by Alcalde Henry SMITH. Group III.

No. 50. J. S. D. BYROM vs. W. T. AUSTIN, October 10, 1833. Petition issued. Group IV.

No. 51. Caleb KEMP vs. Freeman GEORGE, October 15, 1833. Motion for amicable settlement. Group IV.

No. 52. Louis C. MANSON, October 17, 1833. Notice to appear to stand trial in cause brought by T. F. L. PARROTT, issued by Henry SMITH. Group III.

No. 53. Godwin B. COTTEN to Samuel YOUNG, October 29, 1833. Mortgage on two hundred acres of land out of League No. 5, fronting five acres on the west bank of the Colorado River, for $79.00 with interest for the period of one year. Issued by Alcalde Henry SMITH; witnessed by R. R. ROYALL, Henry AUSTIN, W. Barrett TRAVIS, and William H. JACK. Group I.

No. 54. William CLAPP and James CUMMINS, November 12, 1833. Notice to appear as witnesses in case of H. H. LEAGUE vs. Robert H. BOYCE, issued by Alcalde Henry SMITH. Group I.

No. 55. Samuel WILDY, November 12, 1833. Notice to appear to answer cause brought by H. H. LEAGUE, issued by Alcalde Henry SMITH. Included is a promissory note from Samuel WILDY to A. M. CLARE for $540.29, given July 15, 1833, due on or before October 1, 1833. Group I.

No. 56. Samuel WILDY, November 12, 1833. Notice to appear to answer cause brought by Robert H. BOYCE through his agent, H. H. LEAGUE, issued by Alcalde Henry SMITH. Group I.

No. 57. William TATE, William CLAPP, George ROBINSON, and Daniel RAWLS, November 15, 1833. Notice to appear as witnesses in case of H. H. LEAGUE vs. Samuel WILDY, issued by Alcalde Henry SMITH, November 15, 1833, Executed by G. M. COLLINSWORTH. Group I.

No. 58. Henry L. BOYCE, William CLAPP, W. McMAHAN, and Daniel RAWLS, November 16, 1833. Notice to appear in case of Robert H. BOYCE vs. Samuel WILDY, issued by Alcalde Henry SMITH. Group I.

No. 59. Joseph WALKER, D. S. WALTMAN, Joseph MIMS, and John JAMES, November 17, 1833. Notice to appear to give testimony in case of Joseph McGEE vs. Daniel MILLIGAN. Group III.

No. 60. Joseph McGEE vs. Daniel MILLIGAN, November 20, 1833. Notice of trespass, served and acknowledged by G. M. COLLINSWORTH. Group IV.

No. 61. Alvin H. ALLEN, December 2, 1833. Notice that the deposition of Samuel C. DOUGLAS would be taken in the alcalde's court, in suit of D. H. HUNTER and Ann Douglas HUNTER, his wife, vs. P. R. SPLANE. Group III.

No. 62. D. H. HUNTER and Ann Douglas HUNTER, his wife, vs. W. T. AUSTIN and G. B. McKINSTRY, December 3, 1833. Notice that plaintiff would take deposition of Seaborn GOODALL et al., residents of State of Georgia. Group III.

No. 63. J. L. VAUGHAN and Augustus WILLIAMS to Robert H. WILLIAMS, December 24, 1833. Mortgage contract on real property and negroes, subscribed to before Alcalde Henry SMITH, witnessed by Joseph MIMS, W. B. SWEENEY, D. C. CADY, and William H. JACK. Group I.

No. 64. Peyton R. SPLANE, December 29, 1833. Execution issued to sheriff to seize certain property of Peyton R. SPLANE to satisfy debts due creditors, issued by Alcalde John CHAFFIN. Property seized included one bay horse, which was sold at public out-cry to W. D. C. HALL for $109.00; executed July 2, 1834. Group I.

No. 65. Henry KLONNE vs. William HARRIS, 1833. Execution for $168.00. Judgment and costs settled by Augustus WILLIAMS, sheriff. Group IV.

1834

No. 66. H. H. LEAGUE vs. Samuel WILDY, January 1, 1834. Continuance in case granted plaintiff. Group I.

No. 67. H. H. LEAGUE to George HUFF, January 8, 1834. Power of attorney to receive money in possession of CHAMBERS and LEWIS, of San Felipe, to collect all debts and make proper settlements in the name of the grantor. Group I.

No. 68. A. G. MILLS vs. William T. AUSTIN, administrator, and P. R. and Ann D. W. SPLANE, heirs of Sylvester MURPHY, January 14, 1834. Order to make settlemtnt. Group IV.

No. 69. A. G. and R. MILLS vs. P. R. and Ann D. W. SPLANE, January 14, 1834. Order to make settlement. Group IV.

No. 70. John McCASHIN to LEAGUE and AINSWORTH, January 15, 1834. Power of attorney to act in the absence of McCASHIN, subscribed to before Alcalde Edwin WALLER. Badly torn and faded. Group I.

No. 71. A. G. and R. MILLS vs. P. R. and Ann D. W. SPLANE, January 22, 1834. Petition for execution. Group IV.

No. 72. A. G. and R. MILLS vs. G. B. McKINSTRY, W.T. AUSTIN, and P. R. and Ann D. W. SPLANE, January 22, 1834. Execution. Group IV.

No. 73.   Samuel WILDY vs. H. H. LEAGUE and Robert BOYCE, January 24, 1834. All instruments in case. Group IV.

No. 74.   A. G. and R. MILLS vs. P. R. and Ann D. W. SPLANE, January 25, 1834. Execution levied on negro boy, NELSON, and girl, LUCY, by A. WILLIAMS, sheriff. Group IV.

No. 75.   Samuel WILDY, Robert BOYCE and COMPANY, John A. WHARTON, R. M. WILLIAMSON, and LEAGUE and AINSWORTH, January 27, 1834. Notice that he will appear before alcalde of AUSTIN, to take testimony of certain witnesses, issued by Alcalde Edwin WALLER. Group I.

No. 76.   Abram SHULER to G. B. JAMESON, January 31, 1834. Power of attorney. Badly faded. Group I.

No. 77.   Samuel D. WALTMAN, deceased, February 3, 1834. Letter of administration to James P. CALDWELL. Inventory of property, including personal goods and slaves, taken by Gowin HARRIS and William H. CARSON, subscribed to before Alcalde Edwin WALLER, Amount $2,144.00. Group I.

No. 78.   Charlotte JACKSON vs. W. T. AUSTIN, administrator for Edward ROBERTSON, February 5, 1834. Notice of suit. Group IV.

No. 79.   William B. SWEENEY, February 9, 1834. Notice to appear and settle claims for $600.00 due succession of M. HENRY, issued by Edwin WALLER. Group I.

No. 80.   William B. SWEENEY, John SWEENEY, and D. McCORMICK, February 9, 1834. Notice to appear to answer cause brought by J. T. TINSLEY, administrator for succession of James TURNER, issued by Alcalde Edwin WALLER. Group I.

No. 81.   Solomon WILLIAMS, February 9, 1834. Notice to appear to answer cause brought by Samuel HOIT for $270.00. Group I.

No. 82.   Solomon WILLIAMS, February 9, 1834. Notice to appear to answer cause brought by Samuel HOIT, in matter of a judgment of $275.00, which remained unpaid. Alcalde Edwin WALLER ordered WILLIAMS to appear to show cause. Group I.

No. 83.   HALEY and CARSON, February 12, 1834. Notice to appear to answer cause brought by HOWTH and STEVINSON for $100.53, issued by Alcalde Edwin WALLER. Included is promissory note from HALEY and CARSON to HOWTH and WILLIAMS for $100.53, January 18, 1834. Group I.

No. 84.   William TATE, February 13, 1834. Subpoena to appear in action of H. H. LEAGUE vs. Samuel WILDY, issued by Edwin WALLER. Group I.

No. 85.   Phineas SMITH and Asa BRIGHAM, February 14, 1834. Notice to appear to answer cause brought by Jonathan C. PEYTON, administrator for George W. SMITH, issued by Alcalde Edwin WALLER. Group I.

No. 86. P. R. SPLANE, February 18, 1834. Notice to sheriff to summon SPLANE to answer cause brought by Margaret JAMESON on debt of $350.00, issued by Alcalde Edwin WALLER. Group I.

No. 87. Margaret JAMESON vs. P. R. SPLANE, February 18, 1834. Notice to sheriff to summon parties, issued by Alcalde Edwin WALLER. Group I.

No. 88. Margaret JAMESON vs. P. R. SPLANE, February 18, 1834. Plaintiff petitioned for judgment to satisfy mortgage for $305.00 given by P. R. SPLANE on one farm building in town of Brazoria. Group I.

No. 89. Margaret JAMESON vs. P. R. SPLANE, February 18, 1834. Judgment against SPLANE for $305.00. Attached to judgment is promissory note from P. R. SPLANE to Margaret JAMESON, October 20, 1832. Group I.

No. 90. Godwin B. COTTEN vs. succession of D. W. ANTHONY, February 19, 1834. Six instruments in suit to recover wages from estate of D. W. ANTHONY. Included are an itemized list of wages, a petition for suit, and judgment rendered by Alcalde Edwin WALLER. Group I.

No. 91. McNEEL and WOODSON vs. Robert D. MOORE, February 22, 1834. Judgment for $172.00. A pledge on 20 cows and calves was given, and was granted by Alcalde Edwin WALLER, February 22, 1834. Promissory note for $172.09 in favor of McNEEL and WOODSON given by Robert D. MOORE, July 22, 1834, attached to judgment. Group I.

No. 92. Ephriam ANDERSON, February 22, 1834. Notice to appear to settle judgment of $20.00 in favor of E. JEFFERY, issued by Alcalde Edwin WALLER. Group I.

No. 93. Ruben P. T. STONE, February 22, 1834. STONE, under arrest in a criminal offense, petitioned through his counsel, John A. WHARTON, for permission for WHARTON to protect his civil rights. Granted by Alcalde Edwin WALLER. Group I.

No. 94. William H. JACK, February 22, 1834. Notice to Augustus WILLIAMS, sheriff, to summon JACK to appear as witness in suit of George B. McKINSTRY vs. Benjamin F. SMITH, issued by Alcalde Edwin WALLER. Group I.

No. 95. Abram WHEELER to G. B. WHEELER, February, 1834. Power of attorney to settle claims in the province. Badly faded. Group I.

No. 96. Samuel WILDY, March 4, 1834. Petition for new trial in suit brought by H. H. LEAGUE. Group I.

No. 97. O. H. SPENCER, March 6, 1834. Notice to answer cause filed for R. P. T. STONE, under arrest in criminal offense, by S. VANDIVERS, issued by Alcalde Edwin WALLER. VANDIVERS petitioned to attach property of SPENCER, amounting to $175.00. Petition granted. Group I.

No. 98. O. H. SPENCER, March 7, 1834. S. VANDIVERS petitioned through John A. WHARTON, curator for R. P. T. STONE, to recover $145.00 from SPENCER for debt due STONE. Subscribed to before Alcalde Edwin WALLER. Group I.

No. 99. Samuel YOUNG, March 12, 1834. Notice to appear and answer cause brought by George B. McKINSTRY in behalf of McKINSTRY and AUSTIN on note for $239.48, issued by Alcalde Edwin WALLER. Group I.

No. 100. Samuel D. WALTMAN, March 12, 1834. Account with T. F. L. PARROTT for $9.63 for medicines bought in 1833, paid by J. P. CALDWELL. Group I.

No. 101. HOWTH and STEVINSON vs. HALEY and CARSON, March 17, 1834. Execution and order to sheriff by Alcalde Edwin WALLER to seize and sell property of HALEY and CARSON sufficient to cover the amount of judgment. Levied on Blocks 1 and 4 in town of Brazoria, October 23, 1834, by Alex RUSSELL, deputy sheriff. Group I.

No. 102. Asa BRIGHAM to creditors (not named) of BRIGHAM and RICHARDSON, March 21, 1834. Mortgage deed to league of land on Hall's Bayou, on plat League No. 3, East, Jurisdiction of Brazoria, was to remain a pledge to creditors. Group I.

No. 103. Shubael MARSH to William H. JACK, March 28, 1834. Power of attorney to collect money owing MARSH by the succession of Obidiah PITTS. Group I.

No. 104. Charlotte JACKSON, alias ROBERTSON, vs. W. T. AUSTIN, administrator for Edward ROBERTSON, Marvh 30, 1834. Execution served. Group IV.

No. 105. William B. SWEENEY, April 6, 1834. Notice to appear to answer cause brought by M. HENRY, issued by Alcalde Edwin WALLER. Group I.

No. 106. Maurice HENRY, April 8, 1834. Petition to recover $600.00 from W. B. SWEENEY, brought by John A. WHARTON, executor. Group I.

No. 107. William B. SWEENEY, John SWEENEY, and David McCORMICK, April 8, 1834. Notice to appear to answer cause brought by J. T. TINSLEY for debt of $849.43 3/10, issued by Alcalde Edwin WALLER. Group I.

No. 108. Robert H. WILLIAMS, John JONES, George ROBINSON and William TATE, April 8, 1834. Notice to appear in case of LEAGUE vs. WILDY, issued by Alcalde Edwin WALLER. Group I.

No. 109. Warren D. C. HALL, April 9, 1834. Notice to appear and effect amicable settlement with Henry KLONNE in the amount of $440.00, issued by Alcalde Edwin WALLER. Group I.

No. 110. William H. JACK vs. George HUFF, administrator for Samuel SAWYER, April 10, 1834. Petition and commission to take testimony. Group IV.

No. 111. Daniel RAWLS and John JONES, April 12, 1834. Affidavit in the case of H. H. LEAGUE vs. Samuel WILDY, subscribed to before Alcalde Edwin WALLER. Group I.

No. 112. H. S. and N. BROWN vs. Oliver H. ALLEN, April 12, 1834. Petition to sue for $105.06, as per books of the tavern, requesting that action be directed against ALLEN'S property lying in the jurisdiction. Group I.

No. 113. William H. JACK, April 14, 1834. Notice that he would take the testimony of William B. TRAVIS, Ephram RODDY, Ira R. LEWIS and Jonathan C. PEYTON in suit of JACK vs. George HUFF, administrator of the succession of Samuel SAWYER. Group III.

No. 114. Benjamin F. SMITH, April 25, 1834. Affidavit stating that he was not able to procure witnesses to appear in case brought by George B. McKINSTRY. Group I.

No. 115. H. H. LEAGUE, April 30, 1834. Affidavit stating that he could not come to trial without services of William TATE, George ROBINSON, Bert H. WILLIAMS and John JONES, and that on or about April 1, 1833, he (LEAGUE) leased his ferry and tavern on the Colorado River to Samuel WILDY for $35.00 per month, and that WILDY had left the premises to great injury and had not paid rent as stipulated. Subscribed to before Alcalde Edwin WALLER. Group I.

No. 116. William B. SWEENEY, John SWEENEY, and David McCORMICK, April 30, 1834. Notice to answer petition brought by Isaac T. TINSLEY, administrator for James TURNER, on note for $849.43 3/4 signed by John A. WHARTON for petitioner. Included is promissory note from William B. SWEENEY, John SWEENEY, and David McCORMICK to I. T. TINSLEY. Group I.

No. 117. A. W. BREEDLOVE, to A. G. and R. MILLS, June 13, 1834. Transfer of claims held against Alvin H. ALLEN. Account filed for settlement in alcalde's court. Group I.

No. 118. Susan G. BREEDLOVE, to A. G. and R. MILLS, June 13, 1834. Transfer of claims held against Alvin H. ALLEN. Account filed for settlement in alcalde's court. Group I.

No. 119. George HUFF, June 29, 1834. Summons in suit of A. WHARTON vs. R. H. WILLIAMS, served by John HALE. Group III.

No. 120. William H. JACK, to D. HUNTER and WIFE, July 12, 1834. Notice that JACK will take testimony of Luke LOPER, Brazoria. Addressed to John A. WHARTON, attorney. Group III.

No. 121. A. G. and R. MILLS vs. Robert D. MOORE, July 20, 1834. Mortgage and judgment. Group III.

No. 122. William SWEENEY, John SWEENEY, and David McCORMICK, September 11, 1834. Notice to appear to answer cause brought by I. T. TINSLEY for $834.43 3/4, issued by Alcalde Edwin WALLER. Group I.

No. 123. Joseph Bernard HOPPE to F. C. GRAY and A. J. HARRIS, September 18, 1834. Apprentice indenture, in which HOPPE is bound to GRAY and HARRIS, printers, to lear the printing trade. Subscribed to before Alcalde Edwin WALLER, and witnessed by George M. COLLINS-WORTH, Gowin HARRIS, William HALEY, and C. A. BETNER. Group I. Full text:

> This indenture made the 18th day of Sept in the year of our lord one thousand and eight hundred and thirty four witnesseth that Joseph B. HOPPE aged Sixteen years four Months and one day hath, of his own free and voluntary will placd and bound himself apprentice unto GRAY and HARRIS printers of Brazoria, to learn the Sd. profession misstery or occupation of a Printer, which they the Sd. GRAY & HARRIS useth and with them as an apprentice to dwell continue and serve from this day of this date hens, unto the full end and term of four years and and eight months the Sd. apprentice, his Said Masters well and faithfully shall Serve, thir Secrets keep, thir lawful commands gladly do and obay; but to his Sd. Masters he shall not do nor wilfully Suffer to be done by others, but of the Same, to the utmost of his power, Shall forthwith give Notice to his Sd. Masters; the goods of his Sd. Masters he shall not embezzle or waste, nor them lend without thir consent, to any; at Cards, dice, or any other unlawful games he shall not play; Taverns or Ale houses he shall not frequent, Matrimony he shall not contract, from the Service of his Sd. Masters he shall not at any time depart or absent himself without his Sd. Masters leave: but in all things, as a good and faithful apprentice shall and will demean and behave himself towards his Sd. Masters and all thirs, during the said term. And the Sd. Masters doth agree to instruct the Sd. apprentice in the Sd. profession, Mistry or occupation of a printer which they now useth, with all things therunto belonging, shall and will teach, instruct or cause to be well and Sufficiently taught and instructed after the best way and manner he can, and shall and will also find and allow unto this Sd. apprentice Meat, drink, washing, lodging and apparrels both

linnen and woolen and all the necessaries fit and convenient for such an apprentice during the term aforesaid.

Witnesses   Joseph, Bernard, Hoppe
                                             F. C. Gray
Geo. M. Collinsworth   A. J. Harris
Gowin Harris

Asst. Witness   Edwin Waller   Asst. Witness
William Haley   Alcalde   Chas. A. Bettner

No. 124. J. S. D. BYROM vs. Jeremiah BROWN, September 25, 1834. Notice of petition executed. Group IV.

No. 125. Ann M. WALTMAN, October 3, 1834. Bill of goods bought from Thomas I. HAWKS, $8.87. Payment made by J. P. CALDWELL. Group I.

No. 126. Ann M. WALTMAN, October 3, 1834. Bill of goods purchased from Thomas I. HAWKS, 75¢. Payment made by James P. CALDWELL. Group I.

No. 127. Augustus WILLIAMS, sheriff, December 29, 1834. Receipt for costs from A. G. and R. MILLS in the suit brought by them against the succession of Sylvester MURPHY and Peyton R. SPLANE and WIFE. Group III.

1835

No. 128. William P. HARRIS, Robert WILSON, Elisha MATHER, Meriwether W. SMITH, and H. H. LEAGUE, January 2, 1835. Contract relating to steam grist and saw mill in Harrisburg. Group I.

No. 129. James L. VAUGHAN to Augustus WILLIAMS, January 9, 1835. Petition to Alcalde Asa BRIGHAM to summon WILLIAMS to appear in answer to suit brought by plaintiff (not named) to recover for property sold the defendant. Group I.

No. 130. John SWEENEY to S. MARSH, administrator for succession of Obidiah PITTS, January 10, 1835. Mortgage on one negro man, his wife, and four children, for $2,867.00. Group I.

No. 131. Augustus WILLIAMS or Robert H. WILLIAMS, January 15, 1835. Notice to sheriff to summon Augustus WILLIAMS or Robert H. WILLIAMS, his curator, to appear in answer to suit brought by James L. VAUGHAN, issued by Alcalde Asa BRIGHAM. Group I.

No. 132. Samuel HOIT vs. Solomon WILLIAMS, January 25, 1835. Alias execution issued by S. DINSMORE. Group I.

No. 133. J. A. E. PHELPS vs. succession of S. MURPHY, February 11, 1835. All papers in case. Group III.

No. 134.   McKINNEY and WILLIAMS to William H. JACK, March 23, 1835.
Power of attorney.   Group I.

No. 135.   Anthony WINSTON, of Alabama, to Primary Judge Silas
DINSMORE, April 6, 1835.   Complaint that Robert H. WILLIAMS owed
WINSTON $950.00 filed by W. H. JACK, attorney for plaintiff.
Citation issued by S. DINSMORE.   Group III.

No. 136.   Robert H. WILLIAMS, April 7, 1835.   Notice to appear to
answer cause brought by Anthony WINSTON in suit on note for $950.00,
issued by Primary Judge S. DINSMORE.   Printed form.   Group III.

No. 137.   T. F. L. PARROTT, curator for succession of J. AUSTIN, vs.
John W. HALL and W. S. HALL, May 20, 1835.   Notice of petition.
Group III.

No. 138.   Phineas RIPLEY vs. Allen LARRISON, June 2, 1835.   Judgment
in favor of plaintiff on account of $100.50 by court, S. DINSMORE,
primary judge.   Group III.

No. 139.   Theodore BENNETT and John SHARP, June 10, 1835.   Contract
forming a commercial and trading enterprise under the name of
BENNETT and SHARP, stating that they had purchased the goods of
Sterling McNEEL, and had given notes for the amount of purchase,
and agreeing to assume joint responsibility for the indebtedness.
Group I.

No. 140.   Edwin WALLER to John THOMAS, September 22, 1835.   Deed
for two negro slaves, one man and one woman, a bay pony and one
mule, in exchange for two negro slaves, one man and one woman.
Group I.

1836

No. 141. W. C. WHITE to B. C. FRANKLIN, September 1, 1836.   Petition
for probate of estate of Peletin W. GORDON.   Group I.   Full text:

Benj. C. Franklin, Esq: Marion, Sept. 3, 1836

        Dr. Sir Mr. Peletin W. GORDON late a resident of Columbia
was killed in the Alamo and died intestate.   He has some
property in Columbia and as I received a short time since a
letter from his father in the U.S. requesting me to administer
on his estate & also to give him information respects it.   I
have concluded to apply to your honour for letters.   He died
indebted to me a small sum & as he had no blood relation in
the county I presume the application is not improper.

                                    Respectfully yours,
                                    W. C. White

Court Records

No. 142. Walter C. WHITE, District of Brazos, Brazoria, October 18, 1836. Appointment as administrator for estate of Peletin W. GORDON, issued by Judge Benjamin C. FRANKLIN. Group I.

No. 143. James HINES and Edwin WALLER, November 2, 1836. Attest of inventory of property of Jesse STROTHER, deceased. Group I.

No. 144. Patrick FADDIN to Benjamin C. FRANKLIN, November 12, 1836. Petition. Group I. Full text:

    County of Brazoria   To the Honorable Benjamin C.
    District of Brazos   Franklin Judge in and for the
                                District of Brazos

The petition of Patrick FADDIN respectfully submits that his Brother John FADDIN was lately Killed by the Mexican Enemies of the Republic, whilse attached to Capt WESTOVERS Company of Col. FANNIN'S division, that he departed this life intestate, leaving no other relative in the Republic. Wherefore Your Petitioner prays that he may be appointed administrator of the said John FADDIN under such regulations as your Honor may deem right and proper.

                              his
                    Patrick   Faddin
                              mark

To Benjamin C. Franklin
Judge Dist Brazos
At Office Brazoria
12th Nov 1836

The foregoing petition read and the prayer of the Petitioner granted--It is ordered considered and adjudged by the court and Patrick FADDIN is hereby appointed Administrator of John FADDIN and it is ordered that letters of administration issue upon his taking the oath & filing the necessary Bond

                          Benjamin C. Franklin
                          Judge Dist. Brazos

                No date

No. 145. John SUTHERLAND to Benjamin C. FRANKLIN. Application for probation of estate of William WILLS, deceased. Group I. Full text:

    County of Brazoria   To the Honorable Benjamin C.
    District of Brazos   Franklin Judge in and for said
                                District

The petition of John SUTHERLAND respectfully represents

Court Records

that William WILLS late of the Republic of Texas was killed
at the "Alamo" by Mexican enemies of the Republic and departed this life intestate--wherefore your petitioner prays
that he may be appointed administrator of the said William
WILLS dec'd. In the absence of any relative of the dec'd
resident in the Republic of Texas under such regulations as
your honor may deem proper.

John Sutherland (ALS)

No. 146. L. C. MANSON. Affidavit that John AUSTIN, deceased, or
his succession had failed to keep contract and he felt that he should
not be called upon to appear in case. Filed by his attorney,
O. H. ALLEN. Group I.

No. 147. Robert J. CALDER to James P. CALDWELL. Account for
slaves bought from estate (not named). Group I.

No. 148. W. D. C. HALL to H. H. LEAGUE. Application for guardianship. Group I. Full text:

H. H. League, Esq. Sir:

I am requested by my counsel to mention through you the
security I offer for my full and legal administration as Tutor
for Ann E. WILKERSON should I receive the appointment-- is
land & Negroes Twice the amount of the effect of the minor,
with exceptionable personal security.

Warren D. C. Hall (ALS)

Index

12. RECORD (Final), 1828-38. 1 vol. (Book A).
Proceedings in the District Court for the Second Judicial District
in cases either originating in the alcalde or primary courts, or
based on cause prior to February 20, 1837. These proceedings include
copies of instruments introduced as exhibits in the case, copies of
judgments rendered by the District Court, and transcripts of de-
cisions from the Commissioner of Civil Appeals and the Supreme Court
(see Case No. 26). A number of the entries are referred to in the
dockets of the alcalde and primary courts by a notation under the
case "recorded in Book A." This system of recording the proceedings
of the District Court was widely used during the early period of the
courts, but was abandoned in 1879. The entire set consists of
nine volumes. Arr. numer. by case no., with an occasional variation
of entries referring to preceding cases. Direct alph. index by
name of plaintiff to case no. The Historical Records Survey has
prepared a reverse index by name of defendant for this volume.
457 pp. 15 x 9 x 2. D.C., office.

The following cases had their origin in the alcalde or primary
courts or were based on cause prior to 1837; the reference is to
case number.

No. 1. J. W. E. WALLACE vs. J. D. HOLDERMAN, based on cause, December
8, 1835.

No. 2. J. W. E. WALLACE vs. J. D. HOLDERMAN, based on cause, April
7, 1835.

No. 3. McKINNEY and WILLIAMS vs. John THOMAS, based on cause,
March 1, 1836.

No. 4. S. MARSH vs. Elijah CAPLE, James CRUNCK, and S. S. GILLET,
originated in primary court, Municipality of Columbia, March 18, 1835.

No. 5. E. W. GREGORY, endorser, vs. A. BRIGHAM, based on cause,
April 1, 1835.

No. 6. BABCOCK, GARDINER, and CO. vs. Asa BRIGHAM, surviving partner
of the firm of BRIGHAM and RICHARDSON, originated in primary court,
Jurisdiction of Columbia, March 19, 1835.

No. 7. SAYRE and NIXON vs. Asa BRIGHAM, originated in primary
court, Jurisdiction of Columbia, March 19, 1835.

No. 8. PALMER, SMITH, and CO. vs. Asa BRIGHAM et al., originated in
primary court, Jurisdiction of Columbia, March 19, 1835.

No. 9. HILL and HENDERSON vs. Asa BRIGHAM, originated in primary court, Jurisdiction of Columbia, based on cause, April 18, 1832.

No. 10. A. G. and R. MILLS vs. Asa BRIGHAM, originated in primary court, Jurisdiction of Columbia, based on cause, April 18, 1832.

No.10½. A. G. and R. MILLS vs. Asa BRIGHAM, surviving partner, based on cause, October 17, 1832.

No. 11. N. HARRINGTON, Jr. vs. Asa BRIGHAM et al., originated in primary court, Jurisdiction of Columbia, based on cause, September 14, 1832.

No. 12. Samuel YOUNG vs. Asa BRIGHAM, originated in alcalde court, Jurisdiction of Brazoria, January 23, 1834.

No. 13. McKINNEY and WILLIAMS vs. BOWEN and BYROM, originated in alcalde court, Jurisdiction of Brazoria, January 26, 1835.

No. 14. John W. BUCKNER vs. William B. SWEENEY, originated in primary court, Jurisdiction of Columbia, June 5, 1835.

No. 15. Anthony WINSTON vs. Robert W. WILLIAMS, originated in alcalde court, Jurisdiction of Columbia, March 21, 1835.

No. 16. Sterling McNEEL vs. M. W. SMITH, originated in primary court, Jurisdiction of Columbia, April 29, 1835.

No. 17. Walter C. WHITE vs. succession of John AUSTIN, originated in alcalde court, Jurisdiction of Columbia, October 23, 1834.

No. 18. William H. JACK vs. George HUFF, administrator of Samuel SAWYER, originated in alcalde court, April 9, 1834.

No. 19. David AYRES vs. W. B. SWEENEY and John FOSTER et al., based on cause, February 1, 1836.

No. 20. David BREEDING: Guarding & c vs. Wm. S. and Warren D. C. HALL, based on cause, January 1, 1837.

No. 22. Robert SCOBY, administrator of STROTHER, vs. William KENNEDY, based on cause, March 1, 1836.

No. 24. Wyly MARTIN vs. estate of John AUSTIN, originated in alcalde court, Jurisdiction of Brazoria, October 24, 1834.

No. 25. Walter C. WHITE, vs. T.F.L. PARROTT and WIFE, based on cause, December 7, 1833.

No. 26. William B. SWEENEY vs. Joseph H. POLLEY, originated in primary court, Jurisdiction of Columbia, March term, 1835, appealed by plaintiff to the Supreme Court of Texas, which granted injunction in favor of plaintiff, June 18, 1837.

No. 28. Joseph REES, executor for COX, vs. Peyton R. SPLANE, originated in primary court, Jurisdiction of Columbia, June 7, 1835.

No. 29. Charles H. BENNETT vs. Peyton R. SPLANE, originated in alcalde court, Jurisdiction of Columbia, June 2, 1835.

No. 30. Charles H. BENNETT vs. Peyton R. SPLANE, originated in primary court, Jurisdiction of Columbia, June 7, 1835.

No. 35. James F. PERRY, executor, vs. William BARRETT and Abner HARRIS, based on cause, April 4, 1828.

No. 37. Edwin WALLER for Monroe EDWARDS vs. Columbus R. PATTON, based on cause, October 1, 1835.

No. 41. M. W. SMITH vs. George ELLIOTT and Solomon WILLIAMS, originated in alcalde court, Jurisdiction of Brazoria, March 19, 1834.

No. 42. Abner HARRIS vs. Ruth HARRIS, widow of William HARRIS, and Mary Ann, Maria Ann, Elvia and Evelina, children and minors of said William HARRIS by said Ruth, their guardian; based on action sometime during 1830.

No. 43. Monroe EDWARDS vs. Thomas P. CROSBY, based on action, October 7, 1836.

No. 44. Thomas CAYCE vs. George HUFF, based on action, March 2, 1835.

No. 45. George B. McKINSTRY vs. T. F. L. PARROTT and Elizabeth E., his wife, administrators of John AUSTIN, based on cause, February 24, 1834.

No. 48. J. A. E. PHELPS vs. succession of S. MURPHY, originated in alcalde court, Jurisdiction of Columbia, January 26, 1835.

No. 49. Charles H. BURNET vs. W. T. AUSTIN, originated in primary court, Jurisdiction of Columbia, January 26, 1835.

No. 50. L. H. PETERS vs. Robert COCHRANE, originated in primary court, Jurisdiction of Columbia, June 10, 1835.

No. 55. William B. SWEENEY vs. M. W. SMITH and HALL, based on cause, November 7, 1834.

No. 64. Sylvester BOWEN vs. Peyton R. SPLANE, originated in alcalde court, Jurisdiction of Brazoria, April 3, 1834.

No. 77. Monroe EDWARDS vs. J. A. H. CLEVELAND, based on cause, December 6, 1836.

No. 80. R. MILLS and COMPANY vs. John D. and C. R. PATTON, based on cause, August 5, 1836.

No. 81. Gissen CLARK for A. BRISCOE vs. Augustus WILLIAMS and William P. HUFF, based on cause, October 28, 1833.

No. 82. William WARREN vs. Augustus WILLIAMS, based on cause, September 28, 1834.

No. 83. Thomas F. McKINNEY, administrator, vs. Thomas W. GRAYSON, based on cause, March 5, 1836.

No. 97. Isaac VANDORN vs. John A. WHARTON, based on cause, May 8, 1835.

No.100. HUGHES and WATERMAN vs. W. T. AUSTIN, surviving partner, based on cause, March 26, 1833.

No.101. Succession of W. J. EATON vs. succession of William T. AUSTIN, based on cause, February 18, 1836.

No.113. T. F. L. PARROTT, administrator for D. W. ANTHONY, vs. John A. WHARTON, administrator of O. H. ALLEN, Augustus WILLIAMS and Thomas CAYCE, based on cause, November 3, 1833.

The following index, direct by name of plaintiff and reverse by name of defendant, to the preceding list of cases has been prepared by the Historical Records Survey. Reference is to case number.

Direct

(Plaintiff vs. Defendant)

_____Court Records

(Plaintiff vs. Defendant)

Court Records

(Plaintiff vs. Defendant)

YOUNG, Samuel vs. Asa BRIGHAM 12

Reverse

(Defendant vs. Plaintiff)

Court Records

(Defendant vs. Plaintiff)

PARROTT, T.F.L. and Elizabeth E.,
  his wife, adms. of John AUSTIN,
  vs. George B. McKINSTRY   45
PARROTT, T.F.L. and wife vs.
  Walter C. WHITE   25
PATTON, Columbus R. vs. Edwin
  WALLER for Monroe EDWARDS   37
PATTON, C.R. and John D. vs.
  R. MILLS and COMPANY   80
POLLEY, Joseph H. vs.
  William B. SWEENEY   26
SAWYER, Samuel by George HUFF,
  adm. vs. Wm. H. JACK   18
SMITH, M.W. vs. Sterling
  McNEEL   16
SMITH, M.W., and HALL vs.
  William B. SWEENEY   55
SPLANE, Peyton R. vs.
  Charles H. BENNETT   29, 30
SPLANE, Peyton R. vs.
  Sylvester BOWEN   64
SPLANE, Peyton R. vs.
  Joseph REES, exr. for COX   28
SWEENEY, William B. vs.
  John W. BUCKNER   14
SWEENEY, W.B., and John FOSTER,
  et. al., vs. David AYRES   19
THOMAS, John vs.
  McKINNEY and WILLIAMS   3

WHARTON, John A. vs.
  Isaac VANDORN   97
WHARTON, John A., adm. of O.H.
  ALLEN, Augustus WILLIAMS,
  and Thomas CAYCE, vs. T.F.L.
  PARROTT, adm. for D.W.
  ANTHONY   113
WILLIAMS, Augustus, Thomas CAYCE,
  and John A. WHARTON, adm. of
  O.H. ALLEN vs. T.F.L.PARROTT,
  adm. of D.W.ANTHONY   113
WILLIAMS, Augustus, and William
  P. HUFF vs. A. BRISCOE by
  Gissen CLARK   81
WILLIAMS, Augustus vs.
  William WARREN   82
WILLIAMS, Robert W. vs.
  Anthony WINSTON   15
WILLIAMS, Solomon, and George
  ELLIOTT vs. M.W.SMITH   41

13. CIVIL CASES, 1835. 21 cases in 2 file boxes.
Papers of civil cases originating in the primary or alcalde courts
prior to 1837, which were continued in the district court of Brazoria
County. These cases were given numbers to conform with the filing
system of the district court. Each case is filed in a separate
container bearing the case number, name of plaintiff, and name of
defendant. Filed numerically in file boxes marked Civil Cases,
1-100. Case numbers may be secured from the index prepared by the
Historical Records Survey, which follows the list of cases. The
numbers vary from the case numbers in Record (Final), 12.
10½ x 4½ x 15. D.C., office.

No. 2. J. W. E. WALLACE vs. J. and D. HOLDERMAN, originated in
primary court, Jurisdiction of Columbia, March 20, 1835.

No. 3. W. D. C. HALL vs. John GATES, originated in primary court,
Jurisdiction of Columbia, April 24, 1835.

No. 4. J.W.E. WALLACE vs. J. HOLDERMAN, originated in primary
court, Jurisdiction of Columbia, April 27, 1835.

No. 12.   G. McNEAL vs. C. R. PATTON, originated in primary court, Jurisdiction of Columbia, June 12, 1835.

No. 13.   S. MARSH, administrator for Obidiah PITTS, vs. Elijah CAPLE, originated in primary court, Jurisdiction of Columbia, March 18, 1835.

No. 14.   E. W. GREGORY vs. A. BRIGHAM, originated in primary court, Jurisdiction of Columbia, April 7, 1835.

No. 17.   B. WHITING vs. Thomas CAYCE, originated in primary court, Jurisdiction of Columbia, March 19, 1835.

No. 18.   SAYRE and NIXON vs. Asa BRIGHAM, originated in primary court, Jurisdiction of Columbia, March 19, 1835.

No. 19.   PALMER, SMITH, and COMPANY vs. Asa BRIGHAM, originated in primary court, Jurisdiction of Columbia, March 19, 1835.

No. 19.   RICHARDSON and DAVIS vs. G. HUFF, originated in primary court, Jurisdiction of Columbia, March 20, 1835.

No. 21.   Peyton R. SPLANE vs. T. F. L. PARROTT and WIFE, originated in primary court, Jurisdiction of Columbia, March 20, 1835.

No. 22.   Robert D. MOORE vs. Robert H. WILLIAMS, originated in primary court, Jurisdiction of Columbia, June 8, 1835.

No. 23.   McKINNEY and WILLIAMS vs. BOWEN and BYROM, originated in primary court, Jurisdiction of Columbia, April 29, 1835.

No. 28.   R. MILLS et al. vs. Robert D. MOORE, originated in alcalde court, Jurisdiction of Columbia, May 21, 1835.

No. 33.   A. J. HARRIS vs. CAGE et al., based on judgment rendered in primary court, Jurisdiction of Columbia, March 1, 1835.

No. 44.   G. HUFF, curator of S. SAWYER vs. W. D. C. HALL and W. C. WHITE, originated in primary court, Jurisdiction of Columbia, February 11, 1835.

No. 50.   David AYRES vs. Wm. B. SWEENEY, originated in alcalde court, Jurisdiction of Columbia, June 2, 1835.

No. 64.   Almira BOWEN vs. McKINNEY and WILLIAMS, originated in alcalde court, Jurisdiction of Brazoria, April 3, 1834.

No. 84.   BENNETT and SHARP vs. Joshua ABBOTT, originated in primary court, Jurisdiction of Columbia, June 6, 1835.

No. 85.   Charles H. BENNETT vs. P. R. SPLANE, originated in primary court, Jurisdiction of Columbia, June 6, 1835.

Court Records

No. 86.   Charles H. BENNETT vs. P. R. SPLANE, originated in primary
court, Jurisdiction of Columbia, June 6, 1835.

The following index, direct by name of plaintiff and reverse
by name of defendant, has been prepared by the Historical Records
Survey.   Reference is to case number.

Direct

(Plaintiff vs. Defendant)

REVERSE

(Defendant vs. Plaintiff)

Court Records

(Defendant vs. Plaintiff)

HALL, W.D.C., and W.C. WHITE
vs. S. SAWYER by
George HUFF   44
HOLDERMAN, J. vs. J.W.E.
WALLACE   4
HOLDERMAN, J. and D. vs.
J.W.E. WALLACE   2
HUFF, G. vs. RICHARDSON and
DAVIS   19
McKINNEY and WILLIAMS vs.
Almira BOWEN   64
MOORE, Robert D. vs.
R. MILLS, et al.   28

PARROTT, T.F.L., and WIFE
vs. Peyton R. SPLANE   21
PATTON, C.R. vs. G. McNEAL   12
SPLANE, P.R. vs.
Charles H. BENNETT   85, 86
SWEENEY, William B. vs.
David AYRES   50
WHITE, W.C., and W.D.C.
HALL vs. S. SAWYER by
G. HUFF   44
WILLIAMS and McKINNEY
Almira BOWEN   64
WILLIAMS, Robert H. vs.
Robert D. MOORE   22

125

LIST OF COLONIAL RECORDS QUOTED

ABBOT, Joshua 124
ABBOTT, Joshua 123
ABBOTT, Joshua 124
ABERNATHY, Polly 51
ABRAMS, ----- 19
ABRAMS, ----- 98
ACLDWELL, James P. 66
ADAMS, Francis 31
ADAMS, Francis 36
AINSWORTH, ---- 58
AINSWORTH, ----- 104
AINSWORTH, ----- 105
AINSWORTH, ----- 113
AINSWORTH, ----- 114
AINSWORTH, A. C. 72
AINSWORTH, A. C. 73
AINSWORTH, A. C. 76
AINSWORTH, A. C. 78
AINSWORTH, A. C. 80
AINSWORTH, A. C. 89
AINSWORTH, A. C. 92
AINSWORTH, A. C. 93
AINSWORTH, A. C. 95
AJOHNSON, ----- 76
ALCONR, William E. 27
ALCORN, J. H. 41
ALCORN, J.H. 43
ALCORN, John 41
ALCORN, John H. 43
ALCORN, T. J. 41
ALCORN, T. J. 43
ALCORN, William E. 30
ALDRETE, Jose Miguel 7
ALEXANDER, C. R. 78
ALEXANDER, C. R. 80
ALEXANDER, C. R. 92
ALEXANDER, C. R. 93
ALLEN, Alvin H. 104
ALLEN, Alvin H. 108
ALLEN, Alvin H. 113
ALLEN, Mary G. 26
ALLEN, Mary G. 27
ALLEN, Mary G. 30
ALLEN, Mary G. 126
ALLEN, O. H. 54
ALLEN, O. H. 57
ALLEN, O. H. 57
ALLEN, O. H. 58
ALLEN, O. H. 59
ALLEN, O. H. 60
ALLEN, O. H. 61
ALLEN, O. H. 61
ALLEN, O. H. 61
ALLEN, O. H. 71
ALLEN, O. H. 113
ALLEN, O. H. 119
ALLEN, O. H. 120
ALLEN, O. H. 120
ALLEN, O. H. 121
ALLEN, O. H. 122
ALLEN, O.H. 121
ALLEN, Oliver H. 59
ALLEN, Oliver H. 65
ALLEN, Oliver H. 108
ALLEN, Oliver H. 113
ALLEN, Olliver H. 60
ALMY, Leon R. 38
ALPINE, D. W. 45
ALPINE, P. R. 45
ALSBURY, C. G. 24
ALSBURY, G. G. 22
ALSBURY, H. 22
ALSBURY, H. 24
ALSBURY, H. A. 22
ALSBURY, H. A. 22

ALSBURY, H. A. 24
ALSBURY, Hansen 22
ALSBURY, Horatio A. 22
ALSBURY, Horatio A. 25
ALSBURY, L. 76
ALSBURY, L. 80
ALSBURY, Leah Ann 27
ALSBURY, T. J. 74
ALSBURY, T. J. 82
ALSBURY, Thomas J. 74
ALSBURY, Thos. 80
AMITH, Henry 45
ANATHONY, D. W. 82
ANDERSON, E. 41
ANDERSON, E. 42
ANDERSON, E. 42
ANDERSON, E. 43
ANDERSON, E. 47
ANDERSON, E. 56
ANDERSON, E. 56
ANDERSON, E. 59
ANDERSON, E. 65
ANDERSON, E. 66
ANDERSON, E. 67
ANDERSON, E. 68
ANDERSON, E. 71
ANDERSON, E. 72
ANDERSON, E. 73
ANDERSON, E. 76
ANDERSON, E. 80
ANDERSON, E. 80
ANDERSON, E. 81
ANDERSON, E. 82
ANDERSON, E. 90
ANDERSON, Ephriam 31
ANDERSON, Ephriam 36
ANDERSON, Ephriam 50
ANDERSON, Ephriam 51
ANDERSON, Ephriam 54
ANDERSON, Ephriam 57
ANDERSON, Ephriam 59
ANDERSON, Ephriam 61
ANDERSON, Ephriam 62
ANDERSON, Ephriam 63
ANDERSON, Ephriam 64
ANDERSON, Ephriam 65
ANDERSON, Ephriam 71
ANDERSON, Ephriam 71
ANDERSON, Ephriam 89
ANDERSON, Ephriam 93
ANDERSON, Ephriam 106
ANDERSON, Ephriam 113
ANDERSON, Ephrim 47
ANDERSON, Epphriam 54
ANDERSON, M. 41
ANDERSON, M. 43
ANDERSON, M. 44
ANDERSON, Milton 42
ANDERSON. Milton 43
ANDERSON, Milton 46
ANDERSON, Milton 50
ANDERSON, Milton 51
ANDERSON, Milton 62
ANDERSON, Milton 63
ANDERSON, Milton 65
ANDERSON, Milton 66
ANDERSON, Milton 70
ANDERSON, Milton 79
ANDERSON, Milton 80
ANDREWS, E. 22
ANDREWS, E. 22
ANDREWS, E. 23
ANDREWS, E. 24
ANDREWS, E. 24

ANDREWS, E. 24
ANDREWS, E. 25
ANDREWS, E. 26
ANDREWS, E. 41
ANDREWS, E. 43
ANDREWS, E. 44
ANDREWS, E. 56
ANDREWS, E. 72
ANDREWS, E. 80
ANDREWS, E. 81
ANDREWS, E. 83
ANDREWS, E. 95
ANDREWS, E. E. 22
ANDREWS, E. M. B. 22
ANDREWS, E.M. B. 24
ANDREWS, E.M. B. 24
ANDREWS, Edmund 40
ANDREWS, Edmund 57
ANDREWS, Edmund 58
ANDREWS, Edmund 59
ANDREWS, Edmund 67
ANDREWS, Edmund 71
ANDREWS, Edmund 72
ANDREWS, Edmund 88
ANDREWS, Edmund 89
ANDREWS, Edmund 93
ANDREWS, Edmund 126
ANDREWS, H. L. B. 22
ANDREWS, H. L. B. 22
ANDREWS, H.L. B. 24
ANDREWS, Isabella M. 41
ANDREWS, Isabella M. 43
ANDREWS, Mr. Edmund 32
ANGIER, ---- 23
ANGIER, ---- 25
ANGIER, ----- 24
ANGIER, ----- 25
ANGIER, S. F. 23
ANGIER, S. F. 24
ANGIER, S. F. 41
ANGIER, S. F. 41
ANGIER, S. F. 43
ANGIER, S. F. 44
ANGIER, S. F. 72
ANGIER, S. F. 82
ANGIER, S. F. 83
ANGIER, S. F. 84
ANGIER, S. F. 85
ANGIER, S. F. 87
ANGIER, S. F. 87
ANGIER, S. F. 88
ANGIER, S. F. 94
ANGIER, S. F. 95
ANGIER, S. F. 95
ANGIER, S. F. 96
ANGIER, S. F. 97
ANGIER, S. F. 97
ANTHONY, D. W. 31
ANTHONY, D. W. 36
ANTHONY, D. W. 45
ANTHONY, D. W. 59
ANTHONY, D. W. 61
ANTHONY, D. W. 62
ANTHONY, D. W. 66
ANTHONY, D. W. 66
ANTHONY, D. W. 67
ANTHONY, D. W. 69
ANTHONY, D. W. 72
ANTHONY, D. W. 78
ANTHONY, D. W. 80
ANTHONY, D. W. 80
ANTHONY, D. W. 80
ANTHONY, D. W. 81
ANTHONY, D. W. 81

ANTHONY, D. W. 81
ANTHONY, D. W. 81
ANTHONY, D. W. 82
ANTHONY, D. W. 83
ANTHONY, D. W. 84
ANTHONY, D. W. 85
ANTHONY, D. W. 85
ANTHONY, D. W. 86
ANTHONY, D. W. 86
ANTHONY, D. W. 87
ANTHONY, D. W. 88
ANTHONY, D. W. 89
ANTHONY, D. W. 92
ANTHONY, D. W. 93
ANTHONY, D. W. 93
ANTHONY, D. W. 93
ANTHONY, D. W. 94
ANTHONY, D. W. 94
ANTHONY, D. W. 94
ANTHONY, D. W. 95
ANTHONY, D. W. 95
ANTHONY, D. W. 95
ANTHONY, D. W. 96
ANTHONY, D. W. 96
ANTHONY, D. W. 96
ANTHONY, D. W. 97
ANTHONY, D. W. 97
ANTHONY, D. W. 101
ANTHONY, D. W. 103
ANTHONY, D. W. 106
ANTHONY, D. W. 119
ANTHONY, D. W. 120
ANTHONY, D. W. 121
ANTHONY, D. W. 122
ANTHONY, David W. 10-1
ANTHONY, David W. 101
ANTHONY, David W. 113
ANTHONY, W. D. 121
APLANE, Ann D.W. 104
APLANE, Peyton R. 53
ARCHER, ----- 82
ARCHER, B. T. 79
ARCHER, B. T. 80
ARCHER, B. T. 91
ARCHER, B. T. 92
ARCHER, B. T. 93
ARCHER, B. T. 93
ARCHER, B. T. 94
ARCHER, Branch T. 9
ARCHER, Branch T. 77
ARCHER, Branch T. 80
ARCHER, Branch T. 91
ARCHR, Branch T. 93
ARCINIEGA, Miguel 4
ARNOLD, William 31
ARNOLD, William 36
ARUTHERFORD, ----- 96
ARYAN, Isaac 77
ASHARP, ----- 123
ASLBURY, Leah Ann 30
ASUTIN, J. 81
ASUTIN, W. T. 120
ATENNEL, Benjamin 61
ATHOMAS, John 120
ATHOMAS, L. 41
ATHOMPSON, Jesse 54
ATHOMPSON, Jesse 69
ATHOMPSON, Jesse 86
AUSTIN, --- 41
AUSTIN, --- 42
AUSTIN, --- 42
AUSTIN, --- 44
AUSTIN, ---- 6
AUSTIN, ---- 61

AUSTIN, ---- 107
AUSTIN, ----- 41
AUSTIN, ----- 61
AUSTIN, ----- 72
AUSTIN, ----- 75
AUSTIN, ----- 89
AUSTIN, ----- 90
AUSTIN, ----- 100
AUSTIN, ----- 113
AUSTIN, ----- 115
AUSTIN, Capt. 4
AUSTIN, Capt. 5
AUSTIN, E. E. 22
AUSTIN, E. E. 24
AUSTIN, E. E. 24
AUSTIN, E. E. 25
AUSTIN, Elizabeth E. 22
AUSTIN, Elizabeth E. 29
AUSTIN, Elizabeth E. 30
AUSTIN, Emily M, 23
AUSTIN, Emily M. 23
AUSTIN, Emily M. 24
AUSTIN, Emily M. 25
AUSTIN, H. 72
AUSTIN, H. 72
AUSTIN, H. 74
AUSTIN, H. 75
AUSTIN, H. 77
AUSTIN, H. 82
AUSTIN, H. 85
AUSTIN, H. 96
AUSTIN, H.L. B. 24
AUSTIN, Henry 22
AUSTIN, Henry 23
AUSTIN, Henry 23
AUSTIN, Henry 24
AUSTIN, Henry 24
AUSTIN, Henry 25
AUSTIN, Henry 26
AUSTIN, Henry 56
AUSTIN, Henry 59
AUSTIN, Henry 59
AUSTIN, Henry 61
AUSTIN, Henry 66
AUSTIN, Henry 72
AUSTIN, Henry 79
AUSTIN, Henry 80
AUSTIN, Henry 93
AUSTIN, Henry 103
AUSTIN, Henry 113
AUSTIN, J. 22
AUSTIN, J. 24
AUSTIN, J. 25
AUSTIN, J. 26
AUSTIN, J. 41
AUSTIN, J. 43
AUSTIN, J. 51
AUSTIN, J. 73
AUSTIN, J. 79
AUSTIN, J. 85
AUSTIN, J. 86
AUSTIN, J. 86
AUSTIN, J. 87
AUSTIN, J. 88
AUSTIN, J. 111
AUSTIN, John 5
AUSTIN, John 22
AUSTIN, John 24
AUSTIN, John 25
AUSTIN, John 25
AUSTIN, John 26
AUSTIN, John 32
AUSTIN, John 36
AUSTIN, John 40
AUSTIN, John 41

AUSTIN, John 43
AUSTIN, John 46
AUSTIN, John 49
AUSTIN, John 57
AUSTIN, John 59
AUSTIN, John 60
AUSTIN, John 62
AUSTIN, John 64
AUSTIN, John 65
AUSTIN, John 67
AUSTIN, John 68
AUSTIN, John 70
AUSTIN, John 71
AUSTIN, John 72
AUSTIN, John 82
AUSTIN, John 82
AUSTIN, John 83
AUSTIN, John 84
AUSTIN, John 89
AUSTIN, John 89
AUSTIN, John 92
AUSTIN, John 94
AUSTIN, John 96
AUSTIN, John 97
AUSTIN, John 98
AUSTIN, John 99
AUSTIN, John 100
AUSTIN, John 101
AUSTIN, John 113
AUSTIN, John 113
AUSTIN, John 117
AUSTIN, John 117
AUSTIN, John 118
AUSTIN, John 120
AUSTIN, John 120
AUSTIN, John 121
AUSTIN, John 122
AUSTIN, S. F, 25
AUSTIN, S. F. 22
AUSTIN, S. F. 23
AUSTIN, S. F. 23
AUSTIN, S. F. 23
AUSTIN, S. F. 24
AUSTIN, S. F. 24
AUSTIN, S. F. 24
AUSTIN, S. F. 24
AUSTIN, S. F. 25
AUSTIN, S. F. 26
AUSTIN, S. F. 49
AUSTIN, S. F. 53
AUSTIN, S. F. 60
AUSTIN, S. F. 64
AUSTIN, S. F. 69
AUSTIN, S. F. 70
AUSTIN, S. F. 72
AUSTIN, S. F. 78
AUSTIN, S. F. 83
AUSTIN, S. F. 84
AUSTIN, S. F. 89
AUSTIN, Stephen 95
AUSTIN, Stephen F. 1
AUSTIN, Stephen F. 2
AUSTIN, Stephen F. 3
AUSTIN, Stephen F. 7
AUSTIN, Stephen F. 9
AUSTIN, Stephen F. 11
AUSTIN, Stephen F. 15
AUSTIN, Stephen F. 17
AUSTIN, Stephen F. 31
AUSTIN, Stephen F. 36
AUSTIN, Stephen F. 91
AUSTIN, Stephen F. 95
AUSTIN, Stephen F. 101
AUSTIN, Stephen F. 113

AUSTIN, W. C. 24
AUSTIN, W. T. 22
AUSTIN, W. T. 24
AUSTIN, W. T. 24
AUSTIN, W. T. 25
AUSTIN, W. T. 41
AUSTIN, W. T. 41
AUSTIN, W. T. 41
AUSTIN, W. T. 42
AUSTIN, W. T. 43
AUSTIN, W. T. 44
AUSTIN, W. T. 69
AUSTIN, W. T. 72
AUSTIN, W. T. 73
AUSTIN, W. T. 74
AUSTIN, W. T. 74
AUSTIN, W. T. 75
AUSTIN, W. T. 75
AUSTIN, W. T. 75
AUSTIN, W. T. 76
AUSTIN, W. T. 77
AUSTIN, W. T. 78
AUSTIN, W. T. 79
AUSTIN, W. T. 80
AUSTIN, W. T. 80
AUSTIN, W. T. 80
AUSTIN, W. T. 80
AUSTIN, W. T. 81
AUSTIN, W. T. 82
AUSTIN, W. T. 83
AUSTIN, W. T. 85
AUSTIN, W. T. 85
AUSTIN, W. T. 87
AUSTIN, W. T. 88
AUSTIN, W. T. 89
AUSTIN, W. T. 90
AUSTIN, W. T. 90
AUSTIN, W. T. 90
AUSTIN, W. T. 91
AUSTIN, W. T. 91
AUSTIN, W. T. 93
AUSTIN, W. T. 94
AUSTIN, W. T. 96
AUSTIN, W. T. 102
AUSTIN, W. T. 103
AUSTIN, W. T. 104
AUSTIN, W. T. 105
AUSTIN, W. T. 107
AUSTIN, W. T. 118
AUSTIN, W. T. 119
AUSTIN, W. T. 119
AUSTIN, W. T. 120
AUSTIN, William T. 64
AUSTIN, William 113
AUSTIN, William T. 13
AUSTIN, William T. 34
AUSTIN, William T. 45
AUSTIN, William T. 45
AUSTIN, William T. 46
AUSTIN, William T. 47
AUSTIN, William T. 48
AUSTIN, William T. 49
AUSTIN, William T. 53
AUSTIN, William T. 55
AUSTIN, William T. 55
AUSTIN, William T. 60
AUSTIN, William T. 61
AUSTIN, William T. 61
AUSTIN, William T. 64
AUSTIN, William T. 66
AUSTIN, William T. 68
AUSTIN, William T. 76
AUSTIN, William T. 89
AUSTIN, William T. 90
AUSTIN, William T. 93

AUSTIN, William T. 99
AUSTIN, William T. 104
AUSTIN, William T. 121
AUSTIN, Willliam T. 66
AUSTIN, Wm. T. 65
AUSTIN, Wm. T. 69
AUSTIN, Wm. T. 70
AUSTIN, Wm. T. 70
AUSTIN, Wm. T. 90
AYRES, David 117
AYRES, David 119
AYRES, David 121
AYRES, David 122
AYRES, David 123
AYRES, David 124
AYRES, David 125

BABCOCK, ----- 72
BABCOCK, ----- 75
BABCOCK, ----- 81
BABCOCK, ----- 89
BABCOCK, ----- 90
BABCOCK, ----- 93
BABCOCK, ----- 116
BABCOCK, ----- 119
BABCOCK, ----- 120
BABCOCK, ----- 121
BAILEY, --- 43
BAILEY, --- 44
BAILEY, ----- 41
BAILEY, ----- 74
BAILEY, ----- 80
BAILEY, Elizabeth 72
BAILEY, Elizabeth 86
BAILEY, Elizabeth 89
BAILEY, J. B. 22
BAILEY, J. B. 24
BAILEY, J. B. 26
BAILEY, J. B. 26
BAILEY, J. B. 41
BAILEY, J. B. 43
BAILEY, J. B. 45
BAILEY, J. B. 45
BAILEY, J. B. 46
BAILEY, J. B. 46
BAILEY, J. B. 60
BAILEY, J. B. 64
BAILEY, J. B. 64
BAILEY, J. B. 64
BAILEY, J. B. 66
BAILEY, J. B. 66
BAILEY, J. B. 66
BAILEY, J. B. 67
BAILEY, J. B. 68
BAILEY, J. B. 69
BAILEY, J. B. 70
BAILEY, J. B. 70
BAILEY, J. B. 72
BAILEY, J. B. 73
BAILEY, J. B. 78
BAILEY, J. B. 80
BAILEY, J. B. 81
BAILEY, J. B. 84
BAILEY, J. B. 85
BAILEY, J. B. 86
BAILEY, J. B. 89
BAILEY, J. B. 95
BAILEY, J. B. 96
BAILEY, J. B. 97
BAILEY, James B. 32
BAILEY, James B. 36
BAILEY, James B. 42
BAILEY, James B. 43

BAILEY, Mary 72
BAILEY, Mary 86
BAILEY, Mary 86
BAILEY, Mary 89
BAILEY, Mary 96
BAILEY, Nancy 54
BAILEY, Nancy 56
BAILEY, Nancy 60
BAILEY, Nancy 63
BAILEY, Nancy 65
BAILEY, Nancy 65
BAILEY, Nancy 66
BAILEY, Nancy 67
BAILEY, Polly (Mary) 53
BAILEY, Polly (Mary) 60
BAILEY, Polly (Mary) 69
BAILEY, Smith 53
BAILEY, Smith 60
BAILEY, Smith 69
BAILEY, W. P. 90
BAILEY, W. P. 93
BAILEY, William P. 80
BAILEY, Wm. P. 76
BAILEYF, Elizabeth 96
BAIRD, Charles 72
BAIRD, Charles 83
BAIRD, Charles 89
BAIRD, Charles 95
BAIRD, James 22
BAIRD, James 24
BAIRD, James 25
BAIRD, Wiliam 29
BAIRD, William 30
BAIRD, William 55
BAIRD, William 72
BAIRD, William 84
BAIRD, Wm. 60
BAIRD, Wm. 73
BAKER, Mosley 73
BAKER, Mosley 86
BARCLAY, Leah 28
BARCLAY, Leah 30
BARKER, ---- 11
BARKER, ---- 13
BARKER, ---- 14
BARKER, ----- 2
BARKER, ----- 3
BARKER, ----- 7
BARKER, ----- 9
BARKER, Dr. 16
BARKER, Dr. Eugene C. 12
BARKER, E. C. 1
BARKER, Lima 28
BARKER, Lima 30
BARNET, James 31
BARNEY, Jabez 41
BARNEY, Jabez 44
BARRETT, William 27
BARRETT, William 30
BARRETT, William 118
BARRETT, William 121
BARRETT, William 126
BARRETT, Wm. 41
BARRETT, Wm. 43
BARRETT, Wm. 120
BARROW, Stephen 73
BARROW, Stephen 85
BARTLESON, P. R. 51
BARTLESON, P. R. 65
BARTLESON, P. R. 66
BARTLESON, P. R. 71
BARTLESON, P. R. 73
BARTLESON, P. R. 82
BARTLESON, Peter 64
BARTLESON, Peter R. 52
BARTLESON, Peter R. 68

BATTLE, M. 23
BATTLE, M. 24
BATTLE, M. 24
BATTLE, M. 26
BAXTER, W. 87
BAXTER, William 74
BAXTER, William 80
BAXTER, William 90
BAXTER, William 93
BAXTER, William 97
BEAN, Col. Peter Elllis 2
BELL, J. H. 39
BELL, J. H. 73
BELL, J. H. 74
BELL, J. H. 76
BELL, J. H. 77
BELL, J. H. 78
BELL, J. H. 79
BELL, J. H. 79
BELL, J. H. 80
BELL, J. H. 80
BELL, J. H. 81
BELL, J. H. 82
BELL, J. H. 83
BELL, J. H. 85
BELL, J. H. 85
BELL, J. H. 86
BELL, J. H. 86
BELL, J. H. 87
BELL, J. H. 89
BELL, J. H. 91
BELL, J. H. 93
BELL, J. H. 93
BELL, J. H. 95
BELL, J. H. 96
BELL, J. S. 94
BELL, Josiah 73
BELL, Josiah 80
BELL, Josiah A. 89
BELL, Josiah H. 1
BELL, Josiah H. 8
BELL, Josiah H. 23
BELL, Josiah H. 24
BELL, Josiah H. 32
BELL, Josiah H. 36
BELL, Josiah H. 93
BELL, Josiah H. 94
BELL, Pleasant 45
BELL, Pleasant 63
BELL, Pleasant 66
BELL, Pleasant 73
BELL, Pleasant 80
BELL, Thomas B. 49
BELL, Thomas B. 5
BELL, Thomas B. 71
BELL, Thomas B. 80
BENNETT, --- 41
BENNETT, --- 41
BENNETT, --- 44
BENNETT, ---- 42
BENNETT, ----- 73
BENNETT, ----- 85
BENNETT, ----- 89
BENNETT, ----- 96
BENNETT, ----- 123
BENNETT, ----- 124
BENNETT, C. H. 73
BENNETT, C. H. 73
BENNETT, C. H. 74
BENNETT, C. H. 80
BENNETT, C. H. 81
BENNETT, C. H. 84
BENNETT, C. H. 86
BENNETT, C. H. 92
BENNETT, C. H. 93

BENNETT, Charles 66
BENNETT, Charles 89
BENNETT, Charles H. 59
BENNETT, Charles H. 60
BENNETT, Charles H. 80
BENNETT, Charles H. 97
BENNETT, Charles H. 99
BENNETT, Charles H. 101
BENNETT, Charles H. 102
BENNETT, Charles H. 113
BENNETT, Charles H. 119
BENNETT, Charles H. 119
BENNETT, Charles H. 122
BENNETT, Charles H. 123
BENNETT, Charles H. 124
BENNETT, Charles H. 124
BENNETT, Charles H. 125
BENNETT, Theodore 111
BENNETT, Valentine 46
BENNETT, Valentine 60
BENNETT, Valentine 64
BENNETT, Valentine 66
BENNETT, Valentine 70
BENNETT, theasore 113
BENTER, Charles A. 60
BERRY, M. 23
BERRY, M. 24
BERRY, M. 24
BERRY, M. 26
BERRY, Mandey 23
BERRY, Mandey 25
BERRY, P. L. 43
BERRY, P.L. 42
BERRY, Thomas 73
BERRY, Thomas 84
BETNER, C. A. 42
BETNER, C. A. 43
BETNER, C. A. 73
BETNER, C. A. 78
BETNER, C. A. 78
BETNER, C. A. 81
BETNER, C. A. 81
BETNER, C. A. 86
BETNER, C. A. 87
BETNER, C. A. 91
BETNER, C. A. 93
BETNER, C. A. 94
BETNER, C. A. 97
BETNER, C. A. 109
BETNER, C. A. 113
BETNER, Charles 94
BETNER, Charles A. 49
BETNER, Charles A. 51
BETNER, Charles A. 60
BETNER, Charles A. 66
BETNER, Charles A. 89
BETNER, Chas A. 69
BETNER, Chas A. 70
BETTNER, Chas. A. 68
BETTNER, Chas. A. 110
BETTS, Jacob 45
BETTS, Jacob 45
BETTS, Jacob 46
BETTS, Jacob 49
BETTS, Jacob 56
BETTS, Jacob 60
BETTS, Jacob 64
BETTS, Jacob 66
BGARDINER, ----- 120
BIBSON, Wm. 43
BIFFAM, F. 25
BIGGAM, F. 23
BIGGAM, F. 41
BIGGAM, F. 43
BIGGAM, F. 43

BIGGAM, Francis 23
BIGGAM, Francis 24
BIGGAM, Francis 73
BIGGAM, Francis 83
BIGGAM, Francis 89
BIGGAM, Francis 95
BIGGHAM, A. 23
BIGHAM, F. 44
BLAKE, Thomas 66
BLAKE, Thomas M. 48
BLAKE, Thomas M. 61
BLAKE, Thomas M. 64
BLAKLY, Nancy 41
BLAKLY, Nancy 43
BOND, Nicholas D. 99
BOND, Nicholas D. 113
BORDEN, ---- 25
BORDEN, ----- 23
BORDEN, ----- 26
BORDEN, Thomas A. 58
BORDEN, Thomas A. 60
BORDEN, Thomas A. 67
BORDEN, Thomas A. 69
BOSEMAN, H. 75
BOSEMAN, H. 81
BOSEMAN, H. 90
BOSEMAN, H. 93
BOSTWICK, John H. 99
BOSTWICK, John H. 113
BOWEN, ----- 117
BOWEN, ----- 120
BOWEN, ----- 121
BOWEN, ----- 123
BOWEN, Almira 123
BOWEN, Almira 124
BOWEN, Almira 125
BOWEN, S. 28
BOWEN, S. 43
BOWEN, S. 43
BOWEN, S. 72
BOWEN, S. 73
BOWEN, S. 73
BOWEN, S. 74
BOWEN, S. 76
BOWEN, S. 79
BOWEN, S. 84
BOWEN, S. 85
BOWEN, S. 85
BOWEN, S. 86
BOWEN, Sylvester 32
BOWEN, Sylvester 36
BOWEN, Sylvester 41
BOWEN, Sylvester 41
BOWEN, Sylvester 41
BOWEN, Sylvester 41
BOWEN, Sylvester 42
BOWEN, Sylvester 42
BOWEN, Sylvester 44
BOWEN, Sylvester 45
BOWEN, Sylvester 46
BOWEN, Sylvester 48
BOWEN, Sylvester 53
BOWEN, Sylvester 54
BOWEN, Sylvester 57
BOWEN, Sylvester 58
BOWEN, Sylvester 58
BOWEN, Sylvester 60
BOWEN, Sylvester 60
BOWEN, Sylvester 60
BOWEN, Sylvester 52
BOWEN, Sylvester 63
BOWEN, Sylvester 64
BOWEN, Sylvester 64

BOWEN, Sylvester 65	BREEDLOVE, A. W. 91	BRIGHAM, Asa 55
BOWEN, Sylvester 66	BREEDLOVE, A. W. 92	BRIGHAM, Asa 56
BOWEN, Sylvester 69	BREEDLOVE, A. W. 93	BRIGHAM, Asa 57
BOWEN, Sylvester 70	BREEDLOVE, A. W. 94	BRIGHAM, Asa 57
BOWEN, Sylvester 71	BREEDLOVE, A. W. 97	BRIGHAM, Asa 60
BOWEN, Sylvester 72	BREEDLOVE, A. W. 102	BRIGHAM, Asa 64
BOWEN, Sylvester 73	BREEDLOVE, A. W. 108	BRIGHAM, Asa 64-
BOWEN, Sylvester 74	BREEDLOVE, A. W. 113	BRIGHAM, Asa 66
BOWEN, Sylvester 81	BREEDLOVE, S. G. 73	BRIGHAM, Asa 66
BOWEN, Sylvester 89	BREEDLOVE, S. G. 81	BRIGHAM, Asa 68
BOWEN, Sylvester 91	BREEDLOVE, S. G. 82	BRIGHAM, Asa 70
BOWEN, Sylvester 92	BREEDLOVE, S. G. 85	BRIGHAM, Asa 71
BOWEN, Sylvester 93	BREEDLOVE, S. G. 88	BRIGHAM, Asa 73
BOWEN, Sylvester 94	BREEDLOVE, S. G. 89	BRIGHAM, Asa 82
BOWEN, Sylvester 96	BREEDLOVE, S. G. 91	BRIGHAM, Asa 90
BOWEN, Sylvester 118	BREEDLOVE, S. G. 93	BRIGHAM, Asa 99
BOWEN, Sylvester 119	BREEDLOVE, S. W. 97	BRIGHAM, Asa 100
BOWEN, Sylvester 122	BREEDLOVE, Susan 42	BRIGHAM, Asa 105
BOWLS, Sally M. 28	BREEDLOVE, Susan 43	BRIGHAM, Asa 107
BOWLS, Sally M. 30	BREEDLOVE, Susan 45	BRIGHAM, Asa 110
BOWLS, Sally M. 126	BREEDLOVE, Susan 60	BRIGHAM, Asa 110
BOYCE, Henry L. 103	BREEDLOVE, Susan 76	BRIGHAM, Asa 113
BOYCE, Henry L. 113	BREEDLOVE, Susan 81	BRIGHAM, Asa 116
BOYCE, Robert 105	BREEDLOVE, Susan 87	BRIGHAM, Asa 117
BOYCE, Robert 105	BREEDLOVE, Susan 94	BRIGHAM, Asa 119
BOYCE, Robert H. 56	BREEDLOVE, Susan G. 70	BRIGHAM, Asa 120
BOYCE, Robert H. 60	BREEDLOVE, Susan G. 73	BRIGHAM, Asa 121
BOYCE, Robert H. 62	BREEDLOVE, Susan G. 89	BRIGHAM, Asa 123
BOYCE, Robert H. 71	BREEDLOVE, Susan G. 92	BRIGHAM, Asa 124
BOYCE, Robert H. 103	BREEDLOVE, Susan G. 108	BRISCOE, A. 119
BOYCE, Robert H. 113	BREEDLOVE, Susan G. 113	BRISCOE, A. 119
BOYCE, Robert J. 103	BRENAN, Mr. & Mrs. 41	BRISCOE, A. 119
BRADBURN, ----- 3	BRENAN, Mr. & Mrs. 43	BRISCOE, A. 122
BRADBURN, John Davis 2	BRENAN, T. 42	BROWN, --- 41
BRADLEY, ---- 24	BRENAN, T. 43	BROWN, --- 43
BRADLEY, ---- 25	BRENAN, T. H. 41	BROWN, --- 44
BRADLEY, ----- 23	BRENAN, T. H. 43	BROWN, ---- 41
BRADLEY, ----- 25	BRENAN, T. H. 43	BROWN, ---- 42
BRADLEY, James 73	BREWSTER, Adam 73	BROWN, ----- 73
BRADLEY, James 89	BREWSTER, Adam 86	BROWN, ----- 73
BRADLEY, James 95	BRIDGES, Margaret 29	BROWN, ----- 84
BRADLEY, James 96	BRIDGES, Margaret 30	BROWN, ----- 85
BRADLEY, T. H. 41	BRIGHAM, ----- 78	BROWN, ----- 94
BRADLEY, T. H. 43	BRIGHAM, ----- 80	BROWN, ----- 95
BRADLY, James 84	BRIGHAM, ----- 115	BROWN, ----- 96
BRADLY, T. 73	BRIGHAM, A. 25	BROWN, ----- 96
BRADLY, T. 81	BRIGHAM, A. 72	BROWN, Edmund 60
BRADLY, Thomas 74	BRIGHAM, A. 74	BROWN, H. S. 42
BRADLY, Thomas 81	BRIGHAM, A. 77	BROWN, H. S. 43
BRADY, Thomas 40	BRIGHAM, A. 77	BROWN, H. S. 58
BREEDING, David 117	BRIGHAM, A. 78	BROWN, H. S. 59
BREEDING, David 119	BRIGHAM, A. 79	BROWN, H. S. 59
BREEDING, David 120	BRIGHAM, A. 80	BROWN, H. S. 60
BREEDING, David 121	BRIGHAM, A. 81	BROWN, H. S. 61
BREEDING, Wm. S. 121	BRIGHAM, A. 84	BROWN, H. S. 65
BREEDLOVE, A. W. 42	BRIGHAM, A. 84	BROWN, H. S. 66
BREEDLOVE, A. W. 42	BRIGHAM, A. 85	BROWN, H. S. 69
BREEDLOVE, A. W. 43	BRIGHAM, A. 89	BROWN, H. S. 73
BREEDLOVE, A. W. 57	BRIGHAM, A. 90	BROWN, H. S. 75
BREEDLOVE, A. W. 57	BRIGHAM, A. 91	BROWN, H. S. 76
BREEDLOVE, A. W. 60	BRIGHAM, A. 92	BROWN, H. S. 80
BREEDLOVE, A. W. 65	BRIGHAM, A. 116	BROWN, H. S. 81
BREEDLOVE, A. W. 71	BRIGHAM, A. 123	BROWN, H. S. 81
BREEDLOVE, A. W. 72	BRIGHAM, A. 124	BROWN, H. S. 82
BREEDLOVE, A. W. 73	BRIGHAM, Ada 69	BROWN, H. S. 82
BREEDLOVE, A. W. 76	BRIGHAM, Asa 2	BROWN, H. S. 83
BREEDLOVE, A. W. 77	BRIGHAM, Asa 8	BROWN, H. S. 84
BREEDLOVE, A. W. 78	BRIGHAM, Asa 10	BROWN, H. S. 87
BREEDLOVE, A. W. 79	BRIGHAM, Asa 13	BROWN, H. S. 87
BREEDLOVE, A. W. 80	BRIGHAM, Asa 34	BROWN, H. S. 87
BREEDLOVE, A. W. 81	BRIGHAM, Asa 38	BROWN, H. S. 89
BREEDLOVE, A. W. 82	BRIGHAM, Asa 39	BROWN, H. S. 91
BREEDLOVE, A. W. 87	BRIGHAM, Asa 40	BROWN, H. S. 93
BREEDLOVE, A. W. 89	BRIGHAM, Asa 48	

BROWN, H. S. 94
BROWN, H. S. 108
BROWN, H. S. 113
BROWN, Henry 32
BROWN, Henry 36
BROWN, Henry 60
BROWN, Henry S. 7
BROWN, Henry S. 29
BROWN, Henry S. 52
BROWN, Henry S. 58
BROWN, Henry S. 66
BROWN, Henry S. 67
BROWN, Henry S. 68
BROWN, Henry S. 68
BROWN, J. 23
BROWN, J. 41
BROWN, J. 41
BROWN, J. 44
BROWN, J. 72
BROWN, J. 72
BROWN, J. 74
BROWN, J. 78
BROWN, J. 79
BROWN, J. 81
BROWN, J. 81
BROWN, J. 84
BROWN, J. 85
BROWN, J. 87
BROWN, J. 100
BROWN, J. 113
BROWN, Jeremiah 73
BROWN, Jeremiah 80
BROWN, Jeremiah 83
BROWN, Jeremiah 84
BROWN, Jeremiah 89
BROWN, Jeremiah 92
BROWN, Jeremiah 93
BROWN, Jeremiah 93
BROWN, Jeremiah 94
BROWN, Jeremiah 95
BROWN, Jeremiah 95
BROWN, Jeremiah 95
BROWN, Jeremiah 96
BROWN, Jeremiah 97
BROWN, Jeremiah 101
BROWN, Jeremiah 110
BROWN, Jeremiah 113
BROWN, Jesse 74
BROWN, Jesse 84
BROWN, Jesse 86
BROWN, John 25
BROWN, John 44
BROWN, John 98
BROWN, John 113
BROWN, John Henry 2
BROWN, John Henry 7
BROWN, John Henry 16
BROWN, Joseph 56
BROWN, Joseph 61
BROWN, Joseph 69
BROWN, N, 60
BROWN, N. 58
BROWN, N. 59
BROWN, N. 59
BROWN, N. 61
BROWN, N. 65
BROWN, N. 66
BROWN, N. 66
BROWN, N. 68
BROWN, N. 69
BROWN, N. 73
BROWN, N. 80
BROWN, N. 82
BROWN, N. 87
BROWN, N. 98

BROWN, N. 108
BROWN, N. 113
BROWN, Sylvester 95
BROWN, W. 41
BROWN, W. 41
BROWN, W. 42
BROWN, W. 43
BROWN, W. S. 74
BROWN, W. S. 84
BROWN, W. S. 86
BROWN, W. S. 94
BROWN, William S. 59
BROWN, William S. 61
BROWN, William S. 69
BROWN, William S. 74
BROWN, William S. 90
BROWN, William S. 94
BROWN, Wm. S. 82
BROWY, N. 67
BRWON, Henry S. 30
BUCKNER, John W. 117
BUCKNER, John W. 119
BUCKNER, John W. 122
BUCKNER, W. 74
BUCKNER, W. 87
BUCKNER, W. 89
BUCKNER, W. 97
BULLOCK, Capt. 32
BUNDICK, M. H. 74
BUNDICK, M. H. 77
BUNDICK, M. H. 78
BUNDICK, M. H. 83
BURGESS, J. 41
BURGESS, J. 41
BURGESS, J. 43
BURGESS, J. 43
BURLESON, Colonel E. 33
BURNAP, A. L. 41
BURNAP, A. L. 41
BURNAP, A. L. 42
BURNAP, A. L. 42
BURNAP, A. L. 42
BURNAP, A. L. 42
BURNAP, A. L. 43
BURNET, Charles 121
BURNET, Charles H. 118
BURNET, D. G. 81
BURNET, D. G. 89
BURNET, D. G. 94
BURNET, David G. 10
BURNET, David G. 18
BURNET, David G. 23
BURNET, David G. 25
BURNETT, Charles H. 119
BURNETT, David 74
BURNETT, David B. 16
BUSTAMANTE, Anastacio 2
BUTLER, Anthony 74
BUTLER, Anthony 87
BYROM, --- 43
BYROM, ----- 117
BYROM, ----- 121
BYROM, ----- 123
BYROM, J. S.D. 41
BYROM, J. S.D. 42
BYROM, J. S.D. 43
BYROM, J. S.D. 82
BYROM, J. S.D. 93
BYROM, J..S. D. 44
BYROM, J..S. D. 84
BYROM, J..S. D. 110
BYROM, J.S. D. 22
BYROM, J S D. 25

BYROM, J.S. D. 43
BYROM, J.S. D. 43
BYROM, J.S. D. 47
BYROM, J.S. D. 53
BYROM, J.S. D. 55
BYROM, J.S. D. 62
BYROM, J.S. D. 68
BYROM, J.S. D. 71
BYROM, J.S. D. 74
BYROM, J.S. D. 86
BYROM, J.S. D. 86
BYROM, J.S. D. 86
BYROM, J.S. D. 87
BYROM, J.S. D. 88
BYROM, J.S. D. 91
BYROM, J.S. D. 92
BYROM, J.S. D. 94
BYROM, J.S. D. 96
BYROM, J.S. D. 97
BYROM, J.S. D. 97
BYROM, J.S. D. 97
BYROM, J.S. D. 100
BYROM, J.S. D. 100
BYROM, J.S. D. 101
BYROM, J.S. D. 103
BYROM, J.S. D. 113
BYROM, John S. 74
BYROM, John S. D. 9
BYROM, John S. D. 10
BYROM, John S.D. 33
BYROM, John S.D. 36
BYROM, John S.D. 89
BYROME, ----- 120
BYRON, J.S. D. 51
BYRON, J.S. D. 61

CABORN, Nathaniel 99
CABORN, Nathaniel 113
CADY, D. C. 104
CADY, D. C. 113
CAGE, ----- 123
CAGE, ----- 124
CAGE, B. F. 74
CAGE, B. F. 75
CAGE, B. F. 80
CAGE, B. F. 89
CAGE, B. F. 90
CAGE, B. F. 93
CAGE, B. F. 101
CAGE, B. F. 113
CALDER, Robert J. 113
CALDWELL, J. P. 107
CALDWELL, J. P. 110
CALDWELL, J. P. 110
CALDWELL, James P. 57
CALDWELL, James P. 64
CALDWELL, James P. 105
CALDWELL, James P. 113
CALDWELL, James P. 114
CALVERT, Frederick J. 23
CALVERT, J. W. 94
CALVET, F. I. 46
CALVIT, A. 39
CALVIT, A. 81
CALVIT, Alexander 73
CALVIT, Alexander 76
CALVIT, Alexander 81
CALVIT, Alexander 91
CALVIT, Alexander 92
CALVIT, Alexander 94
CALVIT, Alexander 96
CALVIT, Alexander 97
CALVIT, F. I. 65

CALVIT, F. I. 65
CALVIT, F. I. 66
CALVIT, F. I. 66
CALVIT, F. I. 67
CALVIT, F. I. 68
CALVIT, F. I. 70
CALVIT, Frederick 25
CALVIT, Mary Ann 29
CALVIT, Mary ann 30
CAMPBELL, J. 81
CAMPBELL, John 75
CAMPBELL, John 79
CAMPBELL, John 80
CAMPBELL, John 81
CAMPBELL, John 90
CAMPBELL, John 92
CAMPBELL, John 94
CANDAY, Margaret 27
CANDIVERS, S. 52
CAPLE, --- 41
CAPLE, --- 43
CAPLE, --- 44
CAPLE, E. 24
CAPLE, E. 25
CAPLE, E. 25
CAPLE, E. 75
CAPLE, E. 78
CAPLE, E. 81
CAPLE, E. 85
CAPLE, E. 120
CAPLE, E. 121
CAPLE, Elijah 45
CAPLE, Elijah 45
CAPLE, Elijah 46
CAPLE, Elijah 49
CAPLE, Elijah 49
CAPLE, Elijah 49
CAPLE, Elijah 50
CAPLE, Elijah 60
CAPLE, Elijah 61
CAPLE, Elijah 64
CAPLE, Elijah 66
CAPLE, Elijah 77
CAPLE, Elijah 81
CAPLE, Elijah 90
CAPLE, Elijah 94
CAPLE, Elijah 116
CAPLE, Elijah 123
CAPLE, Elijah 124
CAPLE, W. 121
CARSON, ---- 61
CARSON, ----- 48
CARSON, ----- 52
CARSON, ----- 57
CARSON, ----- 58
CARSON, ----- 61
CARSON, ----- 62
CARSON, ----- 65
CARSON, ----- 66
CARSON, ----- 67
CARSON, ----- 71
CARSON, ----- 74
CARSON, ----- 75
CARSON, ----- 76
CARSON, ----- 81
CARSON, ----- 82
CARSON, ----- 90
CARSON, ----- 91
CARSON, ----- 94
CARSON, ----- 94
CARSON, ----- 105
CARSON, ----- 108
CARSON, ----- 114
CARSON, ----- 114

CARSON, Catherine 49
CARSON, Catherine 61
CARSON, Catherine 67
CARSON, W. 76
CARSON, W. H. 69
CARSON, W. H. 73
CARSON, William C. 25
CARSON, William H. 48
CARSON, William H. 52
CARSON, William H. 61
CARSON, William H. 62
CARSON, William H. 64
CARSON, William H. 67
CARSON, William H. 105
CARSON, William H. 114
CARSON, Wm. C. 23
CARSON. ----- 65
CARTER, Samuel 23
CARTER, Samuel 23
CARTER, Samuel 23
CARTER, Samuel 26
CARVER, Martin 42
CARVER, Martin 43
CAVANAH, Charles 67
CAVENAH, Charles 52
CAVENAH, Charles 61
CAYCE, AThomas 118
CAYCE, Thomas 48
CAYCE, Thomas 49
CAYCE, Thomas 50
CAYCE, Thomas 61
CAYCE, Thomas 61
CAYCE, Thomas 62
CAYCE, Thomas 64
CAYCE, Thomas 67
CAYCE, Thomas 74
CAYCE, Thomas 76
CAYCE, Thomas 81
CAYCE, Thomas 82
CAYCE, Thomas 119
CAYCE, Thomas 119
CAYCE, Thomas 120
CAYCE, Thomas 121
CAYCE, Thomas 121
CAYCE, Thomas 122
CAYCE, Thomas 123
CAZNEAU, W. L. 102
CAZNEAU, W. L. 114
CCALDER, Robert J. 114
CHADOWIN, Athomas 52
CHADOWIN, Thomas 61
CHAFFIN, J. 74
CHAFFIN, J. 80
CHAFFIN, J. 83
CHAFFIN, J. 83
CHAFFIN, J. 86
CHAFFIN, J. 87
CHAFFIN, J. 90
CHAFFIN, J. 94
CHAFFIN, John 18
CHAFFIN, John 49
CHAFFIN, John 49
CHAFFIN, John 50
CHAFFIN, John 53
CHAFFIN, John 61
CHAFFIN, John 67
CHAFFIN, John 74
CHAFFIN, John 104
CHAFFIN, John 114
CHAMBERS, ----- 104
CHAMBERS, ----- 114
CHAMBERS, ----- 114
CHAMBERS, Thomas J. 15
CHANCE, S. 23
CHANCE, S. 24

CHANCE, S. 25
CHANCE, Samuel 74
CHANCE, Samuel 87
CHASE, W. W. 83
CHASE, William 84
CHASE, William 84
CHASE, William W. 74
CHEPHAS, ----- 15
CHEPHAS, William 39
CHEPHAS, William 39
CHEPHAS, William 40
CHEPHAS, William 41
CHEPHAS, William 126
CHEPHAS, Wm. 43
CIDIR, Lewis S. 57
CLAPP, William 103
CLAPP, William 114
CLARE, A. M. 103
CLARE, A. M. 114
CLARK, ----- 23
CLARK, ----- 26
CLARK, Gissen 119
CLEVELAND, J. A.H. 56
CLEVELAND, J. A.H. 119
CLEVELAND, J. A.H. 120
CLEVELAND, J..A. H. 61
CLEVELAND, J.A. H. 45
CLEVELAND, J.A. H. 54
CLEVELAND, J.A. H. 63
CLEVELAND, J.A. H. 64
CLEVELAND, J.A. H. 66
CLEVELAND, J.A. H. 67
CLEVELAND, J.A. H. 72
CLEVELAND, J.A. H. 74
CLEVELAND, J.A. H. 74
CLEVELAND, J.A. H. 76
CLEVELAND, J.A. H. 78
CLEVELAND, J.A. H. 81
CLEVELAND, J.A. H. 86
CLEVELAND, J.A. H. 86
CLEVELAND, J.A. H. 89
CLEVELAND, J.A. H. 90
CLEVELAND, J.A. H. 94
CLEVELAND, J.A. H. 96
CLEVELAND, J.S. H. 73
CLEVELAND, Mrs. (Alias) 78
CLEVELAND, Mrs. (Alias) 84
CLEVELAND, Mrs. (Alias) 92
CLEVELAND, Mrs. (MILLIGAN) 9.
CLEVELAND, Wm. 74
CLEVELAND, Wm. 76
CLEVELAND, Wm. 81
CLOKY, Robert 81
CLOKY, Robert 94
CLOSKY, Robert 89
CLOUD, J. W. 40
CLOUD, J. W. 42
CLOUD, J. W. 71
CLOUD, J. W. 72
CLOUD, J. W. 78
CLOUD, J. W. 81
CLOUD, J. W. 85
CLOUD, John W. 39
CLOUD, John W. 43
CLOUD, John W. 45
CLOUD, John W. 61
COCHRANE, R. 73
COCHRANE, R. 78
COCHRANE, R. 83
COCHRANE, R. 87

COCHRANE, R. H. 92
COCHRANE, Robert 73
COCHRANE, Robert 74
COCHRANE, Robert 80
COCHRANE, Robert 80
COCHRANE, Robert 81
COCHRANE, Robert 82
COCHRANE, Robert 82
COCHRANE, Robert 85
COCHRANE, Robert 118
COCHRANE, Robert 120
COCHRANE, Robert 121
COCHRANE, Robert H. 89
COCHRANE, Robert H. 94
COLDRON, Robert 52
COLDRON, Robert 61
COLES, John A. 114
COLES, John P. 23
COLES, John P. 25
COLES, John P. 101
COLLINGSWORTH, G. M. 57
COLLINGSWORTH, G. M. 62
COLLINGSWORTH, G. M. 69
COLLINGSWORTH, George M. 57
COLLINGSWORTH, James 10
COLLINGSWORTH, James 18
COLLINSWORTH G. M. 102
COLLINSWORTH, G. M. 51
COLLINSWORTH, G. M. 67
COLLINSWORTH, G. M. 101
COLLINSWORTH, G. M. 103
COLLINSWORTH, Geo. M. 110
COLLINSWORTH, George M. 61
COLLINSWORTH, George M. 109
COLLINSWORTH, George M. 114
CONLEY, ---- 19
CONLEY, ------ 98
COTTEN, G. B. 54
COTTEN, G. B. 57
COTTEN, G. B. 61
COTTEN, G. B. 61
COTTEN, G. B. 63
COTTEN, G. B. 65
COTTEN, G. B. 67
COTTEN, G. B. 71
COTTEN, G. B. 102
COTTEN, Godwin B. 102
COTTEN, Godwin B. 106
COTTEN, Godwin B. 114
COUNCEL, J. C. 41
COUNCEL, J. S. 41
COUNCEL, J. S. 42
COUNCEL, J. S. 43
COUNCEL, J. S. 43
COUNCEL, J. S. 43
COUNCEL, J. S. 44
COUNCEL, J. S. 56
COUNCEL, J. S. 57
COUNCEL, J. S. 59
COUNCEL, J. S. 60
COUNCEL, J. S. 61
COUNCEL, J. S. 65
COUNCEL, J. S. 67
COUNCEL, J. S. 71
COUNCEL, J. S. 73
COUNCEL, J. S. 74
COUNCEL, J. S. 74
COUNCEL, J. S. 75
COUNCEL, J. S. 82
COUNCEL, J. S. 85
COUNCEL, James S. 32
COUNCEL, James S. 36
COWAN, J. B. 58
COWAN, J. B. 67

COWAN, J. B. 78
COWAN, J. B. 82
COWAN, John 75
COWAN, John 82
COWAN, John B. 30
COWAN, John b. 29
COWAN, Sarah Ann 29
COWAN, Sarah Ann 30
COWAN. J. B. 64
COWEN, S. 74
COX, ----- 118
COX, ----- 120
COX, ----- 122
COX, C. G. 39
COX, C. G. 40
COX, C. G. 41
COX, C. G. 43
COX, C. G. 44
COX, C. G. 49
COX, C. G. 49
COX, C. G. 52
COX, C. G. 56
COX, C. G. 59
COX, C. G. 60
COX, C. G. 60
COX, C. G. 62
COX, C. G. 65
COX, C. G. 69
COX, C. G. 74
COX, C. G. 76
COX, C. G. 80
COX, C. G. 82
COX, C. G. 89
COX, C. G. 90
COX, C. G. 93
COX, C. G. 94
COX, C. G. 96
COX, Christopher 67
COX, Christopher G. 47
COX, Christopher G. 62
COX, Christopher G. 65
COX, Christopher G. 70
COX, Christophr G. 69
COX, Harriet 29
COX, Harriet 30
COX, Harriet H. 30
COX, Harriet H. 30
COX, J. S. 89
COX, J. S. 91
COX, J. S. 94
COX, John S. 32
COX, John S. 36
CRAFT, S. 41
CRAFT, S. 41
CRAFT, S. 42
CRAFT, S. 43
CRANE, J. 41
CRANE, J. 43
CROSBY, T. P. 75
CROSBY, T. P. 82
CROSBY, Thomas 72
CROSBY, Thomas 82
CROSBY, Thomas P. 74
CROSBY, Thomas P. 84
CROSBY, Thomas P. 118
CROSBY, Thomas P. 120
CROSBY, Thomas P. 121
CRUNCK, J. 23
CRUNCK, J. 25
CRUNCK, James 116
CRUNCK, James 120
CRUNCK, James 121
CUMMING, William 25
CUMMINGS, G. B. 78

CUMMINGS, G. B. 82
CUMMINGS, G. B. 85
CUMMINGS, Wm. 23
CUMMINS, James 103
CUMMINS, James 114
CUNNINGHAM, ----- 90
CUNNINGHAM, ------ 93
CUNNINGHAM, ------ 96
CUNNINGHAM, A. C. 80
CUNNINGHAM, K. C. 74
CUNNINGHAM, K. C. 83
CUNNINGHAM, K. C. 85
CURTIS, --- 42
CURTIS, --- 43
CURTIS, H. 26
CURTIS, Hinton 23
CURTIS, Hinton 23
CURTIS, Hinton 44

DAILEY, William 45
DAILEY, William 51
DAILEY, William 57
DAILEY, William 59
DAILEY, William 59
DAILEY, William 61
DAILEY, William 62
DAILEY, William 67
DAILEY, William 67
DAILEY, Wm. 62
DAILEY, Wm. 65
DALE, E. 82
DAMON, Samuel 48
DAMON, Samuel 62
DAMON, Samuel 64
DAMON, Samuel 67
DANIELS, E. 54
DANIELS, Edmund 45
DANIELS, Edmund 45
DANIELS, Edmund 46
DANIELS, Edmund 61
DANIELS, Edmund 67
DANNIELS, Edmund 50
DARST, Abram 32
DARST, Abram 36
DAVIS, ---- 74
DAVIS, ----- 78
DAVIS, ----- 80
DAVIS, ----- 83
DAVIS, ----- 123
DAVIS, ----- 124
DAVIS, ----- 125
DAVIS, Elisha 74
DAVIS, Elisha 81
DAVIS, Eliza 29
DAVIS, Eliza 30
DAVIS, Jesse K. 29
DAVIS, Jesse K. 30
DAVIS, K. W. 23
DAVIS, K. W. 25
DEAL, E. 75
DEAL, E. 79
DELGADO, Juan Jose 38
DEWITT, Green 33
DICHERSON, Edward 23
DICKINSON, Edward 24
DILLARD, John P. 98
DILLARD, John P. 114
DILLARD, N. 42
DILLARD, N. 43
DILLARD, T. 74
DILLARD, Thomas 87

DILLARD, Thomas 87
DILLARD, Thomas 90
DILLARD, Thomas 93
DILLARD, Thomas 97
DILLON, Robert 65
DILLON, T. 80
DINSMORE, S. 53
DINSMORE, S. 110
DINSMORE, Silas 54
DINSMORE, Silas 55
DINSMORE, Silas 56
DINSMORE, Silas 57
DINSMORE, Silas 111
DINSMORE, Silas 114
DOAN, J. 74
DOAN, J. 87
DOAN, J. 90
DOAN, J. 91
DOAN, J. 97
DODSON, A. C. 74
DODSON, A. C. 76
DODSON, A. C. 82
DODSON, A. C. 85
DODSON, A. C. 86
DONAHO, Mortimor 74
DONAHO, Mortimor 85
DONAHO, Mortimor 90
DONAHO, Mortimor 96
DONALSON, ----- 82
DONALSON, D. T. 93
DONALSON, D. T. 94
DONALSON, Daniel T. 79
DONALSON, Daniel T. 80
DONALSON, T. 92
DOUGHERTY, J. 41
DOUGHERTY, J. 43
DOUGLAS, Samuel C. 104
DOUGLAS, Samuel G. 114
DUKE, J. H. 24
DUKE, T. W. 23
DUKE, T. W. 23
DUKE, T. W. 24
DUKE, T. W. 24
DUKE, T. W. 24
DUKE, T. W. 25
DUKE, T. W. 26
DUNAHO, ----- 78
DUNNAHO, ----- 82
DUNNAHO, ----- 85
DUNNAHO, C. R. 82
DUPUY, Pierre 31
DWYER, C. 73
DWYER, C. 74
DWYER, C. 85

EARLY, J. S. 41
EARLY, J. S. 43
EASTON, William J. 32
EATON, J. W. 82
EATON, W. J. 78
EATON, W. J. 92
EATON, W. J. 82
EATON, W. J. 85
EATON, W. J. 85
EATON, W. J. 119
EATON, W. J. 119
EATON, W. J. 121
EATON, William 74
EATON, William J. 36
EATON, Wm. 81
ECKEL, William 4
ECKEL, Wm. 22
ECKEL, Wm. 25
EDWARDS, Amos 23
EDWARDS, Amos 25
EDWARDS, Monroe 118

EDWARDS, Monroe 119
EDWARDS, Monroe 120
EDWARDS, Monroe 120
EDWARDS, Monroe 121
EDWARDS, Monroe 122
EDWARDS, Wm. 76
EDWARDS, Wm. 82
ELAM, D. 76
ELAM, D. 82
ELAM, D. 91
ELAM, D. 94
ELLER, John 74
ELLER, John 87
ELLIOTT, George 74
ELLIOTT, George 114
ELLIOTT, George 118
ELLIOTT, George 121
ELLIOTT, George 122
ELLIOTT, Geroge 99
ERWIN, AT. R. 73
ERWIN, R. T. 88
ERWIN, T. R. 72
ERWIN, T. R. 72
ERWIN, T. R. 73
ERWIN, T. R. 73
ERWIN, T. R. 74
ERWIN, T. R. 75
ERWIN, T. R. 75
ERWIN, T. R. 76
ERWIN, T. R. 77
ERWIN, T. R. 77
ERWIN, T. R. 78
ERWIN, T. R. 79
ERWIN, T. R. 79
ERWIN, T. R. 80
ERWIN, T. R. 81
ERWIN, T. R. 81
ERWIN, T. R. 81
ERWIN, T. R. 81
ERWIN, T. R. 81
ERWIN, T. R. 82
ERWIN, T. R. 82
ERWIN, T. R. 83
ERWIN, T. R. 84
ERWIN, T. R. 85
ERWIN, T. R. 85
ERWIN, T. R. 86
ERWIN, T. R. 87
ERWIN, T. R. 90
ERWIN, T. R. 91
ERWIN, Thomas R. 30
ERWIN, Thomas R. 30
ERWIN, Thomas R. 47
ERWIN, Thomas R. 48
ERWIN, Thomas R. 57
ERWIN, Thomas R. 58
ERWIN, Thomas R. 58
ERWIN, Thomas R. 61
ERWIN, Thomas R. 61
ERWIN, Thomas R. 64
ERWIN, Thomas R. 67
ERWIN, Thomas R. 68
ERWIN, Thomas R. 69
ERWIN, Thomas R. 70
ERWIN, Thomas R. 74
ERWIN, Thomas R. 88
ERWIN, Thomas R. 89
ERWIN, Thomas R. 91
ERWIN, Thomas R. 93
ERWIN, Thomas R. 94
ESTES, Anderson 79
ESTES, Anderson 82
ESTES, Anderson 92
ESTES, Anderson 94
ESTES, Edward 82

ESTES, Edward W. 29
ESTES, Edward W. 30
FADDIN, John 19
FADDIN, John 112
FADDIN, John 114
FADDIN, John 126
FADDIN, John 126
FADDIN, Patrick 112
FADDIN, Patrick 114
FADDIN, Patrick 126
FAIRCHILD, Philo 75
FAIRCHILD, Philo 87
FANNIN, Col. 112
FANNIN, Colonel 114
FANNIN, James W. 32
FANNIN,Jr J. W. 126
FANNIN,Jr. J. W. 33
FANNIN,Jr. James W. 36
FIELDS, J. E. 75
FIELDS, J. E. 87
FIELDS, J. E. 87
FIELDS, J. F. 23
FIELDS, J. F. 25
FIELDS, James 90
FIELDS, James 93
FIELDS, James F. 75
FIELDS, James F. 81
FIELDS, James F. 95
FIELDS, James F. 97
FIELDS, Joseph B. 75
FIELDS, Joseph E. 83
FIELDS, Joseph E. 97
FISHER, S. Rhodes 101
FISHER, S. Rhodes 102
FISHER, S. Rhodes 114
FITCHET, Daniel R. 77
FLETCHER, Daniel R. 82
FORSYTH, John 34
FOSTER, John 54
FOSTER, John 61
FOSTER, John 72
FOSTER, John 82
FOSTER, John 88
FOSTER, John 94
FOSTER, John 117
FOSTER, John 119
FOSTER, John 121
FOSTER, John 122
FOWLER, ----- 23
FOWLER, ----- 26
FOWLER, B. 25
FOWLER, Benjamin 23
FRAM, Wm. 62
FRANKLILN, B. C. 111
FRANKLIN, Benj. C. 111
FRANKLIN, Benjamin C. 10
FRANKLIN, Benjamin C. 112
FRANKLIN, Benjamin C. 112
FRANKLIN, Judge 10
FREAM, William 45
FREAM, William 57
FREAM, William 59
FREAM, William 62
FREAM, William 67
FREAM, William 67
FREAM, Wm. 65
FREEMAN, R. T. 75
FREEMAN, R. T. 77
FREEMAN, R. T. 82
FULCHEAR, Churchill 23
FULCHEAR, Churchill 25
FULCHEAR, Treavy 23
FULCHEAR, Treavy 25
FULLER, S. 55
FULLER, S. 61
FULLER, S. 67
FULLER, S. 71

GALES, G. W. 22
GALLEHER, Edward 29
GALLEHER, Edward 30
GAMMEL, ----- 16
GAMMEL, ----- 17
GAMMEL, H.P.N. 3
GARDINER, ----- 72
GARDINER, ----- 75
GARDINER, ----- 81
GARDINER, ----- 89
GARDINER, ----- 90
GARDINER, ----- 93
GARDINER, ----- 116
GARDINER, ----- 119
GARDINER, ----- 121
GARZA, Gen. Filipe DE LA 11
GATES, John 75
GATES, John 82
GATES, John 90
GATES, John 94
GATES, John 122
GATES, John 124
GAY, F. C. 94
GAY, John J. 57
GAY, John J. 61
GAY, John J. 67
GAY, Thomas 41
GAY, Thomas 41
GAY, Thomas 44
GAY, Thomas 75
GAY, Thomas 80
GAY, Thomas 81
GAY, Thomas 90
GAY, Thomas 93
GAY, Thomas 94
GEORGE, Freeman 103
GEORGE, Freeman 114
GIBSON, Q. 41
GIBSON, Q. 43
GIBSON, W. 74
GIBSON, W. 80
GIBSON, W. 82
GIBSON, Wm.. 41
GILLESPIE, J. 76
GILLESPIE, J. 82
GILLESPIE, J. 91
GILLESPIE, J. 94
GILLESPIE, J. L. 90
GILLESPIE, J. L. 95
GILLESPIE, John L. 75
GILLESPIE, John L. 84
GILLET, S. S. 116
GILLET, S. S. 120
GILLET, S. S. 121
GILLET, S. S. 121
GOODALL, Seaborn 104
GOODALL, Seaborn 114
GORBET, Chester 23
GORBET, Chester 25
GORBET, Mrs. N. 42
GORBET, Mrs. N. 43
GORDON, P. W. 18
GORDON, Peletin W. 111
GORDON, Peletin W. 112
GORDON, Peletin W. 114
GORDON, Peletin W. 126
GRAHAM, John 33
GRAHAM, John 36
GRANT, Diego 38
GRANT, Dr. James 19
GRANT, Dr. James (Diego) 37
GRANT, Dr. James Diego 126

GRAY, A. C. 110
GRAY, F. C. 75
GRAY, F. C. 82
GRAY, F. C. 90
GRAY, F. C. 109
GRAY, F. C. 114
GRAY, F. C. 126
GRAY, Franklin C. 29
GRAY, Franklin C. 30
GRAYSON, Thomas 121
GRAYSON, Thomas W. 119
GRAYSON, Thomas W. 120
GREEN, P. 41
GREEN, P. 44
GREEN, P. 76
GREEN, P. 82
GREEN, P. 91
GREEN, P. 94
GREEN, Patrick 53
GREEN, Patrick 61
GREEN, Patrick 68
GREEN, Patrick 72
GREEN, Patrick 73
GREEN, Patrick 77
GREEN, Patrick 82
GREGORY, E. W. 13
GREGORY, E. W. 53
GREGORY, E. W. 61
GREGORY, E. W. 66
GREGORY, E. W. 75
GREGORY, E. W. 81
GREGORY, E. W. 90
GREGORY, E. W. 93
GREGORY, E. W. 100
GREGORY, E. W. 114
GREGORY, E. W. 116
GREGORY, E. W. 120
GREGORY, E. W. 121
GREGORY, E. W. 123
GREGORY, E. W. 124
GREY, T. 25
GREY, Thomas 23
GRIFFITH, H. 75
GRIFFITH, H. 77
GRIFFITH, H. 81
GRIFFITH, H. 82
GRIFFITH, H. 90
GRIFFITH, H. 91
GRIFFITH, H. 94
GROCE, ----- 59
GROCE, ----- 61
GROCE, Jared 75
GROCE, Jared E. 29
GROCE, Jared E. 30
GROCE, Jared E. 85
GROCE, S. E. 26
GROCE, Sneed E. 23
GTANT, Hugo 38
GUERRERO, Vinente 2

HAALES, C. 82
HALE, John 109
HALE, John 114
HALE, S. M. 90
HALE, S. M. 95
HALE, S. W. 84
HALES, C. 78
HALES, C. 82
HALES, C. 82
HALES, C. 85
HALES, C. 85
HALES, J. M. 74
HALES, J. M. 82
HALEY, ----- 48
HALEY, ----- 52

HALEY, ---- 58
HALEY, ---- 61
HALEY, ----- 61
HALEY, ----- 62
HALEY, ----- 65
HALEY, ----- 65
HALEY, ----- 66
HALEY, ----- 67
HALEY, ----- 71
HALEY, ----- 74
HALEY, ----- 75
HALEY, ----- 76
HALEY, ----- 81
HALEY, ----- 82
HALEY, ----- 90
HALEY, ----- 91
HALEY, ----- 94
HALEY, ----- 94
HALEY, ----- 102
HALEY, ----- 105
HALEY, ----- 107
HALEY, ----- 114
HALEY, ----- 114
HALEY, William 72
HALEY, William 76
HALEY, William 82
HALEY, William 109
HALEY, William 110
HALEY, William 114
HALEY, Wm. 75
HALEY, Wm. 82
HALEY, Wm. 90
HALEY, Wm. 94
HALL, ---- 23
HALL, ---- 24
HALL, ---- 25
HALL, ---- 118
HALL, ----- 25
HALL, ----- 122
HALL, D. C. 117
HALL, D. C. 119
HALL, John J. 91
HALL, John J. 94
HALL, John M. 77
HALL, John W. 75
HALL, John W. 83
HALL, John W. 111
HALL, John W. 114
HALL, Joseph 76
HALL, Joseph 82
HALL, S.D. C. 82
HALL, T. J. 41
HALL, T. J. 43
HALL, Thomas 89
HALL, Thomas 94
HALL, W. D.C. 79
HALL, W. D.C. 84
HALL, W. S. 91
HALL, W. S. 94
HALL, W. S. 111
HALL, W. S. 114
HALL, W..D. C. 60
HALL, W..D. C. 79
HALL, W.D. C. 54
HALL, W.D. C. 59
HALL, W.D. C. 63
HALL, W.D. C. 67
HALL, W.D. C. 69
HALL, W.D. C. 72
HALL, W.D. C. 72
HALL, W.D. C. 73
HALL, W.D. C. 75
HALL, W.D. C. 76
HALL, W.D. C. 78

HALL, W.D. C. 78
HALL, W.D. C. 80
HALL, W.D. C. 82
HALL, W.D. C. 83
HALL, W.D. C. 87
HALL, W.D. C. 88
HALL, W.D. C. 89
HALL, W.D. C. 90
HALL, W.D. C. 90
HALL, W.D. C. 92
HALL, W.D. C. 93
HALL, W.D. C. 94
HALL, W.D. C. 94
HALL, W.D. C. 96
HALL, W.D. C. 97
HALL, W.D. C. 101
HALL, W.D. C. 104
HALL, W.D. C. 113
HALL, W.D. C. 123
HALL, W.D. C. 124
HALL, W.D. C. 125
HALL, W.D. C. 125
HALL, W.D. C. 126
HALL, Warren 82
HALL, Warren 119
HALL, Warren D. C. 8
HALL, Warren D. C. 9
HALL, Warren D.C. 53
HALL, Warren D.C. 102
HALL, Warren D.C. 108
HALL, Warren D.C. 114
HALL, Warren D.C. 120
HALL, Warren D.C. 121
HALL, William 23
HALL, William 25
HALL, William 41
HALL, Wm. 43
HALL, Wm. S. 117
HALL, Wm. S. 119
HALL, Wm. S. 120
HAMELTON, Francis 67
HAMIALTON, Francis 69
HAMILTON, Francis 58
HAMILTON, Francis 60
HARDIN, William 76
HARDIN, Wm. 83
HARRALSON, G. S. 41
HARRALSON, G. S. 43
HARRELL, J. T. 45
HARRELL, J. T. 61
HARRELL, J. T. 66
HARRELL, J. T. 75
HARRELL, J. T. 86
HARRELL, J. T. 90
HARRELL, J. T. 96
HARRELL, Josiah T. 29
HARRELL, Josiah T. 30
HARRINGTON, N. 81
HARRINGTON, N. 117
HARRINGTON,Jr. N. 90
HARRINGTON,Jr. N. 93
HARRINGTON,Jr. N. 120
HARRINGTON,Jr. N. 121
HARRINGTON,Sr. N. 75
HARRIS, A. 41
HARRIS, A. 41
HARRIS, A. 42
HARRIS, A. 43
HARRIS, A. C. 75
HARRIS, A. C. 78
HARRIS, A. C. 82
HARRIS, A. C. 83
HARRIS, A. C. 84
HARRIS, A. J. 90

HARRIS, A. J. 91
HARRIS, A. J. 92
HARRIS, A. J. 94
HARRIS, A. J. 95
HARRIS, A. J. 97
HARRIS, A. J. 109
HARRIS, A. J. 110
HARRIS, A. J. 123
HARRIS, A. J. 124
HARRIS, A. J. 126
HARRIS, Abner 43
HARRIS, Abner 98
HARRIS, Abner 114
HARRIS, Abner 118
HARRIS, Abner 120
HARRIS, Abner 120
HARRIS, Abner 121
HARRIS, Abner 121
HARRIS, Elvia 118
HARRIS, Enoch 57
HARRIS, Enoch 61
HARRIS, Enoch 63
HARRIS, Enoch 67
HARRIS, Evelina 118
HARRIS, G. 43
HARRIS, G. 43
HARRIS, G. 74
HARRIS, G. 75
HARRIS, G. 83
HARRIS, G. 83
HARRIS, G. 83
HARRIS, G. 87
HARRIS, Goin 90
HARRIS, Gowin 52
HARRIS, Gowin 57
HARRIS, Gowin 61
HARRIS, Gowin 75
HARRIS, Gowin 77
HARRIS, Gowin 83
HARRIS, Gowin 90
HARRIS, Gowin 94
HARRIS, Gowin 95
HARRIS, Gowin 97
HARRIS, Gowin 105
HARRIS, Gowin 109
HARRIS, Gowin 110
HARRIS, Gowin 114
HARRIS, Maria Ann 118
HARRIS, Mary Ann 118
HARRIS, Ruth 117
HARRIS, Ruth 120
HARRIS, W. 73
HARRIS, W. 76
HARRIS, William 24
HARRIS, William 42
HARRIS, William 50
HARRIS, William 52
HARRIS, William 63
HARRIS, William 67
HARRIS, William 89
HARRIS, William 95
HARRIS, William 99
HARRIS, William 100
HARRIS, William 100
HARRIS, William 104
HARRIS, William 118
HARRIS, William 126
HARRIS, William P. 110

HARRIS, Wm. 23
HARRIS, Wm. 62
HARRIS, Wm. 65
HARRISON, G. 23
HARRISON, G. 25

HARRISON, George 33
HARRISON, George 36
HARVEY, W. 74
HARVEY, W. 78
HARVEY, W. 80
HARVEY, W. 83
HATCHER, Mattie Austin 3
HAWKINS, E. 67
HAWKINS, E. ST. JOHN 91
HAWKINS, E. ST. JOHN 95
HAWKINS, E. St. John 62
HAWKINS, E. St. John 66
HAWKINS, E. St. John 67
HAWKINS, E. St. John 76
HAWKINS, E. St. John 83
HAWKINS, E. St. John 45
HAWKINS, Edmund 61
HAWKINS, Edmund St. John 33
HAWKINS, Edmund St. John 36
HAWKINS, Edmund St. John 45
HAWKINS, Edmund St. John 52
HAWKINS, Edmund St. John 67
HAWKINS, G. A. 22
HAWKINS, G. A. 25
HAWKINS, J. C. 89
HAWKINS, J. C. 95
HAWKINS, J. H. 22
HAWKINS, J. H. 25
HAWKINS, John 69
HAWKINS, Joseph H. 31
HAWKS, Thomas I. 110
HAWKS, Thomas I. 114
HAYNES, Franklin 75
HAYNES, Frankllin 87
HEAD, E. G. 33
HEAD, E. G. 36
HEDDY, Samuel 75
HEDDY, Samuel 87
HEFFERY, Edmund 41
HENDERSON, ----- 75
HENDERSON, ----- 75
HENDERSON, ----- 81
HENDERSON, ----- 90
HENDERSON, ----- 90
HENDERSON, ----- 93
HENDERSON, ----- 117
HENDERSON, ----- 120
HENDERSON, ----- 121
HENDERSON, Gov.J. Pickney 35
HENDRICK, W. H. 55
HENDRICK, W. H. 63
HENDRICK, W. H. 57
HENDRICK, W. S. 82
HENDRICK, W. S. 82
HENDRICK, W. S. 87
HENDRICKS, W. S. 75
HENDRICKS, W. S. 90
HENDRICKS, W. S. 94
HENRY, M. 47
HENRY, M. 61
HENRY, M. 70
HENRY, M. 75
HENRY, M. 75
HENRY, M. 80
HENRY, M. 80
HENRY, M. 81
HENRY, M. 82
HENRY, M. 83
HENRY, M. 83
HENRY, M. 83
HENRY, M. 85
HENRY, M. 90
HENRY, M. 93
HENRY, M. 94

HENRY, M. 95
HENRY, M. 95
HENRY, M. 96
HENRY, M. 105
HENRY, M. 107
HENRY, Maurice 33
HENRY, Maurice 36
HENRY, Maurice 75
HENRY, Maurice 107
HENRY, Maurice 114
HENSLEY, W. 41
HENSLEY, W. 41
HENSLEY, W. 44
HERNANDEZ, Juan Jose 7
HEWS, Pete M. 69
HEWS, Peter 67
HEWS, Peter M. 45
HEWS, Peter M. 58
HEWS, Peter M. 61
HEWS, Peter M. 64
HEWS, Peter M. 69
HHOSKINS, F. I. 73
HICKS, Milton 48
HICKS, Milton 62
HICKS, Milton 65
HICKS, Milton 67
HIGGINS, James 41
HIGGINS, James 43
HILL, ---- 75
HILL, ---- 117
HILL, ----- 75
HILL, ----- 81
HILL, ----- 90
HILL, ----- 90
HILL, ----- 93
HILL, ----- 121
HINCH, Samuel 27
HINCH, Samuel 30
HINDS, Gerren 46
HINDS, Gerren 60
HINDS, Gerren 64
HINDS, Gerren 67
HINDS, Gerren 70
HINDS, Gerren 72
HINDS, Gerren 83
HINDS, Gerren 88
HINDS, Gerren 95
HINES, James 112
HINES, James 114
HINTON, --- 42
HINTON, --- 43
HODGE, --- 41
HODGE, --- 44
HODGE, ----- 41
HODGE, A. 27
HODGE, A. 75
HODGE, A. 83
HODGE, Alexander 2
HODGE, Alexander 27
HODGE, Arche 59
HODGE, Arche 61
HODGE, Arche 66
HODGE, Arche 75
HODGE, Arche 83
HODGE, Arche 85
HODGE, Arche 90
HODGE, Arche 94
HODGE, James 28
HODGE, James 30
HODGE, John 41
HODGE, John 43
HODGE, R. 48
HODGE, R. 74

HODGE, R. 83
HODGE, R. 89
HODGE, Robert 49
HODGE, Robert 61
HODGE, Robert 76
HODGE, Robert 83
HODGE, Robert 91
HODGE, Robert 95
HODGE, W. S. 86
HODGE, William 90
HODGE, William 97
HODGE, Wm. S. 84
HODGE, Wm. S. 95
HOIT, S. 71
HOIT, Samuel 46
HOIT, Samuel 61
HOIT, Samuel 102
HOIT, Samuel 105
HOIT, Samuel 110
HOIT, Samuel 114
HOLDERMAN, D. 122
HOLDERMAN, D. 125
HOLDERMAN, J. 122
HOLDERMAN, J. 124
HOLDERMAN, J. 125
HOLDERMAN, J. D. 116
HOLDERMAN, J. D. 120
HOLDERMAN, J. D. 121
HOLLEY, Mrs. Mary Austin 3
HOLMES, A. C. 75
HOLMES, A. C. 84
HOOD, ---- 57
HOOD, ----- 63
HOOD, ----- 67
HOOD, ----- 68
HOOD, ----- 69
HOOD, ----- 70
HOPPE, Joseph Benard 109
HOPPE, Joseph Bernard 114
HOPPE, Joseph Bernard 126
HOSKINS, F. I. 72
HOSKINS, F. I. 74
HOSKINS, F. I. 74
HOSKINS, F. I. 75
HOSKINS, F. I. 77
HOSKINS, F. I. 77
HOSKINS, F. I. 78
HOSKINS, F. I. 83
HOSKINS, F. I. 89
HOSKINS, F. I. 90
HOSKINS, F. I. 91
HOSKINS, F. I. 95
HOWETH, ---- 45
HOWETH, ---- 51
HOWETH, ---- 54
HOWETH, ----- 61
HOWETH, William E. 61
HOWTH, ---- 47
HOWTH, ---- 56
HOWTH, ---- 58
HOWTH, ---- 59
HOWTH, ---- 60
HOWTH, ---- 86
HOWTH, ---- 107
HOWTH, ----- 48
HOWTH, ----- 62
HOWTH, ----- 64
HOWTH, ----- 65
HOWTH, ----- 65
HOWTH, ----- 66
HOWTH, ----- 67
HOWTH, ----- 68
HOWTH, ----- 69

HOWTH, ----- 70
HOWTH, ----- 79
HOWTH, ----- 81
HOWTH, ----- 82
HOWTH, ----- 83
HOWTH, ----- 87
HOWTH, ----- 88
HOWTH, ----- 94
HOWTH, ----- 105
HOWTH, ----- 115
HOWTH, ------ 76
HOWTH, ------ 84
HOWTH, H. E. 83
HOWTH, W. E. 46
HOWTH, W. E. 46
HOWTH, W. E. 65
HOWTH, W. E. 66
HOWTH, W. E. 67
HOWTH, W. E. 68
HOWTH, W. E. 74
HOWTH, W. E. 75
HOWTH, W. E. 76
HOWTH, W. E. 77
HOWTH, W. E. 80
HOWTH, W. E. 85
HOWTH, W. E. 86
HOWTH, William E. 55
HOWTH, William E. 69
HOWTH, Wm E. 71
HUFF, F. 83
HUFF, G. 78
HUFF, G. 123
HUFF, G. 123
HUFF, G. 124
HUFF, G. 125
HUFF, Geo. 81
HUFF, George 48
HUFF, George 52
HUFF, George 57
HUFF, George 58
HUFF, George 62
HUFF, George 62
HUFF, George 64
HUFF, George 65
HUFF, George 67
HUFF, George 68
HUFF, George 69
HUFF, George 70
HUFF, George 76
HUFF, George 76
HUFF, George 83
HUFF, George 85
HUFF, George 87
HUFF, George 90
HUFF, George 94
HUFF, George 95
HUFF, George 95
HUFF, George 96
HUFF, George 97
HUFF, George 104
HUFF, George 108
HUFF, George 108
HUFF, George 109
HUFF, George 114
HUFF, George 117
HUFF, George 118
HUFF, George 120
HUFF, George 122
HUFF, George 125
HUFF, William P. 119
HUFF, William P. 119
HUFF, William P. 122
HUGHES, ----- 120
HUGHES, James 93
HUGHES, James 95

HUGHES, Peter 83
HUGHES, Peter M. 76
HUGHES, Peter M. 77
HUGHES, Peter M. 83
HUGHS, ----- 119
HUGHS, ----- 120
HUGHS, ----- 121
HUGHS, James 89
HUNTER, Ann C. 29
HUNTER, Ann C. 30
HUNTER, Ann Douglas 104
HUNTER, Ann Douglas 114
HUNTER, D. 109
HUNTER, D. H. 99
HUNTER, D. H. 101
HUNTER, D. H. 104
HUNTER, D. H. 114
HUSHING, Thomas 41
HUSHING, Thomas 42
HUSHING, Thomas 42
HUSHING, Thomas 43

INGRAM, Ira 49
INGRAM, Ira 62
INGRAM, Ira 67
INGRAM, Ira 69
INGRAM, Seth 101
INGRAM, Seth 102
INGRAM, Seth 114

JACK, Patrick G. 2
JACK, W. H. 76
JACK, W. H. 80
JACK, W. H. 82
JACK, W. H. 83
JACK, W. H. 85
JACK, W. H. 90
JACK, W. H. 95
JACK, W. H. 95
JACK, W. H. 95
JACK, W. H. 96
JACK, W. H. 97
JACK, William H. 8
JACK, William H. 50
JACK, William H. 51
JACK, William H. 54
JACK, William H. 57
JACK, William H. 58
JACK, William H. 62
JACK, William H. 70
JACK, William H. 86
JACK, William H. 101
JACK, William H. 103
JACK, William H. 104
JACK, William H. 106
JACK, William H. 107
JACK, William H. 108
JACK, William H. 108
JACK, William H. 109
JACK, William H. 111
JACK, William H. 114
JACK, William H. 117
JACK, William H. 120
JACK, William H. 121
JACK, Wm. H. 57
JACK, Wm. H. 63
JACK, Wm. H. 67
JACK, Wm. H. 68
JACK, Wm. H. 84
JACK, Wm. H. 122

JACKSON, Charlotte 105
JACKSON, Charlotte 107
JACKSON, Charlotte 114
JACKSON, Charlotte (Alias) 13
JACKSON, Charlotte (Alias) 34
JACKSON, Charlotte (Alias) 55
JACKSON, Charlotte (Alias) 64
JACKSON, Charlotte (Robertson) 62
JACOB, Ann R. 28
JACOB, Ann R. 30
JAMES, John 29
JAMES, John 30
JAMES, John 53
JAMES, John 62
JAMES, John 64
JAMES, John 69
JAMES, John 76
JAMES, John 85
JAMES, John 103
JAMES, John 114
JAMESON, G. B. 53
JAMESON, G. B. 62
JAMESON, G. B. 114
JAMESON, Green B. 33
JAMESON, Green B. 36
JAMESON, Green B. 126
JAMESON, Isaac 41
JAMESON, Isaac 43
JAMESON, Isaac 50
JAMESON, Isaac 62
JAMESON, Isaac 70
JAMESON, Margaret 29
JAMESON, Margaret 30
JAMESON, Margaret 50
JAMESON, Margaret 52
JAMESON, Margaret 55
JAMESON, Margaret 60
JAMESON, Margaret 62
JAMESON, Margaret 63
JAMESON, Margaret 68
JAMESON, Margaret 70
JAMESON, Margaret 72
JAMESON, Margaret 76
JAMESON, Margaret 80
JAMESON, Margaret 83
JAMESON, Margaret 88
JAMESON, Margaret 90
JAMESON, Margaret 93
JAMESON, Margaret 95
JAMESON, Margaret 106
JAMESON, Margaret 114
JAMESON, Mrs. M. 53
JAMESON, Mrs. M. 61
JAMESON, Mrs. M. 68
JAMESON, Thomas 58
JAMESON, Thomas 61
JAMESON, Thomas 68
JEFERY, Edmund 70
JEFFERY, E. 22
JEFFERY, E. 22
JEFFERY, E. 22
JEFFERY, E. 25
JEFFERY, E. 25
JEFFERY, E. 41
JEFFERY, E. 43
JEFFERY, E. 45
JEFFERY, E. 54
JEFFERY, E. 55
JEFFERY, E. 61
JEFFERY, E. 69
JEFFERY, E. 70
JEFFERY, E. 75
JEFFERY, E. 79

JEFFERY, E. 83
JEFFERY, E. 106
JEFFERY, E. 114
JEFFERY, E. E. 22
JEFFERY, Edmund 25
JEFFERY, Edmund 41
JEFFERY, Edmund 41
JEFFERY, Edmund 42
JEFFERY, Edmund 43
JEFFERY, Edmund 43
JEFFERY, Edmund 44
JEFFERY, Edmund 49
JEFFERY, Edmund 51
JEFFERY, Edmund 53
JEFFERY, Edmund 62
JEFFERY, Edmund 66
JEFFERY, Edmund 67
JEFFERY, Edmund 76
JEFFERY, Edmund 76
JEFFERY, Edmund 83
JEFFERY, J. 68
JEFFERY, W. T. 22
JEWELL, Benj. 83
JEWELL, Benjamin 73
JEWETT, Diego 38
JEWETT, Mr. 38
JOHNSON, ----- 23
JOHNSON, ----- 25
JOHNSON, ----- 26
JOHNSON, ----- 78
JOHNSON, ----- 85
JOHNSON, F. W. 101
JOHNSON, Francis W. 101
JOHNSON, Francis W. 114
JOHNSON, S. M. 77
JOHNSON, S. M. 83
JOHNSON, T. W. 91
JOHNSON, T. W. 95
JONES Anson 82
JONES, A. 72
JONES, A. 76
JONES, A. 78
JONES, A. 80
JONES, A. 80
JONES, A. 80
JONES, A. 81
JONES, A. 82
JONES, A. 83
JONES, A. 83
JONES, A. 84
JONES, A. 85
JONES, A. 86
JONES, Anson 75
JONES, Anson 81
JONES, Anson 81
JONES, Anson 82
JONES, Anson 83
JONES, Anson 86
JONES, Anson 88
JONES, Anson 90
JONES, Anson 91
JONES, Anson 93
JONES, Anson 93
JONES, Anson 94
JONES, Anson 94
JONES, Anson 95
JONES, Anson 96
JONES, Henry 41
JONES, Henry 43
JONES, J. 23
JONES, J. 24
JONES, J. 25

JONES, J. 25
JONES, J. R. 81
JONES, J. R. 92
JONES, J. R. 94
JONES, J. R. 97
JONES, John 107
JONES, John 114
JONES, John R. 76
JONES, John R. 84
JONES, John R. 91
JONES, John R. 93
JONES, John R. 93
JONES, John R. 95
JONES, O. 25
JONES, Oliver 24
JONES, Oliver 101
JONES, Oliver 114
JONES. Anson 79
JUNKER, Abraham 58
JUNKER, Abraham 64
JUNKER, Abraham 68

KANADAY, Sally 43
KANADAY, Sally 63
KANADAY, Sally 91
KANADAY, Sally 95
KANADAY, Satanly 77
KANADAY, Stanly 83
KANADY, --- 42
KANADY, Sally 41
KANADY, Sally 63
KEEP, Imla 23
KEEP, Imla 25
KELLER, John 91
KELLER, John 95
KELLER, John 97
KELSEY, L. 90
KELSEY, L. 95
KEMP, Caleb 47
KEMP, Caleb 59
KEMP, Caleb 68
KEMP, Caleb 103
KEMP, Caleb 114
KENADAY, Sally 49
KENADAY, Sally 68
KENNEDY, William 117
KENNEDY, William 120
KENNEDY, Wm. 120
KERETT, S. 22
KERETT, S. 25
KIGANS, Sarah 27
KIGANS, Sarah 30
KINCAID, C. 76
KINCAID, C. 82
KINCAID, C. 83
KINNY, Lawrence 83
KINNY, Lawrence RICHARD 75
KLONNE, H. 83
KLONNE, Henry 42
KLONNE, Henry 44
KLONNE, Henry 54
KLONNE, Henry 59
KLONNE, Henry 62
KLONNE, Henry 64
KLONNE, Henry 65
KLONNE, Henry 68
KLONNE, Henry 69
KLONNE, Henry 70
KLONNE, Henry 75
KLONNE, Henry 90
KLONNE, Henry 95
KLONNE, Henry 99
KLONNE, Henry 104

KLONNE, Henry 108
KLONNE, Henry 114
KLONNE, Mr. 100
KMASS, Charles 75
KMASS, Charles 83
KMASS, Charles 90
KMASS, Charles 95
KNIGHT, James 24
KNIGHT, James 25
KYRKENDALL, Zulema 28
KYRKENDALL, Zulema 30

LACY, William D. 100
LACY, William D. 114
LAMPKIN, William 75
LAMPKIN, William 83
LAMPKIN, William 95
LAMPKIN, Wm. 78
LARKIN, William 90
LARRISON, Allen 29
LARRISON, Allen 30
LARRISON, Allen 62
LARRISON, Allen 76
LARRISON, Allen 78
LARRISON, Allen 83
LARRISON, Allen 85
LARRISON, Allen 91
LARRISON, Allen 92
LARRISON, Allen 95
LARRISON, Allen 96
LARRISON, Allen 100
LARRISON, Allen 111
LARRISON, Allen 114
LASASSIER, Luke 101
LASSIER, --- 43
LASSIER, ---- 42
LAWRENCE, AR. 43
LAWRENCE, R. 41
LAWRENCE, R. 41
LAWRENCE, R. 42
LAWRENCE, R. 42
LAWRENCE, R. 42
LAWRENCE, R. 42
LAWRENCE, R. 42
LAWRENCE, R. 43
LAWRENCE, R. 43
LAWRENCE, Richard 42
LAWRENCE, Richard 43
LEAGUE, ---- 105
LEAGUE, ------ 58
LEAGUE, ------ 104
LEAGUE, ------ 107
LEAGUE, ------ 113
LEAGUE, H. H. 50
LEAGUE, H. H. 52
LEAGUE, H. H. 56
LEAGUE, H. H. 59
LEAGUE, H. H. 60
LEAGUE, H. H. 62
LEAGUE, H. H. 64
LEAGUE, H. H. 66
LEAGUE, H. H. 68
LEAGUE, H. H. 71
LEAGUE, H. H. 76
LEAGUE, H. H. 82
LEAGUE, H. H. 86
LEAGUE, H. H. 91
LEAGUE, H. H. 94
LEAGUE, H. H. 96
LEAGUE, H. H. 103
LEAGUE, H. H. 104
LEAGUE, H. H. 105

LEAGUE, H. H. 106
LEAGUE, H. H. 110
LEAGUE, H. H. 113
LEAGUE, H. H. 114
LEAGUE, H. H. 126
LEE, Joseph 91
LEE, W. H. 74
LEE, W. H. 77
LEE, W. H. 83
LEE, W. H. 83
LEE, W. H. 83
LEE, William 114
LEE, William H. 42
LEE, William H. 42
LEE, William H. 46
LEE, William H. 60
LEE, William H. 64
LEE, William H. 68
LEE, William H. 69
LEE, William H. 98
LEE, Wm. H. 43
LEE, Wm. H. 43
LEE, Wm. H. 44
LESASSIER, L. 101
LESASSIER, Luke 114
LEWIS, ----- 104
LEWIS, ----- 114
LEWIS, ----- 114
LEWIS, Franklin 42
LEWIS, Franklin 43
LEWIS, Ira E. 23
LEWIS, Ira R. 25
LEWIS, Ira R. 108
LEWIS, Ira R. 114
LINDSEY, Benjamin 23
LINDSEY, Benjamin 25
LINDSEY, Lewis 36
LINDSEY, Lewis 36
LIPPENCOTT, Elizabeth 46
LIPPENCOTT, Elizabeth 60
LIPPENCOTT, Elizabeth 64
LIPPENCOTT, Elizabeth 66
LIPPENCOTT, Elizabeth 68
LIPPENCOTT, Elizabeth 70
LITTLE, William H. 45
LITTLE, William H. 46
LITTLE, Wm. H. 62
LOGAN, G. 72
LOGAN, G. 76
LOGAN, G. 83
LOGAN, G. 84
LOGAN, G. 87
LOGAN, Granbury 76
LOGAN, Granbury 91
LOGAN, Granbury 97
LONG Jane H. 75
LONG, J. F. 26
LONG, Jame H. 42
LONG, James 95
LONG, James F. 23
LONG, James F. 23
LONG, Jane H. 43
LONG, Jane H. 83
LONG, Jane H. 91
LONG, Jane H. 95
LONG, Jese 90
LONG, Mrs. Sam H. 76
LONG, Mrs. Sam H. 83
LOPER, Luke 114
LOVEJOY, William 76
LOVEJOY, William 87
LOVEJOY, William 91
LOVEJOY, William 97
LYNCH, H.C. C. 78

LYNCH, H.C. C. 83
LYNCH, James 27
LYNCH, N. 75
LYNCH, N. 83
LYNCH, N. 90
LYNCH, N. 95
LYONS, ---- 50
LYONS, ----- 62
LYONS, ----- 67

MADERO, J. Francisco 2
MAITCHELL, Asa 68
MANSON, L. C. 18
MANSON, L. C. 47
MANSON, L. C. 56
MANSON, L. C. 63
MANSON, L. C. 64
MANSON, L. C. 65
MANSON, L. C. 68
MANSON, L. C. 77
MANSON, L. C. 82
MANSON, L. C. 82
MANSON, L. C. 83
MANSON, L. C. 88
MANSON, L. C. 91
MANSON, L. C. 94
MANSON, L. C. 95
MANSON, L. C. 102
MANSON, L. C. 113
MANSON, L.A C. 54
MANSON, Louis C. 61
MANSON, Louis C. 62
MANSON, Louis C. 68
MANSON, Louis C. 77
MANSON, Louis C. 91
MANSON, Louis C. 97
MANSON, Louis C. 101
MANSON, Louis C. 102
MANSON, Louis C. 103
MANSON, Louis C. 114
MANSON, Louiss C. 55
MARITN, E. H. 43
MARSH, S. 23
MARSH, S. 25
MARSH, S. 25
MARSH, S. 26
MARSH, S. 41
MARSH, S. 42
MARSH, S. 42
MARSH, S. 43
MARSH, S. 43
MARSH, S. 77
MARSH, S. 81
MARSH, S. 110
MARSH, S. 116
MARSH, S. 120
MARSH, S. 121
MARSH, S. 121
MARSH, S. 123
MARSH, S. 124
MARSH, Shubael 23
MARSH, Shubael 42
MARSH, Shubael 43
MARSH, Shubael 50
MARSH, Shubael 51
MARSH, Shubael 57
MARSH, Shubael 63
MARSH, Shubael 64
MARSH, Shubael 70
MARSH, Shubael 107
MARSH, Shubael 114
MARSHALL, ----- 95
MARSHALL, Isaac 33

MARSHALL, Isaac 36
MARSHALL, Isaac 45
MARSHALL, Isaac 45
MARSHALL, Isaac 49
MARSHALL, Isaac 49
MARSHALL, Isaac 58
MARSHALL, Isaac 61
MARSHALL, Isaac 63
MARSHALL, Isaac 63
MARSHALL, Isaac 64
MARSHALL, Isaac 68
MARSHALL, Isaac 68
MARSHALL, Isaac 69
MARSHALL, Isaac 70
MARSHALL, Isaac 70
MARSHALL, Isaac 77
MARSHALL, Isaac 83
MARSHALL, Isaac 87
MARSHALL, Osaac 63
MARTIN, E. H. 42
MARTIN, Elizabeth 78
MARTIN, Elizabeth 92
MARTIN, Elizabeth (POWELL) 79
MARTIN, Elizabeth (POWELL) 84
MARTIN, Elizabeth (POWELL) 95
MARTIN, J. S. 42
MARTIN, J. S. 43
MARTIN, Joseph 62
MARTIN, Joseph S. 58
MARTIN, Joseph S. 59
MARTIN, Joseph S. 61
MARTIN, Joseph S. 64
MARTIN, Joseph S. 69
MARTIN, M. W. 118
MARTIN, R. 73
MARTIN, R. 84
MARTIN, R. 87
MARTIN, Robert 34
MARTIN, Robert 36
MARTIN, Robert 42
MARTIN, Robert 43
MARTIN, Robert 58
MARTIN, Robert 61
MARTIN, Robert 68
MARTIN, Robert 70
MARTIN, Thomas S. 59
MARTIN, Thomas S. 61
MARTIN, Wyley 63
MARTIN, Wyley 99
MARTIN, Wyly 48
MARTIN, Wyly 69
MARTIN, Wyly 70
MARTIN, Wyly 71
MARTIN, Wyly 77
MARTIN, Wyly 84
MARTIN, Wyly 100
MARTIN, Wyly 114
MARTIN, Wyly 117
MARTIN, Wyly 120
MARTIN, Wyly 121
MARTINEZ, Antonio 1
MARTINEZ, Governor 11
MATHER, E. 73
MATHER, E. 75
MATHER, E. 84
MATHER, E. 89
MATHER, E. 95
MATHER, W. E. 77
MATHER, W. E. 77
MATHER, W. E. 80
MATHER, W. E. 82
MATHER, W. E. 91
MATHER, W. E. 93
MATHER, W. E. 93

MATHRE, Elisha 114
MAXEY, Elisha 28
MAXEY, Elisha 30
MAXEY, Elisha 126
MAY, S. 42
MAY, S. 42
MAY, S. 43
MAY, S. 72
MAY, Samuel 33
MAY, Samuel 36
MAY, Samuel 41
MAY, Samuel 43
MAY, Samuel 78
MAY, Samuel 84
MAY, Samuel 92
MAY, Samuel 95
MCCASHIN, John 104
MCCASHIN, John 114
MCCASKLIN, John 76
MCCASKLIN, John 84
MCCLELLAN, T. 76
MCCLELLAN, T. 79
MCCLELLAN, T. 86
MCCLOSKEY, John 23
MCCLOSKEY, John 26
MCCLURE, Robert 75
MCCLURE, Robert 84
MCCORMICK, D. 76
MCCORMICK, D. 87
MCCORMICK, D. 105
MCCORMICK, David 34
MCCORMICK, David 36
MCCORMICK, David 47
MCCORMICK, David 68
MCCORMICK, David 70
MCCORMICK, David 91
MCCORMICK, David 97
MCCORMICK, David 107
MCCORMICK, David 108
MCCORMICK, David 109
MCCORMICK, David 114
MCCORMICK, David G. 65
MCCORMICK, J. 25
MCCORMICK, John 23
MCCORMICK, John 70
MCCRACKEN, H. 77
MCCRACKEN, John 76
MCCRACKEN, John 84
MCCROSKEY, John 52
MCCROSKEY, John 62
MCCROSKEY, John 67
MCCROSKEY, John 69
MCCROSKEY, John 99
MCCROSKEY, John 114
MCCROSKEY, Sally 100
MCCROSKEY, Sally 114
MCCROSKY, John 19
MCDANIEL, Wm. 42
MCDANIEL, Wm. 53
MCDONAL, W. 43
MCFARLAN, A. 24
MCFARLAN, Aechilles 23
MCGEE, ---- 15
MCGEE, Joseph 102
MCGEE, Joseph 114
MCGEE, Joseph 126
MCKINGHT, William 99
MCKINNEY, ---- 59
MCKINNEY, ----- 61
MCKINNEY, ----- 72
MCKINNEY, ----- 79
MCKINNEY, ----- 81
MCKINNEY, ----- 81
MCKINNEY, ----- 83

MCKINNEY, ----- 84
MCKINNEY, ----- 86
MCKINNEY, ----- 88
MCKINNEY, ----- 91
MCKINNEY, ----- 93
MCKINNEY, ----- 94
MCKINNEY, ----- 111
MCKINNEY, ----- 116
MCKINNEY, ----- 117
MCKINNEY, ----- 120
MCKINNEY, ----- 121
MCKINNEY, ----- 122
MCKINNEY, ----- 123
MCKINNEY, ----- 123
MCKINNEY, ----- 124
MCKINNEY, ----- 125
MCKINNEY, Benjamin 75
MCKINNEY, Benjamin 79
MCKINNEY, Benjamin 84
MCKINNEY, Groce 62
MCKINNEY, T. F. 74
MCKINNEY, T. F. 77
MCKINNEY, T. F. 79
MCKINNEY, T. F. 79
MCKINNEY, T. F. 84
MCKINNEY, Thomas 120
MCKINNEY, Thomas F. 57
MCKINNEY, Thomas F. 63
MCKINNEY, Thomas F. 67
MCKINNEY, Thomas F. 68
MCKINNEY, Thomas F. 68
MCKINNEY, Thomas F. 73
MCKINNEY, Thomas F. 76
MCKINNEY, Thomas F. 86
MCKINNEY, Thomas F. 119
MCKINNEY, Thomas F. 121
MCKINNEY, Thos. F. 70
MCKINSTRY, --- 41
MCKINSTRY, --- 42
MCKINSTRY, --- 42
MCKINSTRY, --- 43
MCKINSTRY, ---- 44
MCKINSTRY, ---- 61
MCKINSTRY, ----- 71
MCKINSTRY, ----- 94
MCKINSTRY, ----- 95
MCKINSTRY, ----- 96
MCKINSTRY, ----- 100
MCKINSTRY, ----- 113
MCKINSTRY, G. B. 22
MCKINSTRY, G. B. 23
MCKINSTRY, G. B. 23
MCKINSTRY, G. B. 24
MCKINSTRY, G. B. 25
MCKINSTRY, G. B. 25
MCKINSTRY, G. B. 76
MCKINSTRY, G. B. 82
MCKINSTRY, G. B. 83
MCKINSTRY, G. B. 89
MCKINSTRY, G. B. 91
MCKINSTRY, G. B. 94
MCKINSTRY, G. B. 104
MCKINSTRY, George 58
MCKINSTRY, George 63
MCKINSTRY, George B. 8
MCKINSTRY, George B. 47
MCKINSTRY, George B. 51
MCKINSTRY, George B. 54
MCKINSTRY, George B. 60
MCKINSTRY, George B. 68
MCKINSTRY, George B. 68
MCKINSTRY, George B. 70
MCKINSTRY, George B. 71
MCKINSTRY, George B. 98

MCKINSTRY, George B. 99
MCKINSTRY, George B. 101
MCKINSTRY, George B. 106
MCKINSTRY, George B. 107
MCKINSTRY, George B. 108
MCKINSTRY, George B. 114
MCKINSTRY, George B. 118
MCKINSTRY, George B. 120
MCKINSTRY, George B. 121
MCKINSTRY, George B. 122
MCKINSTRY, George G. 66
MCKNIGHT, William 100
MCKNIGHT, William 114
MCMAHAN, W. 103
MCMAHAN, W. 114
MCNEAL, G. 123
MCNEAL, G. 125
MCNEAL, Greenville 28
MCNEAL, Greenville 30
MCNEEL Polly 95
MCNEEL, ---- 51
MCNEEL, ----- 40
MCNEEL, ----- 62
MCNEEL, ----- 72
MCNEEL, ----- 79
MCNEEL, ----- 82
MCNEEL, ----- 84
MCNEEL, ----- 88
MCNEEL, ----- 89
MCNEEL, ----- 97
MCNEEL, ----- 106
MCNEEL, ----- 116
MCNEEL, G. 124
MCNEEL, J. 49
MCNEEL, J. G. 49
MCNEEL, J. G. 50
MCNEEL, J. G. 60
MCNEEL, J. G. 63
MCNEEL, J. G. 66
MCNEEL, J. G. 68
MCNEEL, J. G. 68
MCNEEL, J. G. 69
MCNEEL, J. G. 70
MCNEEL, J. G. 76
MCNEEL, J. G. 76
MCNEEL, J. G. 81
MCNEEL, J. G. 81
MCNEEL, J. G. 83
MCNEEL, J. G. 85
MCNEEL, J. G. 86
MCNEEL, J. G. 87
MCNEEL, J. G. 87
MCNEEL, J. G. 87
MCNEEL, J. G. 94
MCNEEL, J. G. 94
MCNEEL, J. G. 95
MCNEEL, J. G. 96
MCNEEL, J. G. 97
MCNEEL, J. G. 97
MCNEEL, J. G. 97
MCNEEL, John G. 91
MCNEEL, John G. 93
MCNEEL, John G. 97
MCNEEL, Mary 29
MCNEEL, Mary 30
MCNEEL, Polly 72
MCNEEL, Polly 84
MCNEEL, Polly 88
MCNEEL, S. 22
MCNEEL, S. 24
MCNEEL, S. 25

MCNEEL, S. 26
MCNEEL, S. 86
MCNEEL, S. G. 39
MCNEEL, Sterling 77
MCNEEL, Sterling 82
MCNEEL, Sterling 86
MCNEEL, Sterling 91
MCNEEL, Sterling 97
MCNEEL, Sterling 111
MCNEEL, Sterling 114
MCNEEL, Sterling 117
MCNEEL, Sterling 120
MCNEEL, Sterling 122
MCNEEL, Strling 8
MCNEIL, Pickney S. 29
MCNIEL, Pickney S. 30
MCNOEL, John G. 8
MCSONAL, W. 41
MEEK, Jesse 74
MEEK, Jesse 77
MEEK, Jesse 83
MEEKS, J. 78
MIATCHELL, Asa 42
MIATCHELL, Asa 51
MIATCHELL, Asa 77
MILBURN, D. H. 25
MILBURN, D. H. 25
MILBURN, David H. 23
MILBURN, David H. 24
MILLER, AThomas 77
MILLER, Thomas 91
MILLER, Thomas R. 87
MILLER, Thomas R. 97
MILLER, William H. 50
MILLICAN, A. 79
MILLICAN, A. 84
MILLICAN, Andrew 33
MILLICAN, Andrew 36
MILLICAN, Daniel 15
MILLICAN, John 23
MILLICAN, John 24
MILLICAN, John 25
MILLICAN, Mrs. 78
MILLICAN, Mrs. 84
MILLIGAN, Daniel 102
MILLIGAN, Daniel 114
MILLIGAN, Mrs. 92
MILLIGAN, Mrs. (CLEVELAND) 95
MILLIGAN, Saniel 126
MILLS A. G. 61
MILLS, A. G. 46
MILLS, A. G. 50
MILLS, A. G. 52
MILLS, A. G. 53
MILLS, A. G. 54
MILLS, A. G. 55
MILLS, A. G. 59
MILLS, A. G. 62
MILLS, A. G. 63
MILLS, A. G. 67
MILLS, A. G. 69
MILLS, A. G. 71
MILLS, A. G. 77
MILLS, A. G. 81
MILLS, A. G. 84
MILLS, A. G. 86
MILLS, A. G. 91
MILLS, A. G. 93
MILLS, A. G. 99
MILLS, A. G. 100
MILLS, A. G. 101
MILLS, A. G. 104
MILLS, A. G. 105
MILLS, A. G. 108

MILLS, A. G. 109
MILLS, A. G. 110
MILLS, A. G. 115
MILLS, A. G. 117
MILLS, A. G. 120
MILLS, A. G. 121
MILLS, R. 46
MILLS, R. 50
MILLS, R. 50
MILLS, R. 52
MILLS, R. 55
MILLS, R. 59
MILLS, R. 61
MILLS, R. 62
MILLS, R. 63
MILLS, R. 67
MILLS, R. 69
MILLS, R. 71
MILLS, R. 71
MILLS, R. 81
MILLS, R. 84
MILLS, R. 86
MILLS, R. 91
MILLS, R. 93
MILLS, R. 99
MILLS, R. 100
MILLS, R. 101
MILLS, R. 104
MILLS, R. 105
MILLS, R. 108
MILLS, R. 109
MILLS, R. 110
MILLS, R. 115
MILLS, R. 117
MILLS, R. 119
MILLS, R. 120
MILLS, R. 121
MILLS, R. 122
MILLS, R. 123
MILLS, R. 124
MILLS, R. 125
MILLS, Robert 32
MILLS, Robert 126
MILS, R. 77
MILTON, --- 42
MILTON, --- 43
MILTON, ---- 57
MILTON, ----- 63
MILTON, ----- 67
MILTON, ----- 68
MILTON, ----- 69
MILTON, ----- 70
MIMS, J. 73
MIMS, Joseph 42
MIMS, Joseph 43
MIMS, Joseph 46
MIMS, Joseph 63
MIMS, Joseph 68
MIMS, Joseph 79
MIMS, Joseph 84
MIMS, Joseph 89
MIMS, Joseph 92
MIMS, Joseph 95
MIMS, Joseph 103
MIMS, Joseph 104
MIMS, Joseph 115
MIRO, Estavan 31
MITCHELL, Ada 85
MITCHELL, Asa 23
MITCHELL, Asa 25
MITCHELL, Asa 43
MITCHELL, Asa 43
MITCHELL, Asa 65
MITCHELL, Asa 79

MITCHELL, Asa 80
MITCHELL, Asa 83
MITCHELL, Asa 83
MITCHELL, Asa 83
MITCHELL, Asa 84
MITCHELL, Asa 91
MITCHELL, Asa 93
MITCHELL, Asa 95
MITCHELL, Asa 95
MITCHELL, Asa 96
MOORE, AR. D. 76
MOORE, AR. D. 89
MOORE, F. 49
MOORE, F. 72
MOORE, F. 74
MOORE, F. 78
MOORE, F. 89
MOORE, F. 115
MOORE, F. 126
MOORE, Francis 23
MOORE, Francis 25
MOORE, Francis 48
MOORE, Francis 53
MOORE, Francis 54
MOORE, Francis 55
MOORE, Francis 60
MOORE, Francis 60
MOORE, Francis 64
MOORE, Francis 68
MOORE, Francis 72
MOORE, Francis 73
MOORE, Francis 73
MOORE, Francis 74
MOORE, Francis 84
MOORE, Francis 91
MOORE, Francis 95
MOORE, J. H. 25
MOORE, J. S. 42
MOORE, J. S. 43
MOORE, J. S. 53
MOORE, James 63
MOORE, James 68
MOORE, James 68
MOORE, John H. 23
MOORE, John S. 41
MOORE, John S. 43
MOORE, John S. 44
MOORE, M. W. 101
MOORE, Mr. F. 100
MOORE, R. 75
MOORE, R. D. 68
MOORE, R. D. 73
MOORE, R. D. 73
MOORE, R. D. 74
MOORE, R. D. 74
MOORE, R. D. 76
MOORE, R. D. 78
MOORE, R. D. 78
MOORE, R. D. 79
MOORE, R. D. 84
MOORE, R. D. 91
MOORE, R. D. 95
MOORE, R. D. 102
MOORE, Robert 68
MOORE, Robert 95
MOORE, Robert D. 29
MOORE, Robert D. 30
MOORE, Robert D. 46
MOORE, Robert D. 46
MOORE, Robert D. 50
MOORE, Robert D. 51
MOORE, Robert D. 63

MOORE, Robert D. 65
MOORE, Robert D. 65
MOORE, Robert D. 66
MOORE, Robert D. 67
MOORE, Robert D. 90
MOORE, Robert D. 101
MOORE, Robert D. 106
MOORE, Robert D. 109
MOORE, Robert D. 115
MOORE, Robert D. 123
MOORE, Robert D. 123
MOORE, Robert D. 124
MOORE, Robert D. 125
MOORE, Robert Dillon 51
MOORE, Robert Dillon 62
MOORE, Robert Dillon 65
MORE, Francis 57
MORE, Francis 63
MORSE, Henry 41
MORSE, Henry 43
MOSELEY, R. J. 42
MOSELEY, R. J. 43
MULDOON, Father Michael 34
MUNSON, H. W. 99
MUNSON, H. W. 115
MURPHY, ----- 73
MURPHY, ----- 78
MURPHY, ----- 84
MURPHY, S. 110
MURPHY, S. 118
MURPHY, S. 120
MURPHY, S. 121
MURPHY, Samuel 99
MURPHY, Samuel 115
MURPHY, Sylvester 34
MURPHY, Sylvester 36
MURPHY, Sylvester 98
MURPHY, Sylvester 99
MURPHY, Sylvester 101
MURPHY, Sylvester 102
MURPHY, Sylvester 104
MURPHY, Sylvester 110
MURPHY, Sylvester 115
MYRICK, E. P. 77
MYRICK, E. P. 84
MYRICK, Naomie 77
MYRICK, Naomie 84

NAYLOR, Henry 35
NCNEEL, ----- 65
NCNEEL, J. G. 85
NEU, C. T. 18
NEWELL, J. D. 52
NEWELL, John 68
NEWELL, John D. 48
NEWELL, John D. 55
NEWELL, John D. 62
NEWELL, John D. 64
NEWELL, John D. 65
NEWELL, John D. 70
NEWELL, John D. 79
NEWELL, John D. 84
NICHOLS, Henry F. 28
NICHOLS, Henry F. 30
NIGHT, James 8
NISON, ___ 42
NIXON, --- 42
NIXON, --- 43
NIXON, --- 44
NIXON, ---- 77
NIXON, ----- 78
NIXON, ----- 81
NIXON, ----- 91
NIXON, ----- 92
NIXON, ----- 93

NIXON, ----- 116
NIXON, ----- 120
NIXON, ----- 121
NIXON, ----- 123
NIXON, ----- 124
NUGENT, R. F. 77
NUGENT, R. F. 80
NUGENT, R. F. 83
NUGENT, R. F. 84
NUGENT, R. F. 91
NUGENT, R. F. 92
NUGENT, R. F. 95
NYE, Seth 91
NYE, Seth W. 97
NYE, Steh W. 90

O'CONNER, J. 77
O'CONNOR, J. 85
O'CONNOR, James 91
O'CONNOR, James 96
O'NEAL, John 57
O'NEAL, John 61
O'NEAL, John 63
O'NEAL, John 67
ORGAN, W. 24
ORGAN, W. 25
OSBORN, Maria H. 30
OSBORN, Mariah H. 29
OSBORNE, J. L. 95
OSBORNE, John L. 77
OSBORNE, John L. 84
OSBORNE, Thomas 77
OSBORNE, Thomas 88
OSBORNE, Thomas 91
OSBORNE, Thomas 97

PAGE, E. M. 84
PAGE, Jos. 84
PAGE, Joseph 95
PAGE, Joseph M. 90
PAGE, William 29
PAGE, William 30
PAGE, Wm. 78
PALMER, ---- 77
PALMER, ----- 91
PALMER, ----- 92
PALMER, ----- 93
PALMER, ----- 115
PALMER, ----- 120
PALMER, ----- 120
PALMER, ----- 123
PALMER, ----- 124
PALMRE, ----- 81
PANTALIAN, Mr. 77
PANTALIAN, Mr. 80
PARKER, W. 23
PARKER, W. 23
PARKER, W. 24
PARKER, W. 24
PARKER, W. 24
PARKER, W. 25
PARKER, W. 26
PARKINS, S. 73
PARKINS, Samuel 34
PARKINS, Samuel 36
PARKINS, Samuel 59
PARKINS, Samuel 60
PARKINS, Samuel 67
PARKINS, Samuel 69
PARKS, William 99
PARKS, William 100

PARKS, William 101
PARKS, William 115
PAROTT, T. F.L. 72
PAROTT, T. F.L. 77
PARRON, M. C. 77
PARRON, W.. H. 87
PARROTT, Elizabeth 65
PARROTT, Elizabeth 69
PARROTT, Elizabeth 77
PARROTT, Elizabeth 84
PARROTT, Elizabeth E. 49
PARROTT, Elizabeth E. 66
PARROTT, Elizabeth E. 118
PARROTT, Elizabeth E. 120
PARROTT, Elizabeth E. 121
PARROTT, Elizabeth E. 122
PARROTT, Lady 73
PARROTT, T. F. L. 29
PARROTT, T. F. L. 59
PARROTT, T. F. L. 68
PARROTT, T. F. L. 73
PARROTT, T. F. L. 75
PARROTT, T. F.L. 78
PARROTT, T. F.L. 80
PARROTT, T. F.L. 88
PARROTT, T. F.L. 92
PARROTT, T. F.L. 111
PARROTT, T. F.L. 125
PARROTT, T.F. L. 30
PARROTT, T.F. L. 45
PARROTT, T.F. L. 47
PARROTT, T.F. L. 50
PARROTT, T.F. L. 54
PARROTT, T.F. L. 54
PARROTT, T.F. L. 55
PARROTT, T.F. L. 56
PARROTT, T.F. L. 59
PARROTT, T.F. L. 60
PARROTT, T.F. L. 61
PARROTT, T.F. L. 62
PARROTT, T.F. L. 63
PARROTT, T.F. L. 66
PARROTT, T.F. L. 67
PARROTT, T.F. L. 67
PARROTT, T.F. L. 69
PARROTT, T.F. L. 70
PARROTT, T.F. L. 70
PARROTT, T.F. L. 71
PARROTT, T.F. L. 75
PARROTT, T.F. L. 76
PARROTT, T.F. L. 77
PARROTT, T.F. L. 79
PARROTT, T.F. L. 81
PARROTT, T.F. L. 82
PARROTT, T.F. L. 82
PARROTT, T.F. L. 84
PARROTT, T.F. L. 85
PARROTT, T.F. L. 85
PARROTT, T.F. L. 86
PARROTT, T.F. L. 86
PARROTT, T.F. L. 89
PARROTT, T.F. L. 89
PARROTT, T.F. L. 90
PARROTT, T.F. L. 90
PARROTT, T.F. L. 91
PARROTT, T.F. L. 93
PARROTT, T.F. L. 93
PARROTT, T.F. L. 94
PARROTT, T.F. L. 94
PARROTT, T.F. L. 95
PARROTT, T.F. L. 95
PARROTT, T.F. L. 96
PARROTT, T.F. L. 97
PARROTT, T.F. L. 101

PARROTT, T.F. L. 102
PARROTT, T.F. L. 103
PARROTT, T.F. L. 107
PARROTT, T.F. L. 115
PARROTT, T.F. L. 117
PARROTT, T.F. L. 118
PARROTT, T.F. L. 119
PARROTT, T.F. L. 120
PARROTT, T.F. L. 120
PARROTT, T.F. L. 121
PARROTT, T.F. L. 122
PARROTT, T.F. L. 123
PARTIN, J. P. 86
PARTIN, John P. 77
PATTON M. 73
PATTON, ----- 89
PATTON, A. W. 54
PATTON, A. W. 62
PATTON. Alexander 96
PATTON, C. 85
PATTON, C. R. 75
PATTON, C. R. 76
PATTON, C. R. 77
PATTON, C. R. 77
PATTON, C. R. 78
PATTON, C. R. 80
PATTON, C. R. 81
PATTON, C. R. 82
PATTON, C. R. 82
PATTON, C. R. 82
PATTON, C. R. 85
PATTON, C. R. 85
PATTON, C. R. 87
PATTON, C. R. 90
PATTON, C. R. 91
PATTON, C. R. 92
PATTON, C. R. 94
PATTON, C. R. 96
PATTON, C. R. 96
PATTON, C. R. 97
PATTON, C. R. 119
PATTON, C. R. 120
PATTON, C. R. 122
PATTON, C. R. 123
PATTON, C. R. 124
PATTON, C. R. 125
PATTON, Columbus R. 118
PATTON, Columbus R. 120
PATTON, Columbus R. 120
PATTON, Columbus R. 122
PATTON, John D. 119
PATTON, John D. 120
PATTON, M. 83
PATTON, M. 85
PATTON, M. C. 91
PATTON, M. C. 96
PATTON, Mathew 74
PATTON, Mathew C. 77
PATTON, Mathew C. 83
PATTON, Mrs. 72
PATTON, Mrs. 85
PATTON, St. Clair 85
PATTON, St. Clair 76
PATTON, St. Clair 92
PATTON, St. Clair 96
PATTON, W. H. 66
PATTON, W. H. 73
PATTON, W. H. 76
PATTON, W. H. 76
PATTON, W. H. 79
PATTON, W. H. 79
PATTON, W. H. 85
PATTON, W. H. 87
PATTON, W. H. 91
PATTON, W. H. 92

PATTON, W. H. 93	PERRY, James F. 97	PHELPS, J.A. E. 82
PATTON, W. H. 95	PERRY, James F. 97	PHELPS, J.A. E. 83
PATTON, Willaim H. 77	PERRY, James F. 118	PHELPS, J.A. E. 84
PATTON, William 64	PERRY, James F. 120	PHELPS, J.A. E. 85
PATTON, William H. 45	PERRY, James F. 121	PHELPS, J.A. E. 85
PATTON, William H. 45	PERRY,Sr. James F. 34	PHELPS, J.A. E. 85
PATTON, William H. 45	PERRY,Sr. James F. 36	PHELPS, J.A. E. 95
PATTON, William H. 49	PETERS, ----- 89	PHELPS, J.A. E. 110
PATTON, William H. 54	PETERS, ----- 94	PHELPS, J.A. E. 115
PATTON, William H. 57	PETERS, L. H. 58	PHELPS, J.A. E. 120
PATTON, William H. 58	PETERS, L. H. 64	PHELPS, James A.E. 79
PATTON, William H. 63	PETERS, L. H. 64	PHELPS, James A.E. 86
PATTON, William H. 63	PETERS, L. H. 67	PHELPS, James A.E. 89
PATTON, William H. 68	PETERS, L. H. 67	PHELPS, James A.E. 92
PATTON, William H. 69	PETERS, L. H. 68	PHELPS, James A.E. 96
PATTON, William H. 92	PETERS, L. H. 76	PHILIPS, Sidney 65
PATTON, William H. 96	PETERS, L. H. 78	PHILIPS, Sidney 68
PATTON, Wm. 75	PETERS, L. H. 80	PHILLIPS, Sidney 59
PATTON, Wm. 85	PETERS, L. H. 81	PHILLIPS, Sidney 64
PATTON, Wm. H. 33	PETERS, L. H. 81	PHILLIPS, Zeno 53
PATTON, Wm. H. 61	PETERS, L. H. 84	PHILLIPS, Zeno 62
PATTON, Wm. H. 62	PETERS, L. H. 85	PHILLIPS, Zeno 63
PATTON, Wm. H. 69		PHILLIPS, Zeno 63
PATTON, Wm. H. 70	PETERS, L. H. 85	PHILLIPS, Zeno 64
PATTON, Wm. H. 73	PETERS, L. H. 85	PHILLIPS, Zeno 69
PATTON, Wm. H. 78	PETERS, L. H. 86	PHILLIPS, Zeno 76
PATTON, Wm. H. 85	PETERS, L. H. 86	PHILLIPS, Zeno 85
PATTON, Wm. H. 86	PETERS, L. H. 87	PHILLIPS, Zeon 45
PATTON, Wm. J. 70	PETERS, L. H. 92	PHILLISOHN, --- 44
PATTON, wm. 78	PETERS, L. H. 94	PHILLISOHN, J. 42
PAYTON, J. C. 61	PETERS, L. H. 96	PHILLISOHN, J. 42
PAYTON, Jonathan C. 70	PETERS, L. H. 118	PHILLISOHN, Jacob 78
PAYTON, Jonathan C. 70	PETERS, L. H. 120	PHILLISOHN, Jacob 84
PEEPLES, S. W. 77	PETERS, L. H. 121	PICKERING, R. 73
PEEPLES, S. W. 85	PETERS, S. W. 86	PICKERING, R. 85
PEEPLES, Samuel 91	PETERS, Samuel W. 78	PICKETT, John J. 35
PEEPLES, Samuel W. 96	PETTUS, E. L. 95	PICKETT, John J. 36
PENTICOST, Geo. 85	PETTUS, Edward L. 78	PIEDRAS, Col. 40
PENTICOST, S. 72	PETTUS, Edward L. 79	PIEDRAS, Col. Jose De Las :
PERKINS, S. 83	PETTUS, Edward L. 84	PIEDRAS, J. 39
PERKINS, S. 84	PETTUS, Edward L. 96	PIEDRAS, J. 39
PERRY, J. F. 25	PEVEHOUSE, Jacob 78	PILGRIM, T. J. 42
PERRY, J. F. 72	PEVEHOUSE, Jacob 85	PILGRIM, T. J. 43
PERRY, J. F. 77	PEYTON, J. C. 24	PILGRIM, T. J. 43
PERRY, J. F. 78	PEYTON, J. C. 24	PITTS, --- 41
PERRY, J. F. 83	PEYTON, J. C. 25	PITTS, --- 43
PERRY, J. F. 83	PEYTON, J. C. 26	PITTS, --- 44
PERRY, J. F. 84	PEYTON, J. C. 58	PITTS, ----- 64
PERRY, J. F. 85	PEYTON, J. C. 69	PITTS, ----- 70
PERRY, J. F. 87	PEYTON, J. C. 78	PITTS, Mary Ann 29
PERRY, J. F. 87	PEYTON, J. C. 83	PITTS, Mary Ann 30
PERRY, J. F. 88	PEYTON, J. C. 86	PITTS, O. 24
PERRY, J. F. 95	PEYTON, J. C. 86	PITTS, O. 25
PERRY, James 92	PEYTON, J. C. 93	PITTS, O. 25
PERRY, James F. 8	PEYTON, J. C. 96	PITTS, O. 75
PERRY, James F. 22	PEYTON, Jonathan C. 47	PITTS, O. 78
PERRY, James F. 23	PEYTON, Jonathan C. 48	PITTS, O. 81
PERRY, James F. 23	PEYTON, Jonathan C. 64	PITTS, O. 81
PERRY, James F. 24	PEYTON, Jonathan C. 64	PITTS, O. 85
PERRY, James F. 25	PEYTON, Jonathan C. 66	PITTS, Obediah 51
PERRY, James F. 53	PEYTON, Jonathan C. 99	PITTS, Obediah 63
PERRY, James F. 60	PEYTON, Jonathan C. 106	PITTS, Obediah 64
PERRY, James F. 64	PEYTON, Jonathan C. 108	PITTS, Obediah 70
PERRY, James F. 69	PEYTON, Jonathan C. 115	PITTS, Obediah 110
PERRY, James F. 77	PHARR, Samuel 42	PITTS, Obediah 115
PERRY, James F. 85	PHARR, Samuel 43	PITTS, Obediah 123
PERRY, James F. 89	PHELPS, --- 42	PITTS, Obediah 124
PERRY, James F. 91	PHELPS, --- 43	PITTS, Obidiah 107
PERRY, James F. 92	PHELPS, J. A.E. 72	POLLARD, Amos 74
PERRY, James F. 94	PHELPS, J. A.E. 118	POLLARD, Amos 85
PERRY, James F. 95	PHELPS, J.A. E. 74	POLLARD, Amos 90
PERRY, James F. 95	PHELPS, J.A. E. 78	POLLARD, Amos 92
PERRY, James F. 96	PHELPS, J.A. E. 82	POLLARD, Amos 96
	PHELPS, J.A. E. 82	

POLLEY, H. 25
POLLEY, J. H. 23
POLLEY, J. H. 24
POLLEY, J. H. 25
POLLEY, Joseph 45
POLLEY, Joseph 46
POLLEY, Joseph 60
POLLEY, Joseph 60
POLLEY, Joseph 64
POLLEY, Joseph 66
POLLEY, Joseph 68
POLLEY, Joseph 69
POLLEY, Joseph H. 42
POLLEY, Joseph H. 43
POLLEY, Joseph H. 55
POLLEY, Joseph H. 64
POLLEY, Joseph H. 68
POLLEY, Joseph H. 70
POLLEY, Joseph H. 72
POLLEY, Joseph H. 85
POLLEY, Joseph H. 89
POLLEY, Joseph H. 96
POLLEY, Joseph H. 117
POLLEY, Joseph H. 120
POLLEY, Joseph H. 122
POLLOCK, Carlie 31
PORTER, B. A. 34
PORTER, B. A. 34
PORTER, B. A. 36
PORTER, B. A. 41
PORTER, B. A. 43
PORTER, B. A. 44
PORTER, B. A. 48
PORTER, B. A. 63
PORTER, B. A. 69
PORTER, B. A. 69
PORTER, B. A. 70
PORTER, B. A. 71
PORTER, B. A. 78
PORTER, B. A. 79
PORTER, B. A. 81
PORTER, B. A. 84
PORTER, B. A. 84
PORTER, B. A. 85
PORTER, B. A. 92
PORTER, B. A. 93
PORTER, B. A. 95
PORTER, B. A. 95
PORTER, B. A. 96
PORTER, J. M. 85
PORTER, John M. 34
PORTER, John M. 36
PORTER, John M. 48
PORTER, John M. 63
PORTER, John M. 69
PORTER, John M. 70
PORTER, John M. 71
PORTER, Pamelia 63
PORTER, Pamilia 48
PORTER, Pamilia 69
PORTER, Pamilia 70
PORTER, Pamilia 71
POWELL, E. 89
POWELL, E. 89
POWELL, E. 96
POWELL, E. (MARTIN) 96
POWELL, Elizabeth 56
POWELL, Elizabeth 57
POWELL, Elizabeth 61
POWELL, Elizabeth 62
POWELL, Elizabeth 65
POWELL, Elizabeth 74
POWELL, Elizabeth 90

POWELL, Elizabeth 92
POWELL, Elizabeth 96
POWELL, Elizabeth (Alias) 78
POWELL, Elizabeth (Alias) 92
POWELL, Joseph 58
POWELL, Joseph 64
POWELL, Joseph 69
POWELL, Mrs. Elizabeth 73
POWELL, Mrs. Elizabeth 73
POWELL, Mrs. Elizabeth 78
POWELL, Mrs. Elizabeth 85
POWELL, Peter 52
POWELL, Peter 61
POWELL, Peter 69
POWELL, W. E. 73
POWELL, W. E. 85
PRATER, William 24
PRATER, William 25
PRICE, John 36
PROCTOR, S. M. 82
PUGH, Spencer 41
PUGH, Spencer 41
PUGH, Spencer 42
PUGH, Spencer 44
PUGH, Spencer A. 41
PUGH, Spencer A. 42

RAINES, C. B. 97
RAINES, Dr. 92
RAINES, Dr. 94
RAINS, C. B. 78
RAINS, C. B. 83
RAINS, C. B. 84
RAINS, C. B. 85
RAINS, C. B. 88
RAINS, C. B. 91
RAINS, C. B. 92
RAINS, C. B. 94
RAINS, C. B. 95
RAINS, Dr. 95
RAMSBURGH, Jacob 41
RAMSBURGH, Jacob 44
RAMSEY, L. 102
RAMSEY, L. 115
RAMSEY, Sally 77
RAMSEY, Sally 85
RANDOM, David 85
RANDOM, David 97
RANDOM, David 97
RANDOM, John 36
RANDON, David 54
RANDON, David 64
RANDON, David 72
RANDON, David 89
RANDON, David 92
RANDON, David 92
RANDON, David 93
RANDON, David 94
RANDON, David 96
RANDON, David 99
RANDON, David 115
RANDON, John 34
RAWLS, Daniel 103
RAWLS, Daniel 108
RAWLS, Daniel 115
RECTOR, Nancy C. 29
RECTOR, Nancy C. 30
RECTOR, S. M. 78
RECTOR, S. M. 82
RECTOR, S. M. 85
RECTOR, S. M. 85
RED, William Stuart 16
REEDING, R. L. 57

REEDING, R. L. 64
REEL, R. H.W. 65
REEL, R. H.W. 85
REEL, R. H. W. 76
REEL, R.H.W. 52
REEL, R.H. W. 50
REEL, R.H. W. 53
REEL, R.H. W. 54
REEL, R.H. W. 62
REEL, R.H. W. 64
REEL, R.H. W. 69
REEL, R.H. W. 72
REEL, R.H. W. 79
REEL, R.H. W. 91
REEL, R.H. W. 92
REEL, R.H. W. 96
REES, J. 75
REES, J. 79
REES, J. 85
REES, J. 92
REES, J. R. 93
REES, J. R. 94
REES, J. R. 97
REES, J.65 76
REES, Joseph 42
REES, Joseph 43
REES, Joseph 47
REES, Joseph 47
REES, Joseph 49
REES, Joseph 49
REES, Joseph 50
REES, Joseph 52
REES, Joseph 56
REES, Joseph 60
REES, Joseph 61
REES, Joseph 62
REES, Joseph 62
REES, Joseph 65
REES, Joseph 65
REES, Joseph 67
REES, Joseph 69
REES, Joseph 70
REES, Joseph 76
REES, Joseph 77
REES, Joseph 78
REES, Joseph 80
REES, Joseph 86
REES, Joseph 91
REES, Joseph 93
REES, Joseph 96
REES, Joseph 96
REES, Joseph 119
REES, Joseph 120
REES, Joseph 122
RES, Joseph 118
REYNOLDS, --- 42
REYNOLDS, --- 42
REYNOLDS, --- 43
REYNOLDS, ---- 53
REYNOLDS, ----- 61
REYNOLDS, ----- 66
REYNOLDS, ----- 72
REYNOLDS, ----- 75
REYNOLDS, ----- 85
REYNOLDS, ----- 89
REYNOLDS, ----- 90
REYNOLDS, ----- 93
REYNOLDS, ----- 96
REYNOLDS, ----- 100
REYNOLDS, ----- 113
REYNOLDS, ----- 115
REYNOLDS, ------ 80
REYNOLDS, Albert G. 34

REYNOLDS, Albert G. 36
RIANS, C. B. 73
RICE, John 34
RICHARDSON, ----- 73
RICHARDSON, ----- 74
RICHARDSON, ----- 78
RICHARDSON, ----- 80
RICHARDSON, ----- 83
RICHARDSON, ----- 107
RICHARDSON, ----- 113
RICHARDSON, ----- 115
RICHARDSON, ----- 116
RICHARDSON, ----- 123
RICHARDSON, ----- 124
RICHARDSON, ----- 125
RICHARDSON, S. 25
RICHARDSON, Stephen 24
RICHARDSON, Stephen 73
RICHARDSON, Stephen 74
RICHARDSON, Stephen 78
RICHARDSON, Stephen 78
RICHARDSON, Stephen 80
RICHARDSON, Stephen 85
RICHERSON, Edwin 40
RICHESON, Edwin 34
RICHESON, Edwin 36
RICHESON, Edwin 39
RICHESON, Stephen 57
RICHESON, Stephen 64
RIPLEY, Phinas 83
RIPLEY, Phineas 78
RIPLEY, Phineas 92
RIPLEY, Phineas 95'
RIPLEY, Phineas 111
RIPLEY, Phineas 115
RIVERS, Manson D. 83
RIVERS, Mason 78
ROBERTS, ----- 90
ROBERTS, ----- 96
ROBERTS, A. 42
ROBERTS, A. 42
ROBERTS, A. 43
ROBERTS, A. 44
ROBERTS, A. 75
ROBERTS, A. 85
ROBERTS, Andrew 24
ROBERTS, Andrew 26
ROBERTS, Andrew 43
ROBERTS, W. 24
ROBERTS, W. 26
ROBERTS, W. 75
ROBERTS, W. 80
ROBERTS, W. 85
ROBERTS, William 24
ROBERTS, William 26
ROBERTSON, A. 53
ROBERTSON, A. 64
ROBERTSON, Andrew 96
ROBERTSON, Charles 41
ROBERTSON, Charles 44
ROBERTSON, Charlotte 13
ROBERTSON, Charlotte 34
ROBERTSON, Charlotte 55
ROBERTSON, Charlotte 64
ROBERTSON, Charlotte 66
ROBERTSON, Charlotte 100
ROBERTSON, Charlotte 115
ROBERTSON, Charlotte (Alias) 107
ROBERTSON, Charlotte (Jackson) 69
ROBERTSON, E. 42
ROBERTSON, E. E. 41
ROBERTSON, E. E. 42
ROBERTSON, E. E. 44
ROBERTSON, Edward 13

ROBERTSON, Edward 34
ROBERTSON, Edward 37
ROBERTSON, Edward 41
ROBERTSON, Edward 42
ROBERTSON, Edward 42
ROBERTSON, Edward 43
ROBERTSON, Edward 55
ROBERTSON, Edward 62
ROBERTSON, Edward 64
ROBERTSON, Edward 66
ROBERTSON, Edward 69
ROBERTSON, Edward 100
ROBERTSON, Edward 105
ROBERTSON, Edward 107
ROBERTSON, Edward 115
ROBERTSON, Mrs. C. 42
ROBERTSON, Mrs. C. 43
ROBINSON, A. 74
ROBINSON, A. 86
ROBINSON, Andrew 26
ROBINSON, Andrew 27
ROBINSON, Andrew 30
ROBINSON, Andrew 72
ROBINSON, Andrew 79
ROBINSON, Andrew 85
ROBINSON, Andrew 88
ROBINSON, Andrew 126
ROBINSON, F. 24
ROBINSON, F. 25
ROBINSON, F. 25
ROBINSON, F. 25
ROBINSON, F. 42
ROBINSON, F. 44
ROBINSON, G. 24
ROBINSON, G. 25
ROBINSON, George 47
ROBINSON, George 64
ROBINSON, George 65
ROBINSON, George 103
ROBINSON, George 107
ROBINSON, George 108
ROBINSON, George 115
ROBINSON, Wm. 74
RODDY, Ephram 108
RODDY, Ephram 115
ROLSEY, L. 76
ROLSEY, L.. 85
ROSS, --- 41
ROSS, --- 43
ROSS, --- 44
ROSS, ---- 41
ROSS, W. M. 27
ROYAL, R. R. 4
ROYAL, R. R. 5
ROYAL, R. R. 103
ROYALL, R. R. 115
RUNNELLS, E. M. 82
RUNNELS, E. M. 78
RUSSEL, Wm. J. 70
RUSSELL, Ales 115
RUSSELL, Alex 107
RUSSELL, W. J. 66
RUSSELL, W. J. 72
RUSSELL, W. J. 75
RUSSELL, W. J. 77
RUSSELL, W. J. 78
RUSSELL, W. J. 81
RUSSELL, W. J. 86
RUSSELL, W. J. 90
RUSSELL, W. J. 96
RUSSELL, William H. 63
RUSSELL, William J. 45
RUSSELL, William J. 46
RUSSELL, William J. 49

RUSSELL, William J. 53
RUSSELL, William J. 56
RUSSELL, William J. 58
RUSSELL, William J. 59
RUSSELL, William J. 60
RUSSELL, William J. 60
RUSSELL, William J. 60-
RUSSELL, William J. 63
RUSSELL, William J. 64
RUSSELL, William J. 64
RUSSELL, William J. 68
RUSSELL, Wm. J. 60
RUSSELL, Wm. J. 67
RUSSELL, Wm. J. 69
RUSSELL, Wm. J. 69
RUSSELL, Wm. R. 77
RUTHERFORD, ----- 78
RUTHERFORD, ----- 80
RUTHERFORD, ----- 92
RUTHERFORD, ----- 93
RUTHERFORD, W. H. 69
RUTHERFORD, William H. 51
RUTHERFORD, William H. 67
RUTHERFORD, Wm. H. 62
RYAN, Isaac 74
RYAN, Isaac 78
RYAN, Isaac 83

SAAYRE, C. D. 96
SAMPIER, ----- 86
SAMPIER, ----- 86
SAMPIER, Joseph 35
SAMPIER, Wm. 78
SAMPLIER, Wm. 87
SANDES, William R. 28
SANTA ANNA, ----- 9
SAURE, --- 42
SAWYER, ----- 124
SAWYER, S. 48
SAWYER, S. 62
SAWYER, S. 64
SAWYER, S. 67
SAWYER, S. 76
SAWYER, S. 78
SAWYER, S. 83
SAWYER, S. 85
SAWYER, S. 87
SAWYER, S. 123
SAWYER, S. 125
SAWYER, S. 125
SAWYER, Samuel 35
SAWYER, Samuel 37
SAWYER, Samuel 58
SAWYER, Samuel 62
SAWYER, Samuel 68
SAWYER, Samuel 70
SAWYER, Samuel 101
SAWYER, Samuel 108
SAWYER, Samuel 115
SAWYER, Samuel 117
SAWYER, Samuel 120
SAWYER, Samuel 122
SAWYER, W. B. 122
SAYARE, C. D. 93
SAYER, ----- 121
SAYER, ----- 123
SAYER, ----- 124
SAYER, C. D. 22
SAYER, Charles D. 68
SAYLES, ----- 7
SAYLES, Henry 2
SAYLES, John 2

SAYRE, --- 42
SAYRE, --- 43
SAYRE, --- 44
SAYRE, ----- 77
SAYRE, ----- 78
SAYRE, ----- 81
SAYRE, ----- 91
SAYRE, ----- 92
SAYRE, ----- 93
SAYRE, ----- 116
SAYRE, ----- 120
SAYRE, C. D. 22
SAYRE, C. D. 22
SAYRE, C. D. 22
SAYRE, C. D. 22
SAYRE, C. D. 23
SAYRE, C. D. 24
SAYRE, C. D. 24
SAYRE, C. D. 24
SAYRE, C. D. 25
SAYRE, C. D. 26
SAYRE, C. D. 90
SAYRE, Charles D. 47
SAYRE, Charles D. 55
SAYRE, Charles D. 57
SAYRE, Charles D. 62
SAYRE, Charles D. 64
SAYRE, Charles D. 65
SAYRE, Charles D. 69
SAYRE, Charles D. 70
SAYRE, Charles D. 100
SAYRE, Charles D. 114
SAYRE, Chas. D. 63
SAYRE, Chas. D. 67
SAYRE, S. F. 22
SCLOKY, Robert 74
SCOBY, Robert 117
SCOBY, Robert 120
SCOBY, Robert 120
SCOBY, Robert 121
SCOTS, W. P. 55
SCOTT, Capt. Wm. P. 37
SCOTT, Capt. William P. 35
SCOTT, Caroline 29
SCOTT, Caroline 30
SELKIRK, Wm. 24
SELKIRK, Wm. 24
SETTLE, W. H. 45
SETTLE, W. H. 64
SHANNON, Jacob 52
SHANNON, Jacob 64
SHANNON, Jacob 66
SHANNON, Jacob 68
SHARP, ----- 124
SHARP, John 30
SHARP, John 30
SHARP, John 72
SHARP, John 73
SHARP, John 86
SHARP, John 89
SHARP, John 89
SHARP, John 96
SHARP, John 111
SHARP, John 115
SHAW, George D. 100
SHAW, George D. 100
SHAW, George D. 101
SHAW, George D. 115
SHELBY, D. 41
SHELBY, D. 44
SHELBY, David 23
SHELBY, David 26
SHELBY, David 46
SHELBY, David 60

SHELBY, David 64
SHELBY, David 67
SHELBY, David 70
SHIPMAN, John M. 42
SHIPMAN, John M. 44
SHOON, E. D. 53
SHOON, E. D. 62
SHOON, E. D. 64
SHOON, E. D. 69
SHULER, Abram 115
SLAYTON, Robert G. 35
SLAYTON, Robert G. 37
SLEDGE, Samuel 35
SLEDGE, Samuel 37
SLEDGE, W. H. 8
SLEDGE, W. H. 47
SLEDGE, W. H. 48
SLEDGE, W. H. 49
SLEDGE, W. H. 50
SLEDGE, W. H. 52
SLEDGE, W. H. 53
SLEDGE, W. H. 54
SLEDGE, W. H. 55
SLEDGE, W. H. 56
SLEDGE, W. H. 57
SLEDGE, W. H. 58
SMIATH, Henry 60
SMISTH, C. 25
SMITH ----- 81
SMITH, ----- 72
SMITH, ----- 74
SMITH, ----- 77
SMITH, ----- 80
SMITH, ----- 81
SMITH, ----- 84
SMITH, ----- 86
SMITH, ----- 92
SMITH, ----- 93
SMITH, ----- 94
SMITH, ----- 95
SMITH, ----- 96
SMITH, ----- 116
SMITH, ----- 120
SMITH, ----- 120
SMITH, ----- 123
SMITH, ----- 124
SMITH, Adam 78
SMITH, Adam 86
SMITH, Alcalde Henry 103
SMITH, Alcalde Henry 104
SMITH, Arlclde Henry 101
SMITH, B. F. 72
SMITH, B. F. 77
SMITH, B. F. 86
SMITH, B. F. 89
SMITH, B. F. 96
SMITH, Benjamin 62
SMITH, Benjamin F. 51
SMITH, Benjamin F. 52
SMITH, Benjamin F. 64
SMITH, Benjamin F. 68
SMITH, Benjamin F. 70
SMITH, Benjamin F. 106
SMITH, Benjamin F. 108
SMITH, Benjamin F. 115
SMITH, C. 24
SMITH, C. 24
SMITH, C. 25
SMITH, C. 26
SMITH, C. C. 24
SMITH, C. C. 26

SMITH, F. 86
SMITH, Francis 41
SMITH, Francis 44
SMITH, George 35
SMITH, George 37
SMITH, George 48
SMITH, George 64
SMITH, George 64
SMITH, George 66
SMITH, George B. 70
SMITH, George M. 99
SMITH, George W. 106
SMITH, George W. 115
SMITH, H. W. 75
SMITH, Henry 2
SMITH, Henry 3
SMITH, Henry 4
SMITH, Henry 5
SMITH, Henry 6
SMITH, Henry 7
SMITH, Henry 9
SMITH, Henry 12
SMITH, Henry 13
SMITH, Henry 15
SMITH, Henry 22
SMITH, Henry 24
SMITH, Henry 26
SMITH, Henry 28
SMITH, Henry 42
SMITH, Henry 44
SMITH, Henry 45
SMITH, Henry 46
SMITH, Henry 51
SMITH, Henry 60
SMITH, Henry 60
SMITH, Henry 63
SMITH, Henry 64
SMITH, Henry 64
SMITH, Henry 66
SMITH, Henry 66
SMITH, Henry 67
SMITH, Henry 68
SMITH, Henry 69
SMITH, Henry 70
SMITH, Henry 70
SMITH, Henry 74
SMITH, Henry 86
SMITH, Henry 89
SMITH, Henry 96
SMITH, Henry 98
SMITH, Henry 99
SMITH, Henry 100
SMITH, Henry 102
SMITH, Henry 115
SMITH, Henry 126
SMITH, M. W. 53
SMITH, M. W. 62
SMITH, M. W. 72
SMITH, M. W. 73
SMITH, M. W. 74
SMITH, M. W. 74
SMITH, M. W. 76
SMITH, M. W. 77
SMITH, M. W. 78
SMITH, M. W. 81
SMITH, M. W. 82
SMITH, M. W. 83
SMITH, M. W. 83
SMITH, M. W. 86
SMITH, M. W. 86
SMITH, M. W. 86
SMITH, M. W. 88
SMITH, M. W. 89

SMITH, M. W. 90
SMITH, M. W. 91
SMITH, M. W. 95
SMITH, M. W. 101
SMITH, M. W. 102
SMITH, M. W. 117
SMITH, M. W. 118
SMITH, M. W. 120
SMITH, M. W. 120
SMITH, M. W. 121
SMITH, M. W. 122
SMITH, M. W. 122
SMITH, Meriwether 115
SMITH, Meriwether W. 110
SMITH, P. 78
SMITH, P. 78
SMITH, P. 80
SMITH, P. 86
SMITH, Palmer 78
SMITH, Phimeas 115
SMITH, Phineas 48
SMITH, Phineas 55
SMITH, Phineas 63
SMITH, Phineas 64
SMITH, Phineas 66
SMITH, Phineas 75
SMITH, Phineas 76
SMITH, Phineas 86
SMITH, Phineas 92
SMITH, Phineas 93
SMITH, Phineas 99
SMITH, Phineas 105
SMITH, Sally 29
SMITH, Sally 30
SMITH, Thomas 92
SMITH, Thomas 93
SMITH, Thomas 96
SMITH, William 78
SMITH, William 87
SMITH, William 115
SMITH, William B. 115
SMITHERS, L. 42
SMITHERS, L. 42
SMITHERS, L. 43
SMITHERS, L. 43
SMITHERS, L. 44
SMITHERS, L. 96
SMITHERS, S. 73
SMITHERS, S. 73
SMITHERS, S. 76
SMITHERS, S. 76
SMITHERS, S. 77
SMITHERS, S. 79
SMITHERS, S. 79
SMITHERS, S. 79
SMITHERS, S. 86
SMITHERS, S. 86
SMOTHERS, S. 78
SMSITH, Phineas 70
SNIDER, A. 58
SNIDER, A. 60
SNIDER, A. 70
SPENCER, O. H. 52
SPENCER, O. H. 65
SPENCER, O. H. 65
SPENCER, O. H. 70
SPENCER, O. H. 70
SPENCER, O. H. 107
SPENCER, O. H. 115
SPLANCE, Peyton R. 7
SPLANE, Ann 100
SPLANE, Ann D.W. 105
SPLANE, Ann D.W. 115
SPLANE, Ann S.W. 64
SPLANE, Douglas 86

SPLANE, Douglas C. 77
SPLANE, P. R. 49
SPLANE, P. R. 50
SPLANE, P. R. 60
SPLANE, P. R. 62
SPLANE, P. R. 64
SPLANE, P. R. 72
SPLANE, P. R. 73
SPLANE, P. R. 73
SPLANE, P. R. 73
SPLANE, P. R. 74
SPLANE, P. R. 74
SPLANE, P. R. 75
SPLANE, P. R. 76
SPLANE, P. R. 77
SPLANE, P. R. 78
SPLANE, P. R. 78
SPLANE, P. R. 79
SPLANE, P. R. 79
SPLANE, P. R. 81
SPLANE, P. R. 86
SPLANE, P. R. 89
SPLANE, P. R. 89
SPLANE, P. R. 91
SPLANE, P. R. 92
SPLANE, P. R. 93
SPLANE, P. R. 94
SPLANE, P. R. 96
SPLANE, P. R. 97
SPLANE, P. R. 100
SPLANE, P. R. 104
SPLANE, P. R. 105
SPLANE, P. R. 106
SPLANE, P. R. 123
SPLANE, P. R. 124
SPLANE, P. R. 125
SPLANE, Peyton 96
SPLANE, Peyton 115
SPLANE, Peyton R. 46
SPLANE, Peyton R. 46
SPLANE, Peyton R. 60
SPLANE, Peyton R. 60
SPLANE, Peyton R. 52
SPLANE, Peyton R. 64
SPLANE, Peyton R. 65
SPLANE, Peyton R. 65
SPLANE, Peyton R. 66
SPLANE, Peyton R. 66
SPLANE, Peyton R. 68
SPLANE, Peyton R. 9
SPLANE, Peyton R. 104
SPLANE, Peyton R. 110
SPLANE, Peyton R. 118
SPLANE, Peyton R. 118
SPLANE, Peyton R. 119
SPLANE, Peyton R. 120
SPLANE, Peyton R. 122
SPLANE, Peyton R. 123
SPLANE, Peyton R. 125
SPLANE, T. 73
SPLANE, T. 74
SPLANE, T. 79
SPLANE, T. 85
SPLANE, T. 86
SPLANE, Thomas 79
SPLANE, Thomas 86
STAFFORD, W. 78
STAFFORD, William 46
STAFFORD, William 56
STAFFORD, William 64
STAFFORD, William 66
STAFFORD, Wm. 86
STANDEFORD, Elizabeth 30

STANDFIELD, Elizabeth 28
STEVENSON, ----- 61
STEVENSON, ----- 65
STEVENSON, R. 72
STEVENSON, R. 81
STEVENSON, R. 86
STEVENSON, Robert 51
STEVENSON, Robert 77
STEVENSON, Robert 78
STEVENSON, Robert 84
STEVENSON, Robert 89
STEVENSON, Robert 97
STEVINSON ----- 67
STEVINSON, ---- 45
STEVINSON, ---- 47
STEVINSON, ----- 48
STEVINSON, ----- 62
STEVINSON, ----- 64
STEVINSON, ----- 70
STEVINSON, ----- 71
STEVINSON, ----- 105
STEVINSON, ----- 107
STEVINSON, ----- 114
STEVINSON, ----- 115
STEVINSON, ------ 86
STEVINSON, _____ 66
STEWART, C. B. 41
STEWART, C. B. 41
STEWART, C. B. 41
STEWART, C. B. 41
STEWART, C. B. 41
STEWART, C. B. 42
STEWART, C. B. 42
STEWART, C. B. 43
STEWART, C. B. 43
STEWART, C. B. 44
STEWART, C. B. 44
STEWART, C. B. 47
STEWART, C. B. 56
STEWART, C. B. 56
STEWART, C. B. 64
STEWART, C. B. 64
STEWART, C. B. 67
STEWART, C. B. 68
STEWART, Charles B. 51
STEWART, Charles B. 57
STEWART, Charles B. 64
STEWART, Charles B. 66
STIFF, Thomas R. 30
STIFF, thomas R. 30
STIFFLER, ----- 76
STIFFLER, ----- 78
STIFFLER, ----- 85
STIFFLER, Jacob 77
STIFFLER, Jacob 87
STIFFLER, Jacob 91
STIFFLER, Jacob 97
STILES, W. 85
STILES, William 78
STILES, Wm. 81
STILES, Wm. 81
STILES, Wm. 85
STONE, R.P. T. 52
STONE, R.P. T. 65
STONE, R.P. T. 65
STONE, R.P. T. 70
STONE, R.P. T. 70
STONE, R.P. T. 107
STONE, Ruben 70
STONE, Ruben P.T. 15
STONE, Ruben P.T. 51
STONE, Ruben P.T. 60

STONE, Ruben P.T. 62
STONE, Ruben P.T. 106
STONE, Ruben P.T. 115
STOUT, O. H. 91
STOUT, O. H. 97
STOUT, Owen H. 76
STOUT, Owen H. 87
STRATTON, A. R. 74
STRATTON, A. R. 87
STRATTON, Ann Rebecca 78
STRATTON, Ann Rebecca 87
STRATTON, H. 52
STRATTON, H. 57
STRATTON, H. B. 53
STRATTON, Horace 28
STRATTON, Horace 30
STRATTON, Horace 58
STRATTON, Horace 65
STRATTON, Horace B. 35
STRATTON, Horace B. 37
STRATTON, Rebecca 75
STRATTON, Wm. 75
STRATTON, Wm. 87
STRINGFELLOW, Susan 29
STRINGFELLOW, Susan 30
STRODER(?), Edmund 35
STROTHER, ----- 117
STROTHER, ----- 120
STROTHER, Edmund 35
STROTHER, Edmund (STRODER) 37
STROTHER, Jesse 112
STROTHER, Jesse 115
STROWDER, Jesse STROTHER- 37
SUTHERLAND, John 112
SUTHERLAND, John 113
SUTHERLAND, John 115
SUTHERLAND, John 126
SWEENEY, Em. B. 70
SWEENEY, Henry 70
SWEENEY, John 47
SWEENEY, John 49
SWEENEY, John 63
SWEENEY, John 63
SWEENEY, John 65
SWEENEY, John 68
SWEENEY, John 70
SWEENEY, John 105
SWEENEY, John 107
SWEENEY, John 108
SWEENEY, John 109
SWEENEY, John 110
SWEENEY, John 115
SWEENEY, W. B. 54
SWEENEY, W. B. 62
SWEENEY, W. B. 65
SWEENEY, W. B. 72
SWEENEY, W. B. 74
SWEENEY, W. B. 74
SWEENEY, W. B. 76
SWEENEY, W. B. 76
SWEENEY, W. B. 77
SWEENEY, W. B. 78
SWEENEY, W. B. 78
SWEENEY, W. B. 79
SWEENEY, W. B. 79
SWEENEY, W. B. 79
SWEENEY, W. B. 87
SWEENEY, W. B. 87
SWEENEY, W. B. 89
SWEENEY, W. B. 89
SWEENEY, W. B. 91
SWEENEY, W. B. 91
SWEENEY, W. B. 92

SWEENEY, W. B. 96
SWEENEY, W. B. 97
SWEENEY, W. B. 97
SWEENEY, W. B. 104
SWEENEY, W. B. 107
SWEENEY, W. B. 117
SWEENEY, W. B. 119
SWEENEY, W. B. 121
SWEENEY, W. B. 124
SWEENEY, William 109
SWEENEY, William B. 47
SWEENEY, William B. 55
SWEENEY, William B. 61
SWEENEY, William B. 65
SWEENEY, William B. 68
SWEENEY, William B. 105
SWEENEY, William B. 107
SWEENEY, William B. 108
SWEENEY, William B. 117
SWEENEY, William B. 117
SWEENEY, William B. 118
SWEENEY, William B. 119
SWEENEY, William B. 120
SWEENEY, William B. 122
SWEENEY, William B. 125
SWEENEY, Wm. B. 123
SWENEY, Wm. B. 64
SYNDICO, William Eckel 5

TALBOT, John 52
TALBOT, John 65
TALBOT, John 67
TALLEY, D. 26
TALLEY, Davis 73
TALLEY, Davis 74
TALLEY, Davis 79
TALLEY, Davis 87
TATE, William 103
TATE, William 105
TATE, William 107
TATE, William 108
TATE, William 115
TAYLOR, J. B. 92
TAYLOR, J. B. 96
TAYLOR, Jesse 75
TAYLOR, Jesse 79
TAYLOR, Jesse 87
TAYLOR, Jesse 87
TAYLOR, Jesse 90
TAYLOR, Jesse 97
TAYLOR, John B. 75
TAYLOR, John B. 85
TAYLOR, John B. 87
TAYLOR, John B. 90
TAYLOR, John B. 97
TAYLOR, Samuel 79
TAYLOR, Samuel 80
TAYLOR, Samuel 86
TENNEL, B. 78
TENNEL, B. 84
TENNEL, Benjamin 58
TENNEL, Benjamin 61
TENNEL, Benjamin 69
TENNEL, Benjamin 70
TENNEL, Benjamin 73
TENNEL, Benjamin 74
TENNEL, Benjamin 76
TENNEL, Benjamin 79
TENNEL, Benjamin 87
TENNEL, Benjamin 89
TENNEL, Benjamin 97
TENNEL, Geo. 76

TENNEL, George 24
TENNEL, George 26
TENNEL, George 45
TENNEL, George 48
TENNEL, George 63
TENNEL, George 69
TENNEL, George 77
TENNEL, George 77
TENNEL, George 87
TENNEL, George 91
TENNEL, George 97
TENNEL, H. S. 97
TENNELL, Benjamin 61
TENNELL, George 63
TENNELL, George 69
TENNELL, George 71
TENORIO, Capt. Antonio 8
TERCERO, Sello 37
THOMAS, J. 75
THOMAS, J. 79
THOMAS, John 42
THOMAS, John 43
THOMAS, John 43
THOMAS, John 45
THOMAS, John 46
THOMAS, John 49
THOMAS, John 60
THOMAS, John 62
THOMAS, John 65
THOMAS, John 70
THOMAS, John 90
THOMAS, John 97
THOMAS, John 111
THOMAS, John 115
THOMAS, John 116
THOMAS, John 120
THOMAS, John 122
THOMAS, John B. 79
THOMAS, L. 41
THOMAS, L. 44
THOMPSON, Jesse 53
THOMPSON, Jesse 62
THOMPSON, Jesse 65
THOMPSON, Jesse 70
THOMPSON, Jesse 76
THOMPSON, Jesse 79
THOMPSON, William 59
THOMPSON, William 64
THOMPSON, William 65
THOMPSON, William 68
TINSLEY, A. B. 79
TINSLEY, A. B. 84
TINSLEY, Isaac T. 108
TINSLEY, Isaac T. 115
TINSLEY, J. T. 47
TINSLEY, J. T. 65
TINSLEY, J. T. 68
TINSLEY, J. T. 70
TINSLEY, J. T. 105
TINSLEY, J. T. 107
TINSLEY, J. T. 115
TINSLEY, James 52
TINSLEY, James 61
TINSLEY, James 61
TOMILINSON, J. 41
TOMILINSON, J. 42
TOMILINSON, James 41
TOMILINSON, James 42
TOMILINSON, James 43
TOMILINSON, James 44
TOMILNSON, James 42

TOMLINSON, J. 42
TONE, Thomas 79
TONE, Thomas 87
TONE, Thomas 92
TONE, Thomas 97
TOUCHON, F. 22
TOWNES, Martin 74
TOWSON, Jacob 78
TOWSON, Jacob 87
TOWSON, Jacob 92
TOWSON, Jacob 97
TRAVIS, Barrett 32
TRAVIS, W. Barrett 103
TRAVIS, William B. 50
TRAVIS, William B. 65
TRAVIS, William B. 108
TRAVIS, William Barrett 2
TRAVIS, William Barrett 36
TRAVIS, William Barrett 37
TRAVIS, William Barrett 115
TRESPALACIOS, Jose Felex 1
TURNER, James 36
TURNER, James 37
TURNER, James 105
TURNER, James 108
TURNER, James 115

UGARTECHEA, Col. Domingo DE 3
VANDIVERS, S. 65
VANDIVERS, S. 65
VANDIVERS, S. 70
VANDIVERS, S. 107
VANDIVERS, S. 115
VANDIVRS, S. 70
VANDORN, Isaac 119
VANDORN, Isaac 120
VANDORN, Isaac 122
VAUGHAN, J. L. 104
VAUGHAN, James L. 110
VAUGHN, James L. 110
VAUGHN, James L. 115
VAUGHN, R. 101
VAUGHN, R. 115
VELASCO, ---- 94
VELASCO, ----- 81
VELASCO, ----- 93
VELASCO, ----- 95
VELASCO, ----- 96
VERNON, Alexander 79
VERNON, Alexander 82
VERNON, Alexander 92
VERNON, Alexander 94
VIDIR, Lewis S. 62
VIDIR, Lewis S. 65
VIDIR, Lewis S. 69
VINCE, Jesse 36
VINCE, Jesse 37
VINCE, Robert 51
VINCE, Robert 65
VINCE, Robert 66
VINCE, Robert 71

WAKEFIELD, N. 79
WAKEFIELD, N. 82
WALKER, ---- 25
WALKER, ----- 23
WALKER, ----- 26
WALKER, Joseph 79
WALKER, Joseph 84
WALKER, Joseph 103
WALKER, Joseph 115
WALLACE, J.W. E. 116
WALLACE, J.W. E. 120

WALLACE, J.W. E. 121
WALLACE, J.W. E. 122
WALLACE, J.W. E. 122
WALLACE, J.W. E. 125
WALLACE, J.W. E. 125
WALLACE, John Y. 36
WALLACE, John Y. 37
WALLACH, William D. 35
WALLER, --- 41
WALLER, --- 43
WALLER, Byrd B. 8
WALLER, E. 43
WALLER, E. 43
WALLER, E. 72
WALLER, E. 72
WALLER, E. 74
WALLER, E. 75
WALLER, E. 76
WALLER, E. 77
WALLER, E. 78
WALLER, E. 79
WALLER, E. 79
WALLER, E. 79
WALLER, E. 80
WALLER, E. 81
WALLER, E. 83
WALLER, E. 84
WALLER, E. 84
WALLER, E. 86
WALLER, E. 91
WALLER, Edwin 7
WALLER, Edwin 9
WALLER, Edwin 10
WALLER, Edwin 14
WALLER, Edwin 44
WALLER, Edwin 46
WALLER, Edwin 48
WALLER, Edwin 49
WALLER, Edwin 50
WALLER, Edwin 55
WALLER, Edwin 56
WALLER, Edwin 65
WALLER, Edwin 66
WALLER, Edwin 67
WALLER, Edwin 70
WALLER, Edwin 79
WALLER, Edwin 87
WALLER, Edwin 89
WALLER, Edwin 90
WALLER, Edwin 92
WALLER, Edwin 92
WALLER, Edwin 93
WALLER, Edwin 94
WALLER, Edwin 94
WALLER, Edwin 94
WALLER, Edwin 95
WALLER, Edwin 97
WALLER, Edwin 104
WALLER, Edwin 106
WALLER, Edwin 107
WALLER, Edwin 108
WALLER, Edwin 109
WALLER, Edwin 110
WALLER, Edwin 111
WALLER, Edwin 112
WALLER, Edwin 115
WALLER, Edwin 118
WALLER, Edwin 120
WALLER, Edwin 120
WALLER, Edwin 122
WALLER, Mr. 10
WALLEY, Edwin 68
WALLIS, John G. 36

WALLIS, John G. 37
WALTMAN, Ann M. 110
WALTMAN, Ann M. 115
WALTMAN, D. S. 103
WALTMAN, D. S. 115
WALTMAN, David S. 19
WALTMAN, Samuel D. 105
WALTMAN, Samuel D. 107
WALTMAN, Samuel D. 115
WARE, James 22
WARE, James 24
WARE, James 26
WARE, James 77
WARE, James 87
WARREN, William 119
WARREN, William 120
WARREN, William 122
WATERMAN, ---- 120
WATERMAN, ----- 120
WATERMAN, ----- 121
WATRMAN, ----- 119
WEATHERBAY, Alvan 70
WESTALL, ----- 89
WESTALL, A. 92
WESTALL, A. E. 87
WESTALL, Adm 97
WESTALL, Andrew 73
WESTALL, Andrew 79
WESTALL, Andrew 83
WESTALL, Andrew 87
WESTALL, Andrew 87
WESTALL, Andrew 92
WESTALL, Andrew 97
WESTALL, Andrew E. 72
WESTALL, Andrew E. 97
WESTALL, Ann A. 28
WESTALL, Ann A. 30
WESTALL, J. M. 78
WESTALL, J. M. 84
WESTALL, James 60
WESTALL, James 63
WESTALL, James 65
WESTALL, James 66
WESTALL, James 68
WESTALL, James 70
WESTALL, James 87
WESTALL, James M. 36
WESTALL, James M. 37
WESTALL, James M. 50
WESTALL, James M. 51
WESTALL, James M. 79
WESTALL, James M. 85
WESTALL, James M. 92
WESTALL, James M. 96
WESTALL, Thomas 82
WESTALL, Thomas 97
WESTOVER, Capt. 112
WESTOVER, Captain 115
WESTSIDES, James 79
WETHEBAY, Alvan 64
WETHERBAY, Alvan 47
WHARTON, A. 109
WHARTON, J. A. 73
WHARTON, J. A. 76
WHARTON, J. A. 86
WHARTON, J. A. 87
WHARTON, John 6
WHARTON, John 65
WHARTON, John A. 8
WHARTON, John A. 9
WHARTON, John A. 48
WHARTON, John A. 54
WHARTON, John A. 57

WHARTON, John A. 58
WHARTON, John A. 60
WHARTON, John A. 61
WHARTON, John A. 61
WHARTON, John A. 61
WHARTON, John A. 63
WHARTON, John A. 65
WHARTON, John A. 65
WHARTON, John A. 65
WHARTON, John A. 69
WHARTON, John A. 70
WHARTON, John A. 71
WHARTON, John A. 89
WHARTON, John A. 91
WHARTON, John A. 97
WHARTON, John A. 105
WHARTON, John A. 106
WHARTON, John A. 107
WHARTON, John A. 107
WHARTON, John A. 108
WHARTON, John A. 115
WHARTON, John A. 119
WHARTON, John A. 119
WHARTON, John A. 120
WHARTON, John A. 120
WHARTON, John A. 121
WHARTON, John A. 121
WHARTON, John A. 122
WHARTON, Sarah Jane 30
WHARTON, Sarah Jane 30
WHARTON, W. H. 84
WHARTON, William H. 4
WHARTON, William H. 5
WHARTON, William H. 7
WHARTON, William H. 9
WHATRTON, John A. 59
WHEELER, Abram 106
WHEELER, Abram 115
WHEELER, G. B. 106
WHEELER, G. B. 115
WHITE, W. C. 23
WHITE, W. C. 23
WHITE, W. C. 23
WHITE, W. C. 24
WHITE, W. C. 26
WHITE, W. C. 26
WHITE, W. C. 76
WHITE, W. C. 76
WHITE, W. C. 77
WHITE, W. C. 78
WHITE, W. C. 79
WHITE, W. C. 79
WHITE, W. C. 83
WHITE, W. C. 87
WHITE, W. C. 90
WHITE, W. C. 94
WHITE, W. C. 97
WHITE, W. C. 111
WHITE, W. C. 111
WHITE, W. C. 123
WHITE, W. C. 124
WHITE, W. C. 125
WHITE, W. C. 125
WHITE, W. C. 126
WHITE, Walter 73
WHITE, Walter 80
WHITE, Walter C. 79
WHITE, Walter C. 80
WHITE, Walter C. 86
WHITE, Walter C. 112
WHITE, Walter C. 115
WHITE, Walter C. 117

WHITE, Walter C. 120
WHITE, Walter C. 121
WHITE, Walter C. 122
WHITESIDES, G. W. 74
WHITESIDES, G. W. 80
WHITESIDES, G. W. 87
WHITESIDES, Geo. 90
WHITESIDES, George 87
WHITESIDES, George 93
WHITESIDES, George 97
WHITESIDES, James 87
WHITING, B. 123
WHITING, B. 124
WHITING, Samuel 85
WHITING, Samuel 92
WHITING, Samuel 96
WHITMAN, E. R. 69
WHORTON, John A. 47
WHORTON, John A. 52
WIENT, Elizabeth 27
WIENT, Elizabeth 30
WIENT, Elizabeth 126
WIGHTMAN, E. R. 49
WIGHTMAN, E. R. 49
WIGHTMAN, E. R. 65
WIGHTMAN, E. R. 65
WIGHTMAN, E. R. 66
WIGHTMAN, E. R. 69
WIGHTMAN, E. R. 85
WIGJTMAN, E. R. 67
WILDY, ----- 108
WILDY, Samuel 52
WILDY, Samuel 56
WILDY, Samuel 60
WILDY, Samuel 62
WILDY, Samuel 71
WILDY, Samuel 103
WILDY, Samuel 104
WILDY, Samuel 105
WILDY, Samuel 105
WILDY, Samuel 106
WILDY, Samuel 108
WILDY, Samuel 115
WILIAMS, Mrs. A.C. 41
WILIAMS, Napoleon D. 62
WILIAMS, Robert H. 124
WILIAMS, Solomon 122
WILISMS, A. 73
WILKERSON, Ann E. 113
WILKERSON, Ann E. 115
WILKERSON, Ann E. 126
WILKINSON, Gen. James 31
WILLAIMS, Agustus 73
WILLIAMS, --- 42
WILLIAMS, --- 43
WILLIAMS, ---- 51
WILLIAMS, ---- 54
WILLIAMS, ---- 56
WILLIAMS, ---- 58
WILLIAMS, ---- 59
WILLIAMS, ---- 60
WILLIAMS, ---- 79
WILLIAMS, ----- 65
WILLIAMS, ----- 68
WILLIAMS, ----- 69
WILLIAMS, ----- 76
WILLIAMS, ----- 81
WILLIAMS, ----- 82
WILLIAMS, ----- 83
WILLIAMS, ----- 84
WILLIAMS, ----- 86
WILLIAMS, ----- 87
WILLIAMS, ----- 88

WILLIAMS, ----- 91
WILLIAMS, ----- 93
WILLIAMS, ----- 94
WILLIAMS, ----- 102
WILLIAMS, ----- 111
WILLIAMS, ----- 116
WILLIAMS, ----- 117
WILLIAMS, ----- 120
WILLIAMS, ----- 121
WILLIAMS, ----- 122
WILLIAMS, ----- 123
WILLIAMS, ----- 123
WILLIAMS, ----- 124
WILLIAMS, ----- 125
WILLIAMS, A. 50
WILLIAMS, A. 63
WILLIAMS, A. 71
WILLIAMS, A. 79
WILLIAMS, A. 85
WILLIAMS, A. 87
WILLIAMS, A. 88
WILLIAMS, A. 92
WILLIAMS, A. 105
WILLIAMS, A. 120
WILLIAMS, A. 120
WILLIAMS, Agustus 71
WILLIAMS, Augustus 55
WILLIAMS, Augustus 61
WILLIAMS, Augustus 67
WILLIAMS, Augustus 74
WILLIAMS, Augustus 75
WILLIAMS, Augustus 89
WILLIAMS, Augustus 91
WILLIAMS, Augustus 94
WILLIAMS, Augustus 97
WILLIAMS, Augustus 104
WILLIAMS, Augustus 104
WILLIAMS, Augustus 106
WILLIAMS, Augustus 110
WILLIAMS, Augustus 110
WILLIAMS, Augustus 115
WILLIAMS, Augustus 119
WILLIAMS, Augustus 119
WILLIAMS, Augustus 119
WILLIAMS, Augustus 120
WILLIAMS, Augustus 121
WILLIAMS, Augustus 121
WILLIAMS, Augustus 122
WILLIAMS, Bert H. 108
WILLIAMS, Bert H. 115
WILLIAMS, D. H. 23
WILLIAMS, D. H. 23
WILLIAMS, D. H. 26
WILLIAMS, Elliott 78
WILLIAMS, Elliott 88
WILLIAMS, Henry 52
WILLIAMS, Henry 71
WILLIAMS, J. 23
WILLIAMS, J. 24
WILLIAMS, J. 24
WILLIAMS, J. 26
WILLIAMS, J. S. 25
WILLIAMS, Jesse 100
WILLIAMS, Jesse 115
WILLIAMS, John 23
WILLIAMS, John 26
WILLIAMS, John A. 9
WILLIAMS, John S. 24
WILLIAMS, Mrs. A. C. 44
WILLIAMS, Napoleon D. 45
WILLIAMS, Napoleon D. 65
WILLIAMS, Napoleon D. 71
WILLIAMS, R. H. 77

WILLIAMS, R. H. 77
WILLIAMS, R. H. 79
WILLIAMS, R. H. 79
WILLIAMS, R. H. 87
WILLIAMS, R. H. 88
WILLIAMS, R. H. 88
WILLIAMS, R. H. 91
WILLIAMS, R. H. 92
WILLIAMS, R. H. 97
WILLIAMS, R. H. 109
WILLIAMS, Robert H. 98
WILLIAMS, Robert H. 102
WILLIAMS, Robert H. 104
WILLIAMS, Robert H. 107
WILLIAMS, Robert H. 110
WILLIAMS, Robert H. 111
WILLIAMS, Robert H. 116
WILLIAMS, Robert H. 123
WILLIAMS, Robert W. 117
WILLIAMS, Robert W. 120
WILLIAMS, Robert W. 122
WILLIAMS, S. 72
WILLIAMS, S. 88
WILLIAMS, S. M. 42
WILLIAMS, S. M. 44
WILLIAMS, S. M. 76
WILLIAMS, S. M. 79
WILLIAMS, S. M. 79
WILLIAMS, Sam 73
WILLIAMS, Sam M. 86
WILLIAMS, Samuel M. 5
WILLIAMS, Samuel M. 101
WILLIAMS, Samuel M. 116
WILLIAMS, Solomon 46
WILLIAMS, Solomon 52
WILLIAMS, Solomon 53
WILLIAMS, Solomon 60
WILLIAMS, Solomon 61
WILLIAMS, Solomon 63
WILLIAMS, Solomon 71
WILLIAMS, Solomon 98
WILLIAMS, Solomon 105
WILLIAMS, Solomon 110
WILLIAMS, Solomon 116
WILLIAMS, Solomon 118
WILLIAMS, Solomon 120
WILLIAMS, Solomon 121
WILLIAMS, W. C. 77
WILLIAMSON, R. M. 74
WILLIAMSON, R. M. 78
WILLIAMSON, R. M. 88
WILLIAMSON, R. M. 89
WILLIAMSON, R. M. 92
WILLIAMSON, R. M. 94
WILLIAMSON, R. M. 96
WILLIAMSON, R. M. 97
WILLIAMSON, R. M. 101
WILLIAMSON, R. M. 105
WILLIAMSON, R. M. 116
WILLS, William 31
WILLS, William 37
WILLS, William 112
WILLS, William 113
WILLS, William 116
WILLS, William 126
WILSON, Abraham S. 77
WILSON, Abraham S. 88
WILSON, James 79
WILSON, James 86
WILSON, Mrs. Amelia 29
WILSON, Mrs. Amelia 30
WILSON, R. 72
WILSON, R. 88
WILSON, Robert 110

WILSON, Robert 116
WILSON, Thomas 35
WILSON, Thomas 37
WILSON, Thomas 41
WILSON, Thomas 44
WILSON, William 87
WILSON, Wm. 75
WILSON, Wm. 88
WILSON, Wm.. 79
WINSON, Ann W. 30
WINSON, Ann W. 30
WINSTON, A. 92
WINSTON, A. 97
WINSTON, Anthony 79
WINSTON, Anthony 88
WINSTON, Anthony 111
WINSTON, Anthony 116
WINSTON, Anthony 117
WINSTON, Anthony 120
WINSTON, Anthony 122
WITGHTMAN, E. R. 66
WJARTON, John A. 57
WLLIOTT, George 120
WOGHTMAN, E. R. 79
WOODRUFF, John 29
WOODRUFF, John 30
WOODRUFF, John 30
WOODRUFF, John 42
WOODRUFF, John 44
WOODRUFF, John 79
WOODRUFF, John 85
WOODRUFF, William 88
WOODRUFF, Wm. 76
WOODSON, ----- 51
WOODSON, ----- 63
WOODSON, ----- 65
WOODSON, ----- 72
WOODSON, ----- 77
WOODSON, ----- 79
WOODSON, ----- 82
WOODSON, ----- 84
WOODSON, ----- 88
WOODSON, ----- 89
WOODSON, ----- 97
WOODSON, ----- 106
WOODSON, ----- 116
WOODSON, ------ 95
WOODSON, James M. 35
WOODSON, James M. 37
WRAY, Edward 79
WRAY, Edward 86
WRIGHT, Claiborne 41
WRIGHT, Claiborne 44
WRIGHT, I. G. 51
WRIGHT, I. G. 65
WRIGHT, I. G. 66
WRIGHT, I. G. 71
WRIGHT, R. T. 72
WRIGHT, R. T. 88
YOUNG, James 50
YOUNG, James 65
YOUNG, James 69
YOUNG, Samuel 42
YOUNG, Samuel 43
YOUNG, Samuel 47
YOUNG, Samuel 47
YOUNG, Samuel 50
YOUNG, Samuel 54
YOUNG, Samuel 61
YOUNG, Samuel 63
YOUNG, Samuel 63
YOUNG, Samuel 65
YOUNG, Samuel 68

YOUNG, Samuel 71
YOUNG, Samuel 79
YOUNG, Samuel 80
YOUNG, Samuel 80
YOUNG, Samuel 81
YOUNG, Samuel 81
YOUNG, Samuel 84
YOUNG, Samuel 92
YOUNG, Samuel 93
YOUNG, Samuel 95
YOUNG, Samuel 99
YOUNG, Samuel 100
YOUNG, Samuel 103
YOUNG, Samuel 107
YOUNG, Samuel 116
YOUNG, Samuel 117
YOUNG, Samuel 121
YOUNG, Samuel 121
YOUNG, T. 22
YOUNG, T. 26